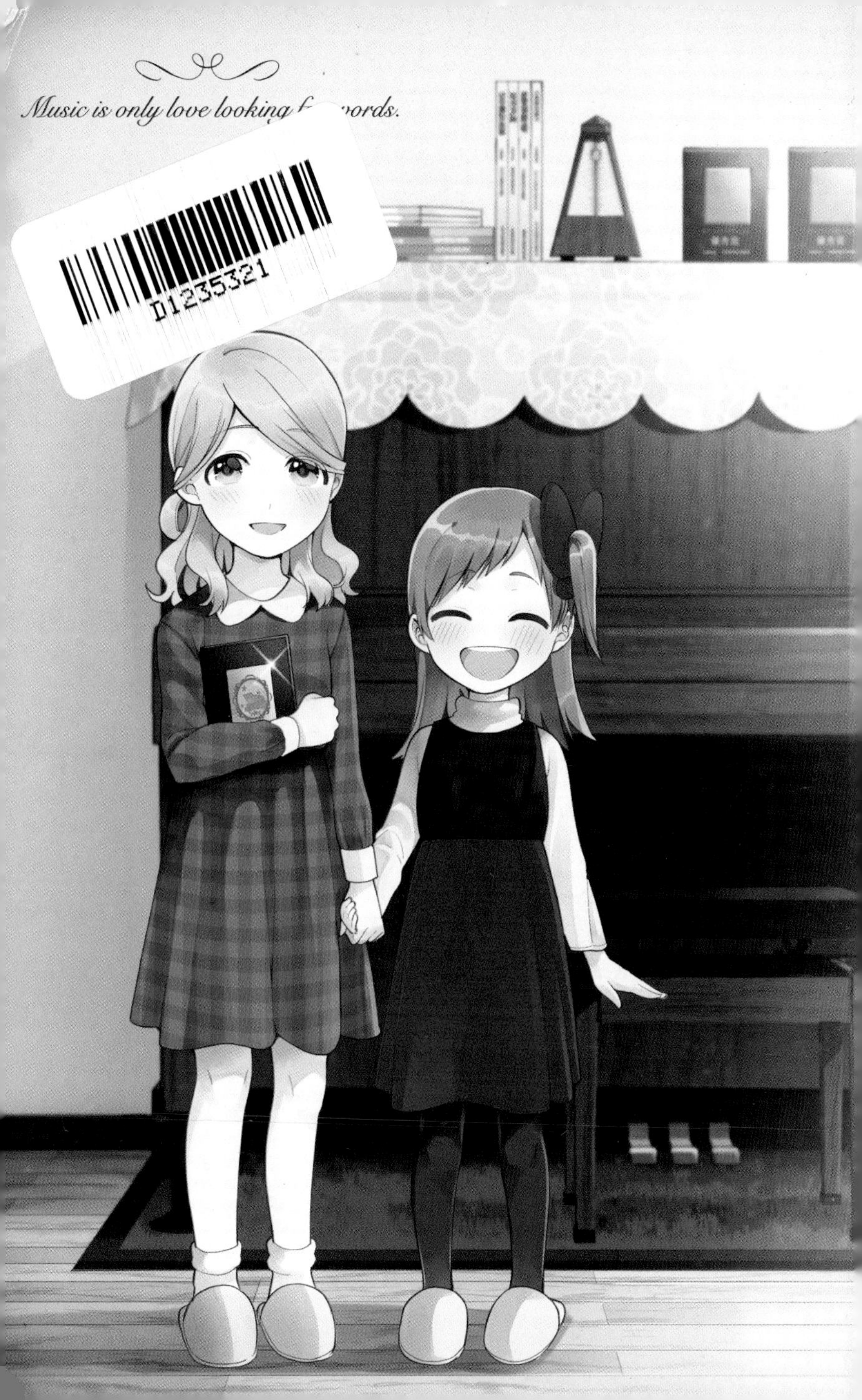
Music is only love looking f
words.

Kiss and White Lily for My Dearest Girl

Kiss & White Lily for My Dearest Girl

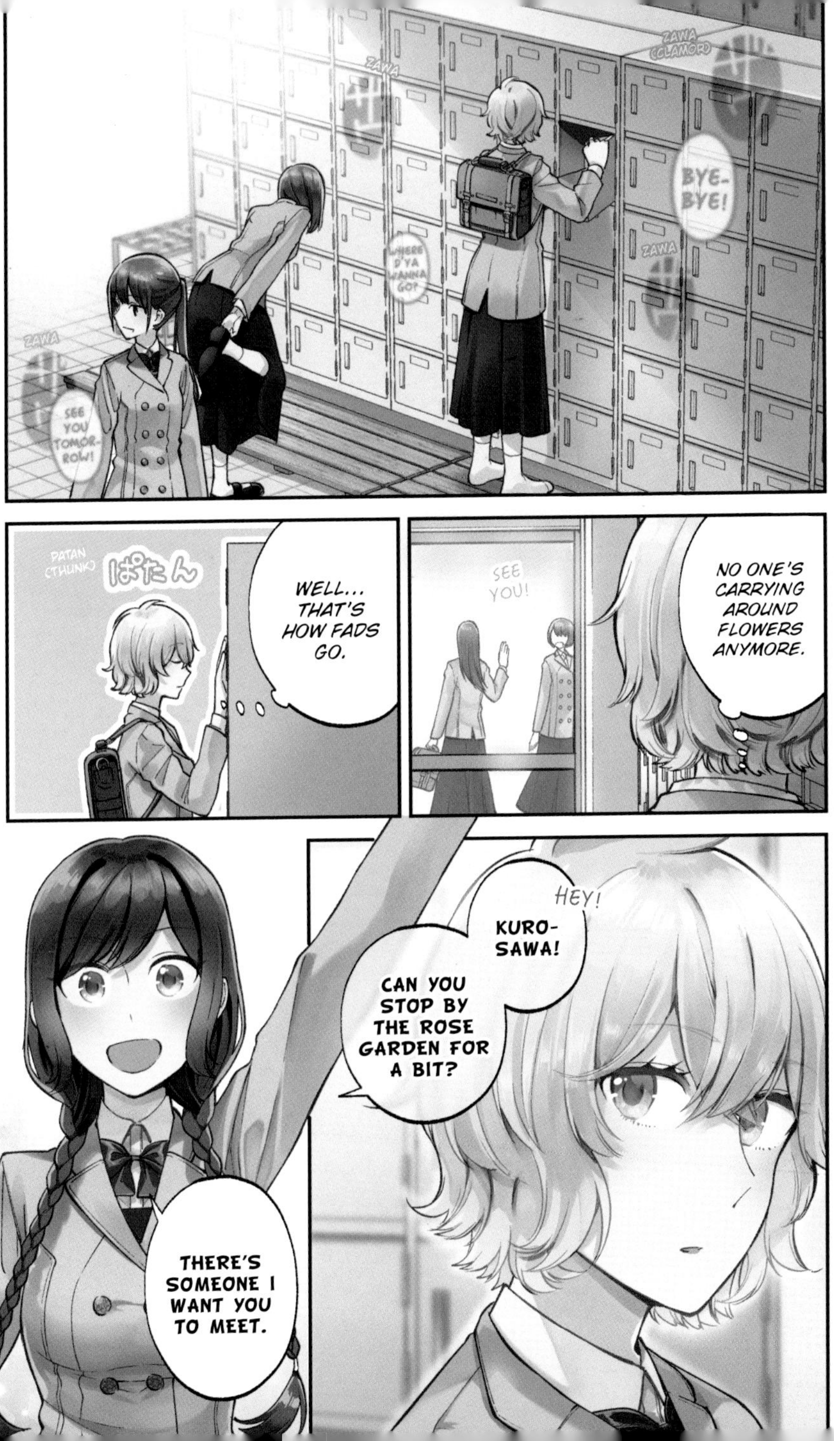

ZAWA (CLAMOR)
BYE-BYE!
ZAWA
ZAWA
WHERE D'YA WANNA GO?
ZAWA
SEE YOU TOMOR-ROW!
NO ONE'S CARRYING AROUND FLOWERS ANYMORE.
SEE YOU!
WELL... THAT'S HOW FADS GO.
PATAN (THUNK)
ぱたん
HEY!
KURO-SAWA!
CAN YOU STOP BY THE ROSE GARDEN FOR A BIT?
THERE'S SOMEONE I WANT YOU TO MEET.

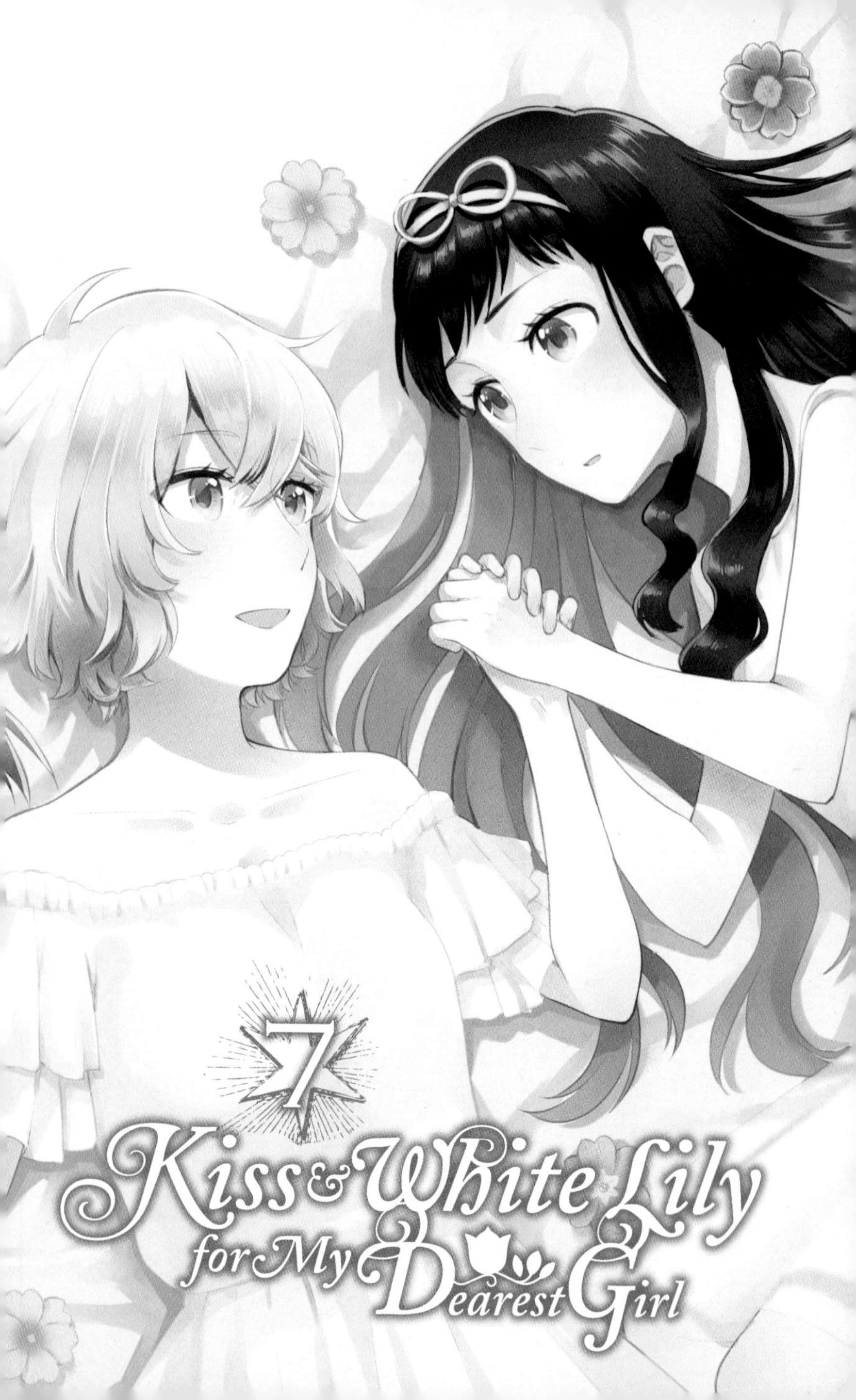
7
Kiss & White Lily
for My Dearest Girl

Chapter 31: *Solitary Girl*

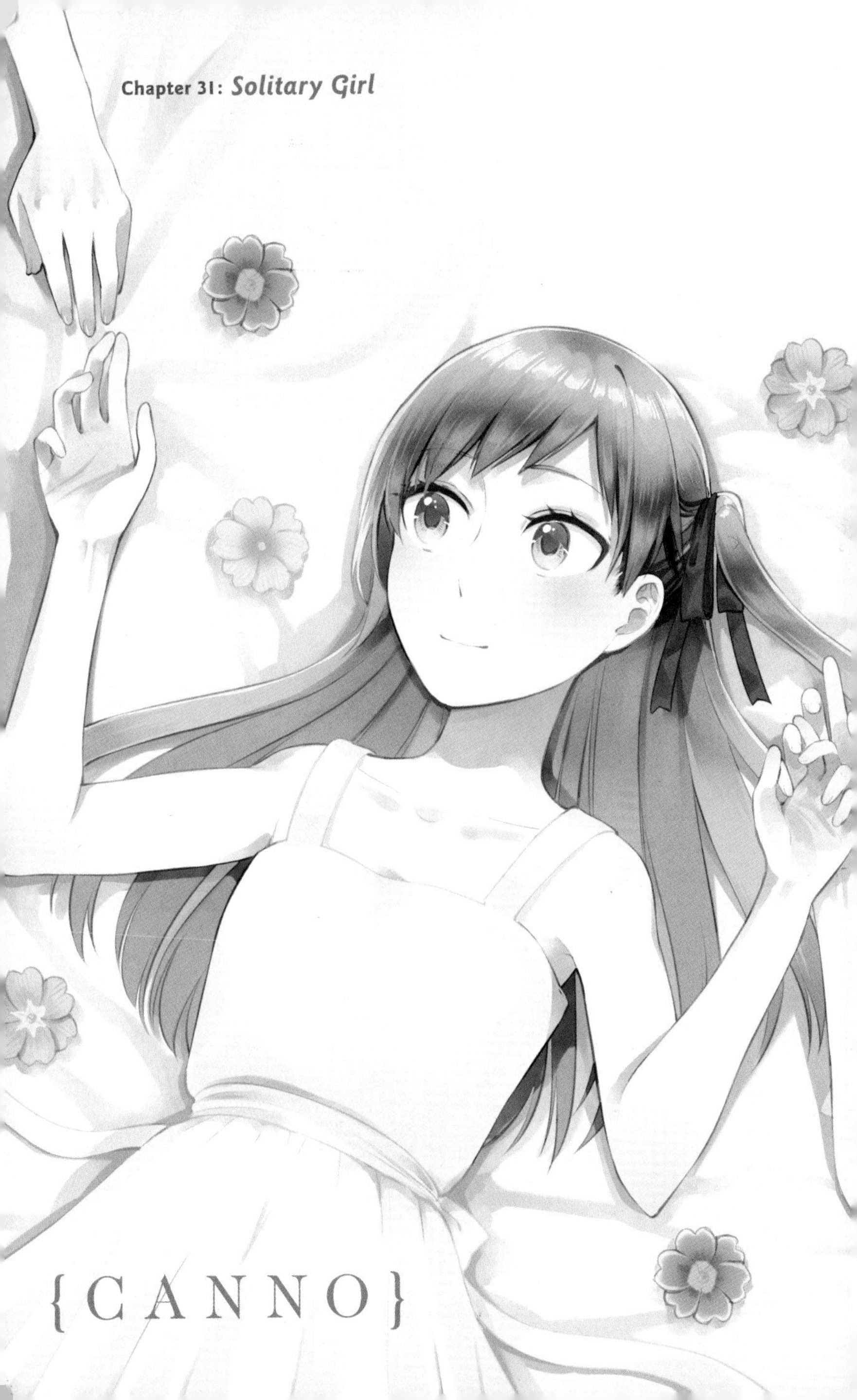
{CANNO}

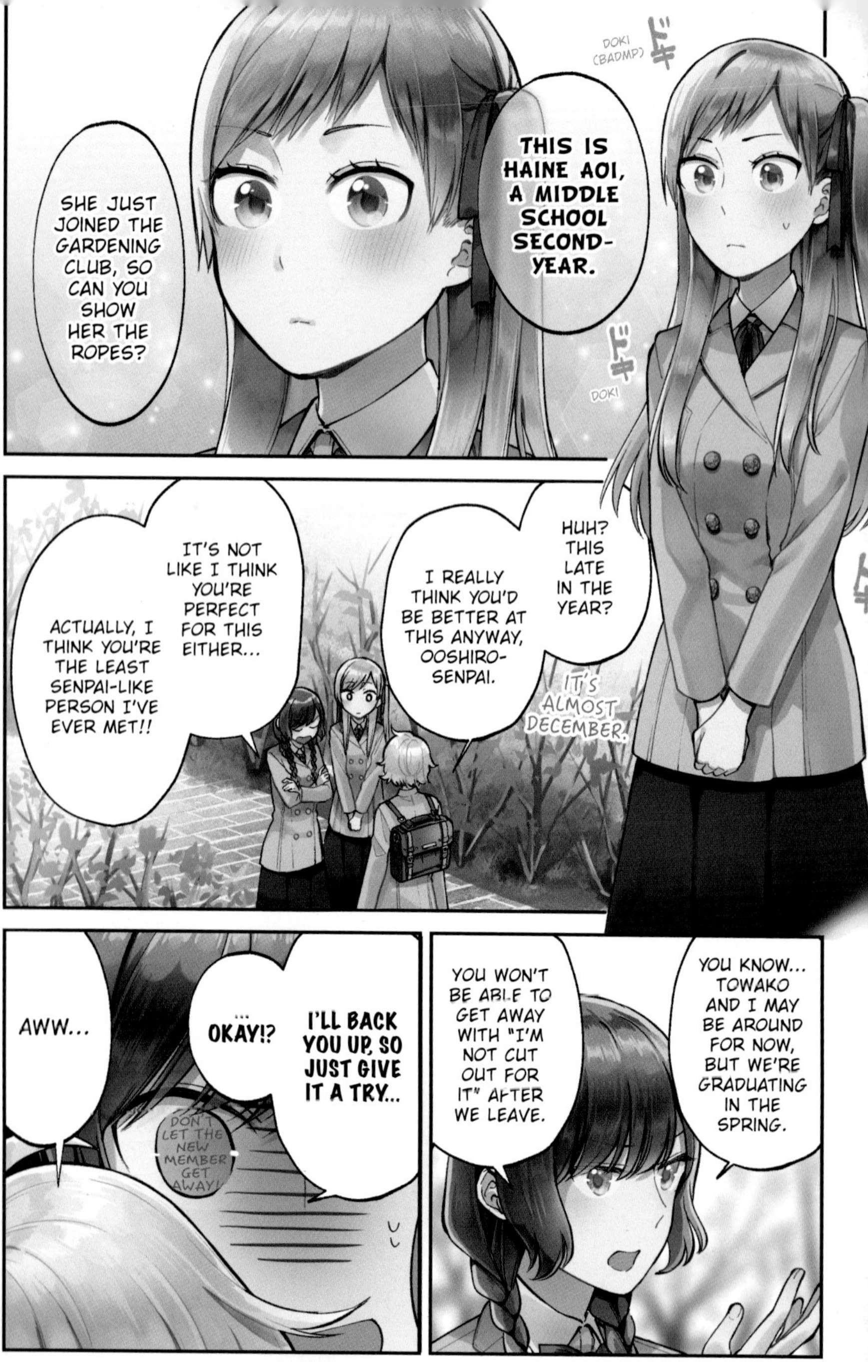
DOKI (BADMP)
THIS IS HAINE AOI, A MIDDLE SCHOOL SECOND-YEAR.
SHE JUST JOINED THE GARDENING CLUB, SO CAN YOU SHOW HER THE ROPES?
DOKI
HUH? THIS LATE IN THE YEAR?
IT'S ALMOST DECEMBER.
I REALLY THINK YOU'D BE BETTER AT THIS ANYWAY, OOSHIRO-SENPAI.
IT'S NOT LIKE I THINK YOU'RE PERFECT FOR THIS EITHER...
ACTUALLY, I THINK YOU'RE THE LEAST SENPAI-LIKE PERSON I'VE EVER MET!!
YOU KNOW... TOWAKO AND I MAY BE AROUND FOR NOW, BUT WE'RE GRADUATING IN THE SPRING.
YOU WON'T BE ABLE TO GET AWAY WITH "I'M NOT CUT OUT FOR IT" AFTER WE LEAVE.
I'LL BACK YOU UP, SO JUST GIVE IT A TRY...
...OKAY!?
DON'T LET THE NEW MEMBER GET AWAY!
AWW...

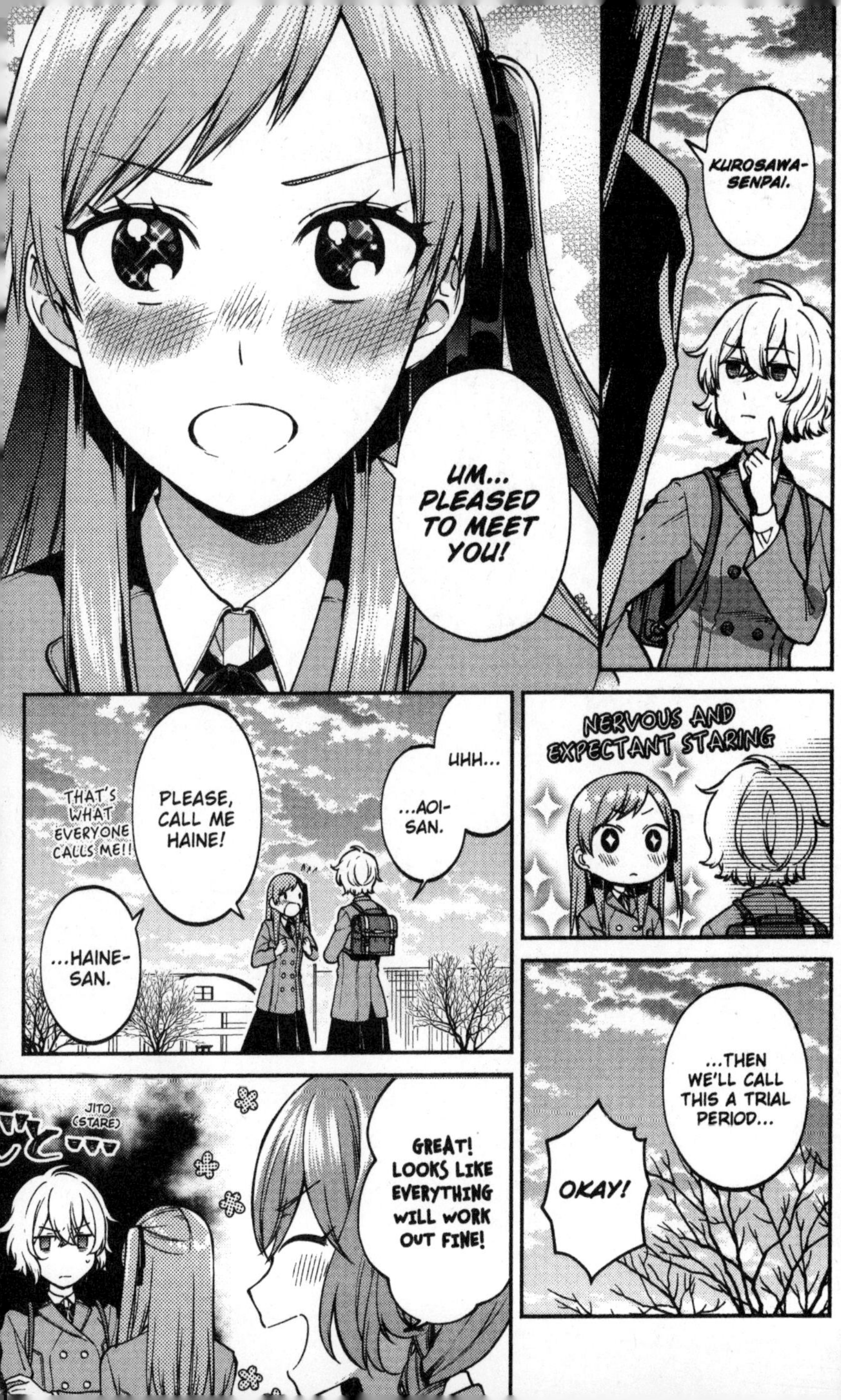
KUROSAWA-SENPAI.
UM... PLEASED TO MEET YOU!
NERVOUS AND EXPECTANT STARING
UHH...
...AOI-SAN.
PLEASE, CALL ME HAINE!
THAT'S WHAT EVERYONE CALLS ME!!
...HAINE-SAN.
...THEN WE'LL CALL THIS A TRIAL PERIOD...
OKAY!
GREAT! LOOKS LIKE EVERYTHING WILL WORK OUT FINE!
JITO (STARE)

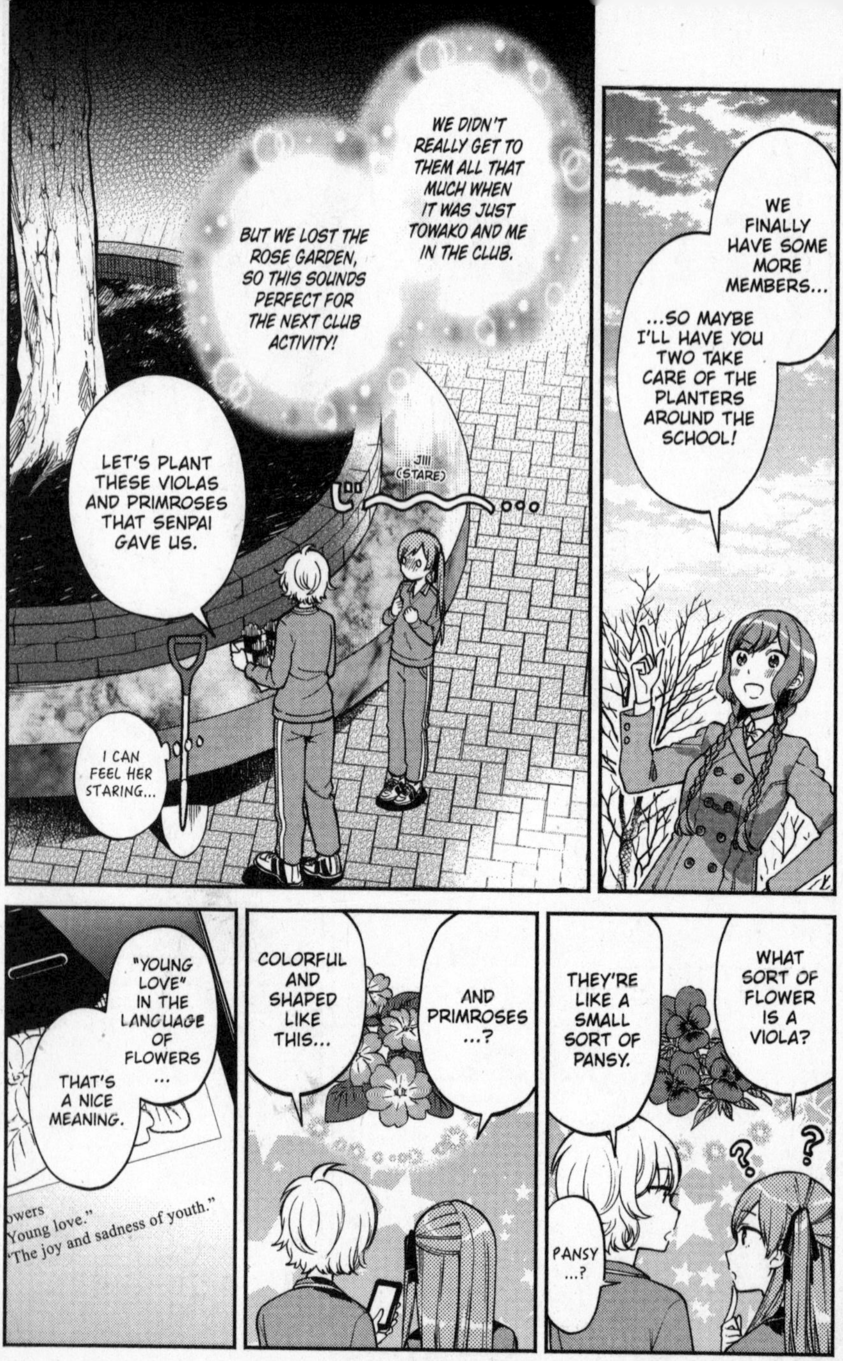
WE FINALLY HAVE SOME MORE MEMBERS...
...SO MAYBE I'LL HAVE YOU TWO TAKE CARE OF THE PLANTERS AROUND THE SCHOOL!
WE DIDN'T REALLY GET TO THEM ALL THAT MUCH WHEN IT WAS JUST TOWAKO AND ME IN THE CLUB.
BUT WE LOST THE ROSE GARDEN, SO THIS SOUNDS PERFECT FOR THE NEXT CLUB ACTIVITY!
LET'S PLANT THESE VIOLAS AND PRIMROSES THAT SENPAI GAVE US.
JIII (STARE)
I CAN FEEL HER STARING...
WHAT SORT OF FLOWER IS A VIOLA?
THEY'RE LIKE A SMALL SORT OF PANSY.
PANSY ...?
AND PRIMROSES ...?
COLORFUL AND SHAPED LIKE THIS...
owers
"Young love."
"The joy and sadness of youth."
"YOUNG LOVE" IN THE LANGUAGE OF FLOWERS...
THAT'S A NICE MEANING.

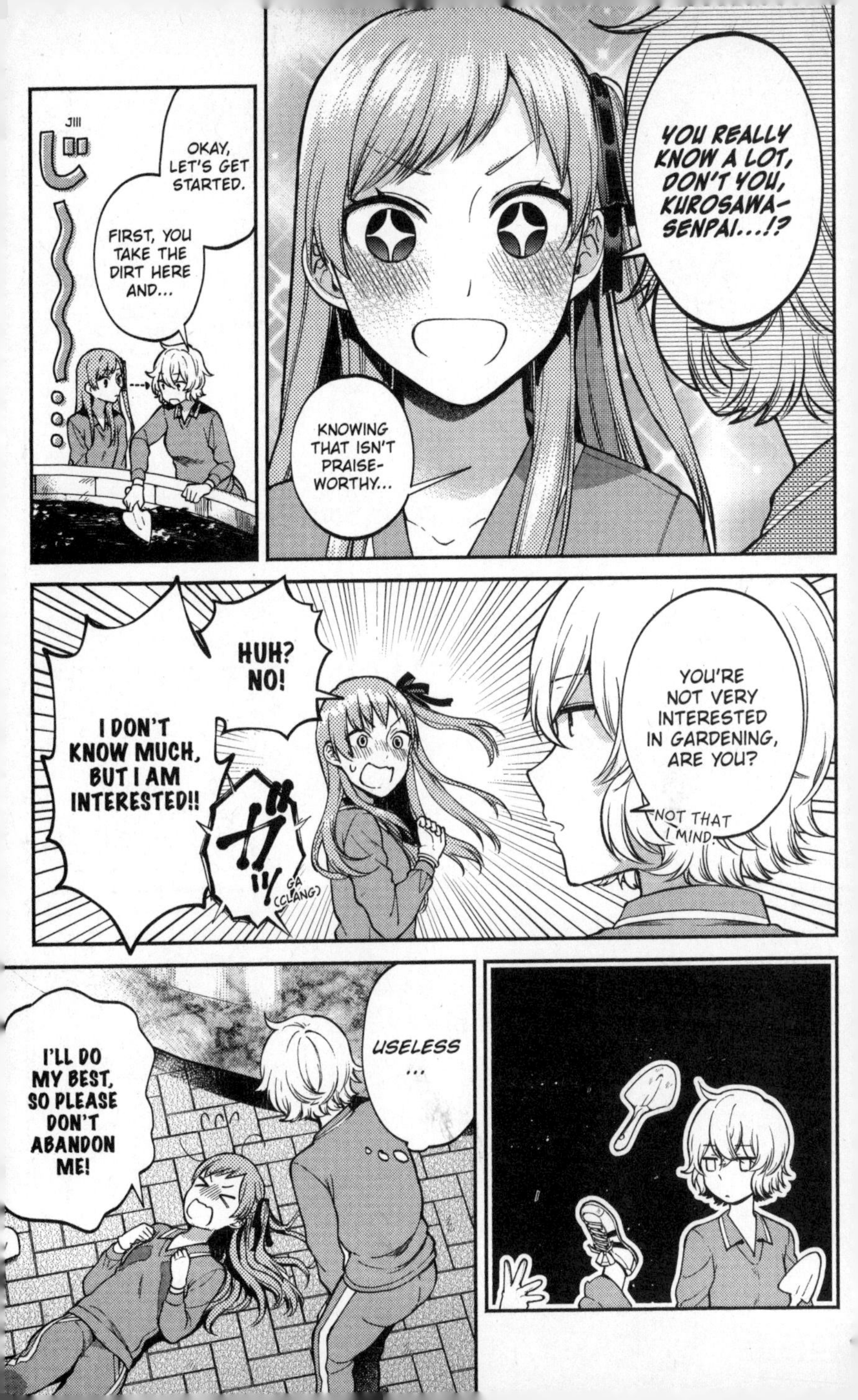
YOU REALLY KNOW A LOT, DON'T YOU, KUROSAWA-SENPAI...!?
KNOWING THAT ISN'T PRAISE-WORTHY...
OKAY, LET'S GET STARTED.
FIRST, YOU TAKE THE DIRT HERE AND...
JIII
YOU'RE NOT VERY INTERESTED IN GARDENING, ARE YOU?
NOT THAT I MIND.
HUH? NO!
GA (CLANG)
I DON'T KNOW MUCH, BUT I AM INTERESTED!!
USELESS...
I'LL DO MY BEST, SO PLEASE DON'T ABANDON ME!

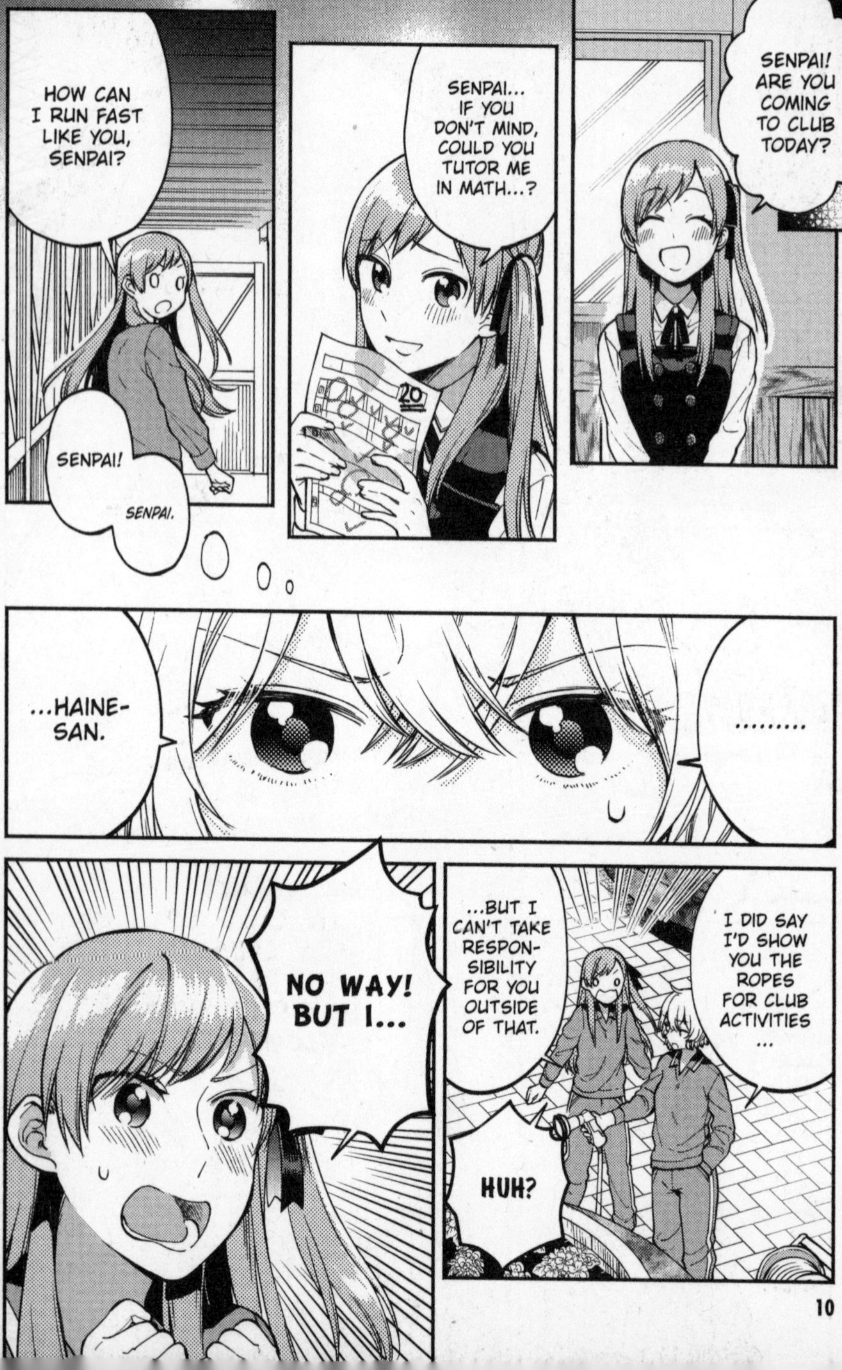

SENPAI! ARE YOU COMING TO CLUB TODAY?
SENPAI... IF YOU DON'T MIND, COULD YOU TUTOR ME IN MATH...?
HOW CAN I RUN FAST LIKE YOU, SENPAI?
SENPAI!
SENPAI.
....
...HAINE-SAN.
I DID SAY I'D SHOW YOU THE ROPES FOR CLUB ACTIVITIES ...
...BUT I CAN'T TAKE RESPON-SIBILITY FOR YOU OUTSIDE OF THAT.
HUH?
NO WAY! BUT I...

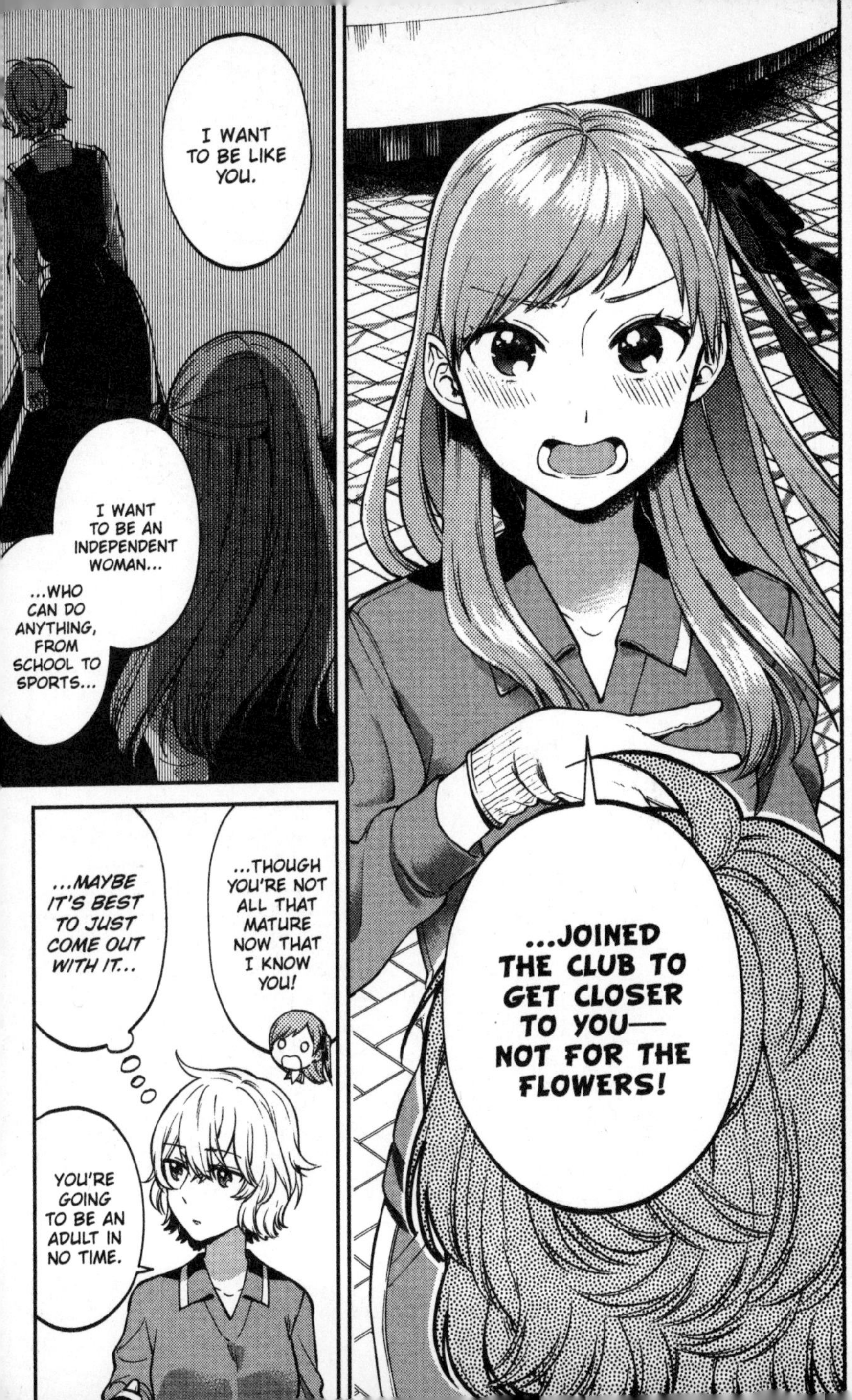
...JOINED THE CLUB TO GET CLOSER TO YOU— NOT FOR THE FLOWERS!
I WANT TO BE LIKE YOU.
I WANT TO BE AN INDEPENDENT WOMAN...
...WHO CAN DO ANYTHING, FROM SCHOOL TO SPORTS...
...THOUGH YOU'RE NOT ALL THAT MATURE NOW THAT I KNOW YOU!
...MAYBE IT'S BEST TO JUST COME OUT WITH IT...
YOU'RE GOING TO BE AN ADULT IN NO TIME.

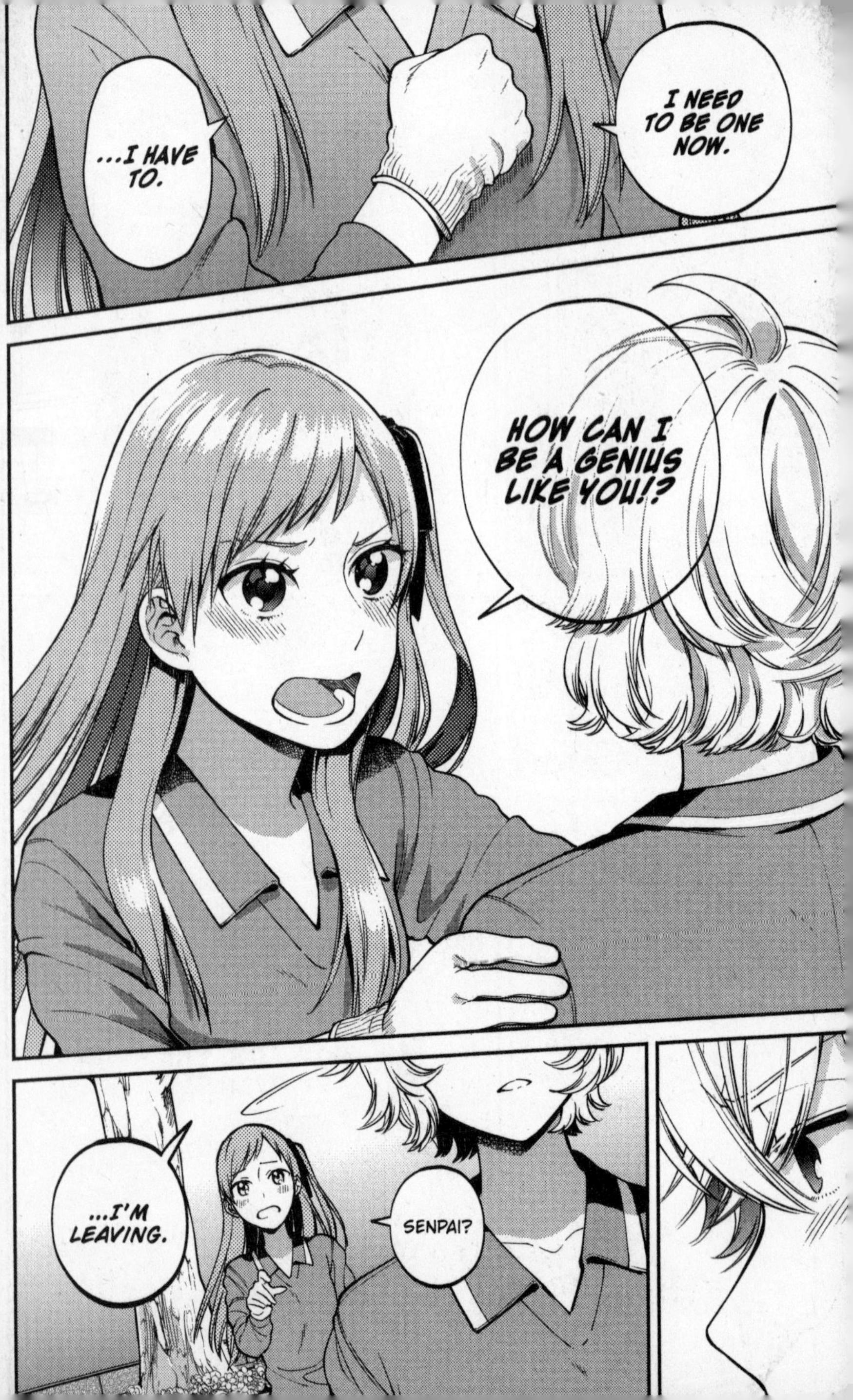
I NEED TO BE ONE NOW.
...I HAVE TO.
HOW CAN I BE A GENIUS LIKE YOU!?
SENPAI?
...I'M LEAVING.

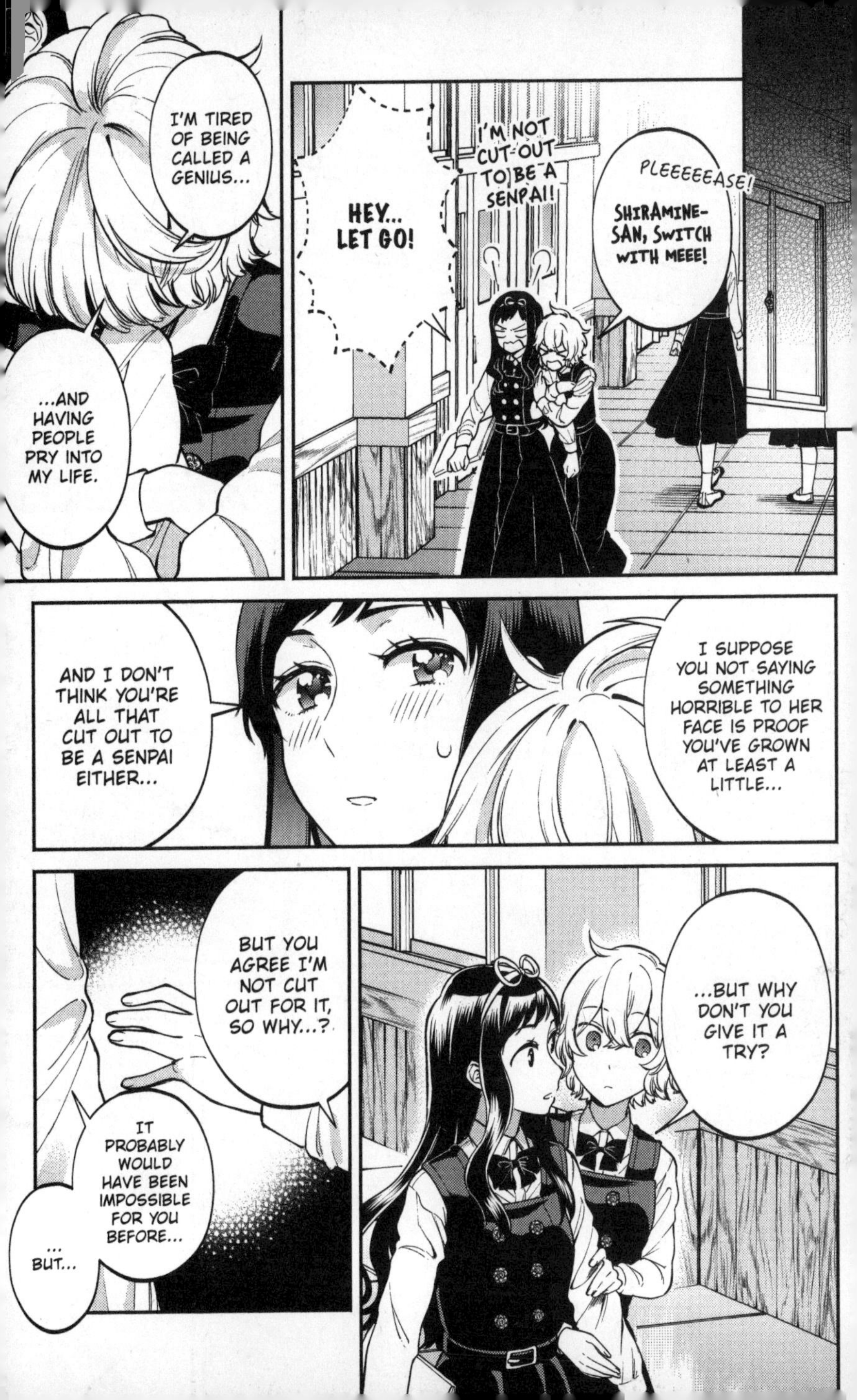
PLEEEEEASE! SHIRAMINE-SAN, SWITCH WITH MEEE!
I'M NOT CUT OUT TO BE A SENPAI!
HEY... LET GO!
I'M TIRED OF BEING CALLED A GENIUS...
...AND HAVING PEOPLE PRY INTO MY LIFE.
I SUPPOSE YOU NOT SAYING SOMETHING HORRIBLE TO HER FACE IS PROOF YOU'VE GROWN AT LEAST A LITTLE...
AND I DON'T THINK YOU'RE ALL THAT CUT OUT TO BE A SENPAI EITHER...
...BUT WHY DON'T YOU GIVE IT A TRY?
BUT YOU AGREE I'M NOT CUT OUT FOR IT, SO WHY...?
IT PROBABLY WOULD HAVE BEEN IMPOSSIBLE FOR YOU BEFORE...
... BUT...

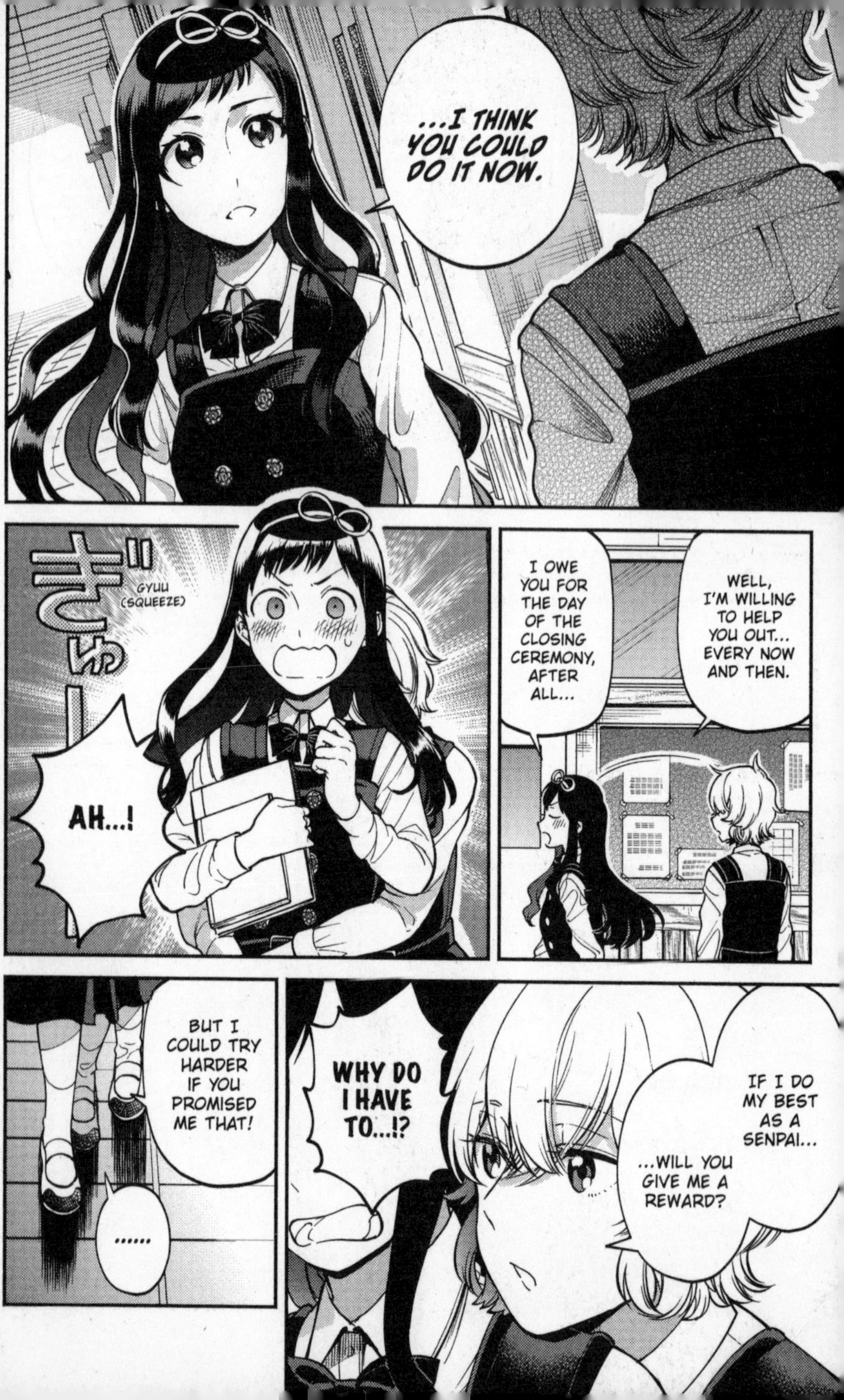
...I THINK YOU COULD DO IT NOW.
WELL, I'M WILLING TO HELP YOU OUT... EVERY NOW AND THEN.
I OWE YOU FOR THE DAY OF THE CLOSING CEREMONY, AFTER ALL...
ぎゅー
GYUU (SQUEEZE)
AH...!
IF I DO MY BEST AS A SENPAI...
...WILL YOU GIVE ME A REWARD?
WHY DO I HAVE TO...!?
BUT I COULD TRY HARDER IF YOU PROMISED ME THAT!
......

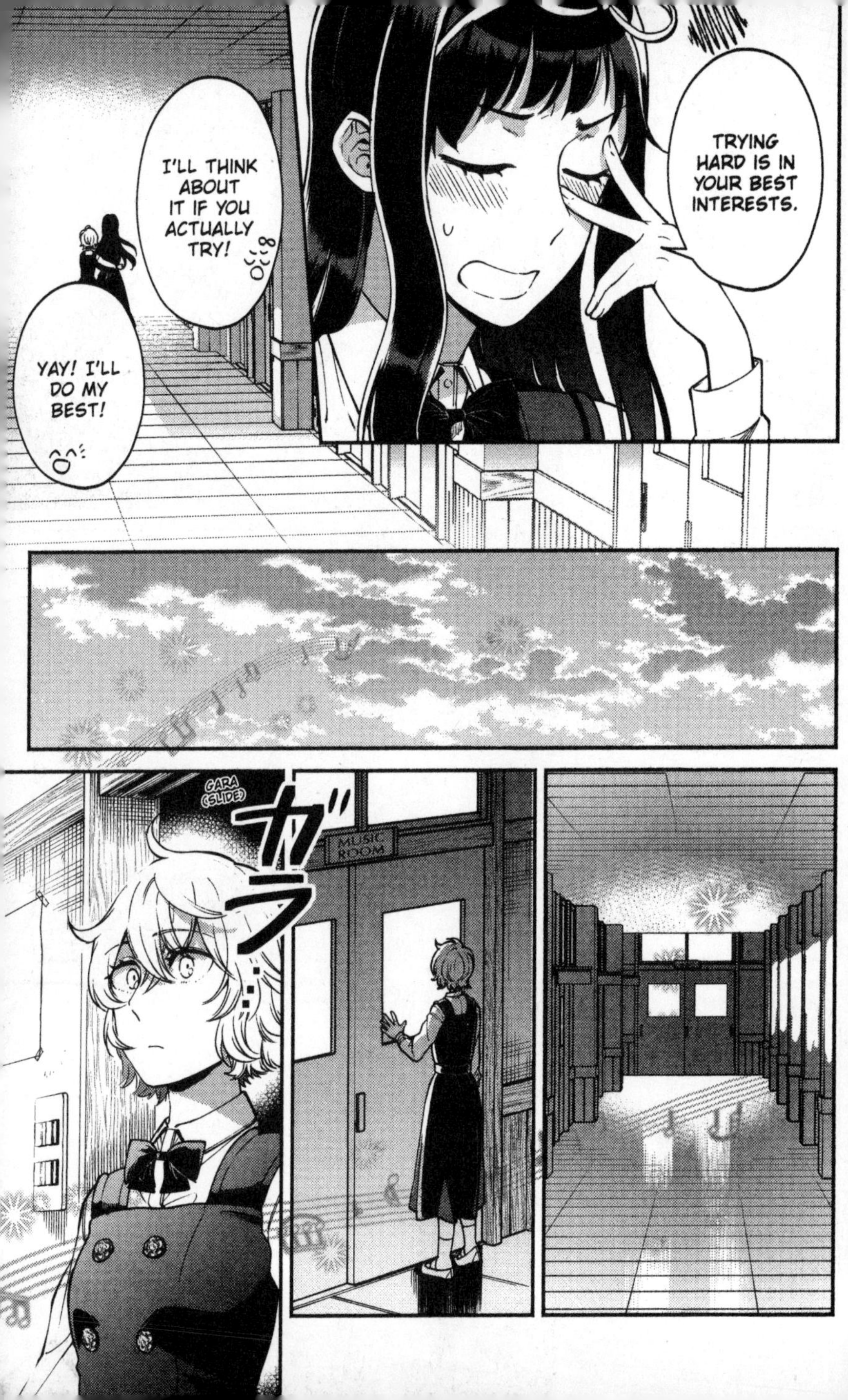
TRYING HARD IS IN YOUR BEST INTERESTS.
I'LL THINK ABOUT IT IF YOU ACTUALLY TRY!
YAY! I'LL DO MY BEST!
MUSIC ROOM
GARA (SLIDE)

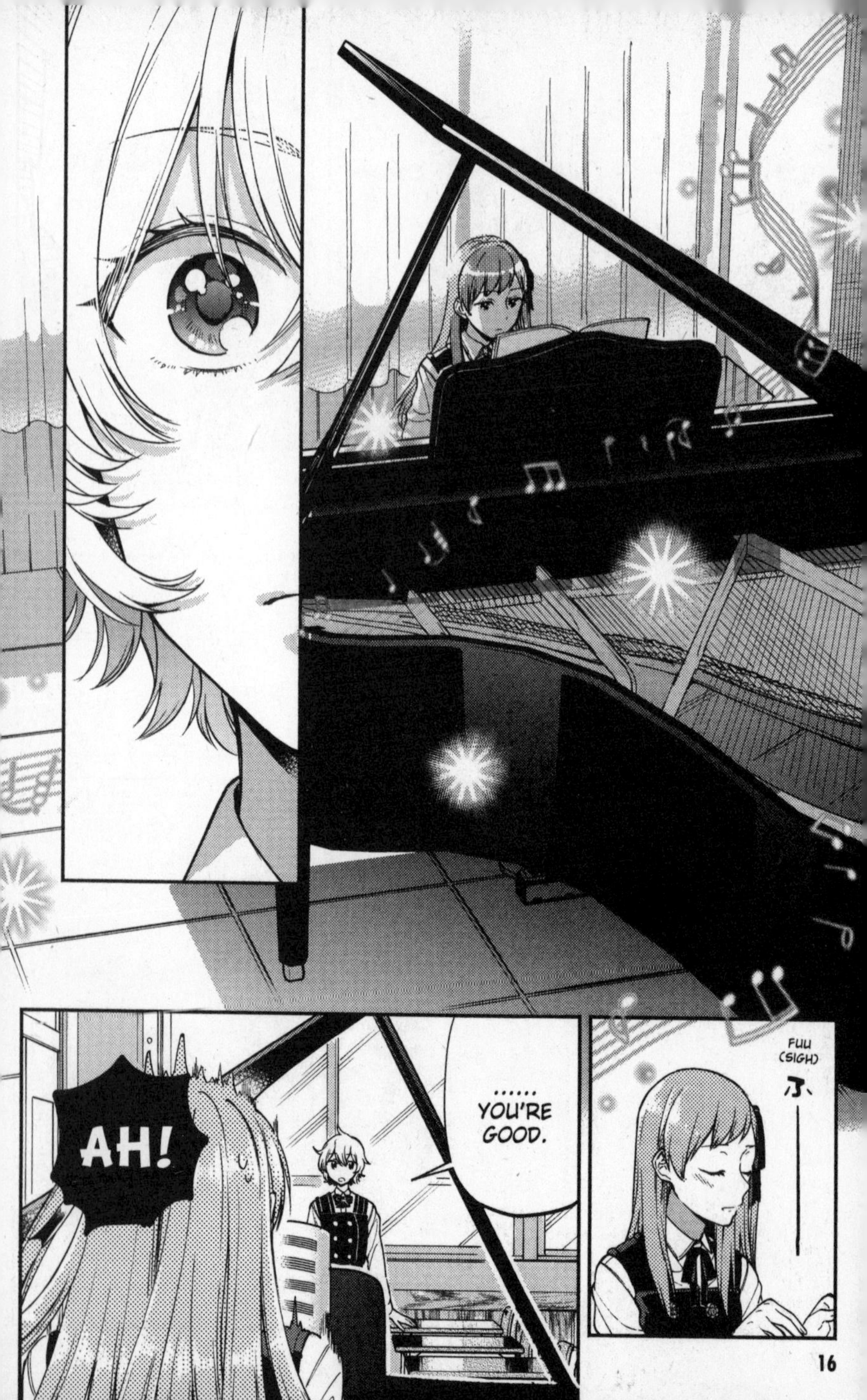
FUU (SIGH)
ふー
...... YOU'RE GOOD.
AH!

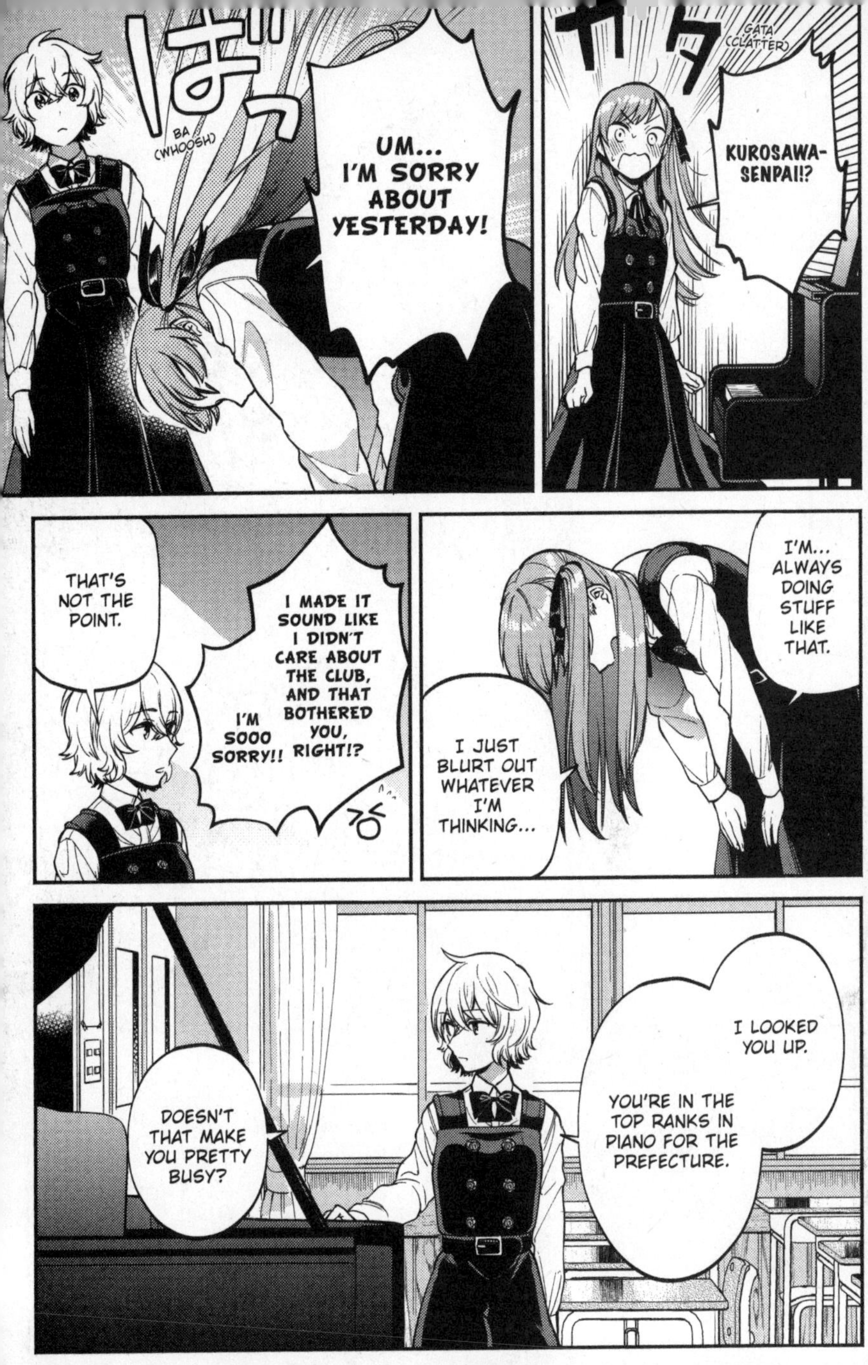
ガタ
GATA (CLATTER)
KUROSAWA-SENPAI!?
ばっ
BA (WHOOSH)
UM... I'M SORRY ABOUT YESTERDAY!
I'M... ALWAYS DOING STUFF LIKE THAT.
I JUST BLURT OUT WHATEVER I'M THINKING...
I MADE IT SOUND LIKE I DIDN'T CARE ABOUT THE CLUB, AND THAT BOTHERED YOU, RIGHT!?
I'M SOOO SORRY!!
THAT'S NOT THE POINT.
I LOOKED YOU UP.
YOU'RE IN THE TOP RANKS IN PIANO FOR THE PREFECTURE.
DOESN'T THAT MAKE YOU PRETTY BUSY?

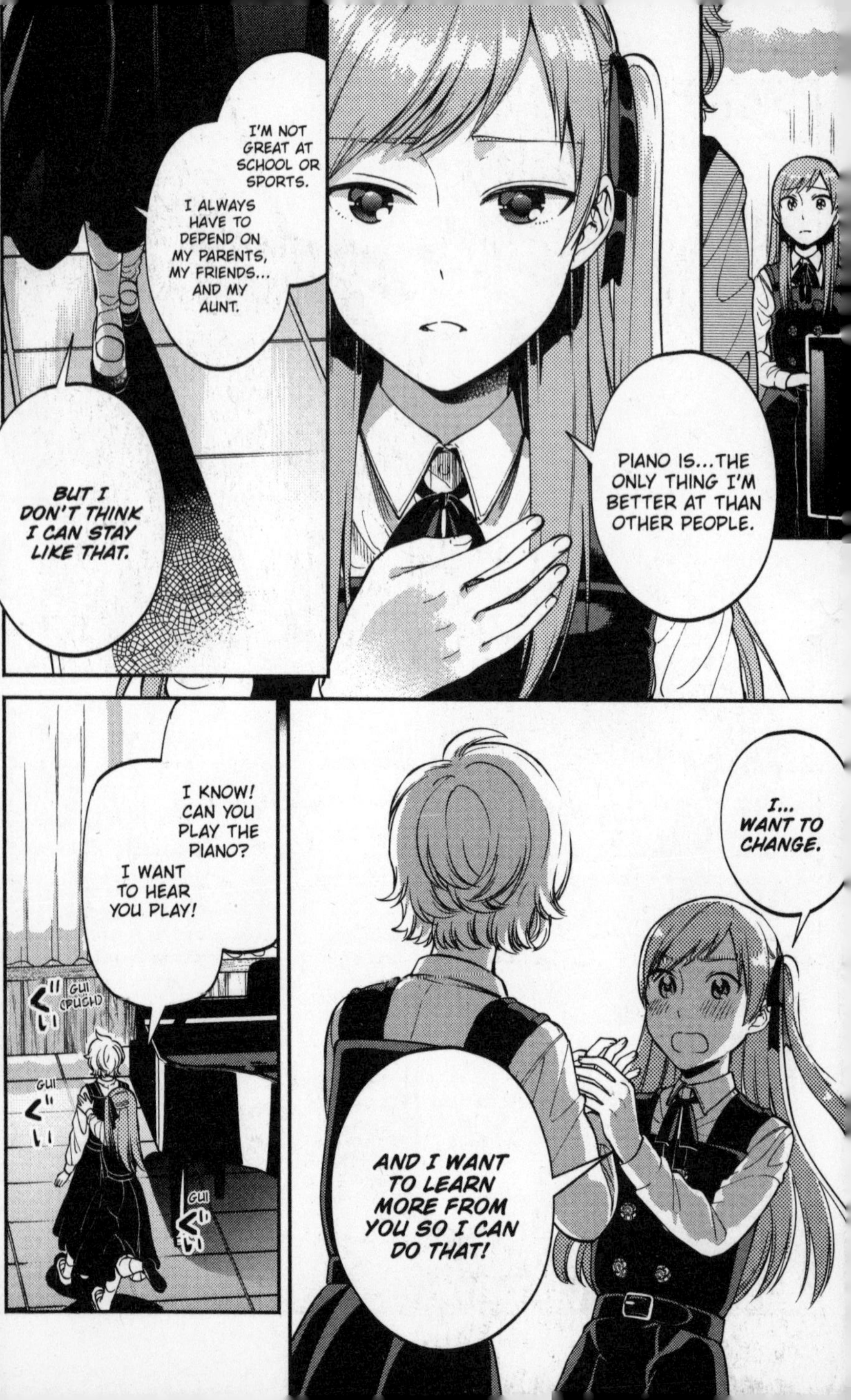
PIANO IS...THE ONLY THING I'M BETTER AT THAN OTHER PEOPLE.
I'M NOT GREAT AT SCHOOL OR SPORTS.
I ALWAYS HAVE TO DEPEND ON MY PARENTS, MY FRIENDS... AND MY AUNT.
BUT I DON'T THINK I CAN STAY LIKE THAT.
I... WANT TO CHANGE.
AND I WANT TO LEARN MORE FROM YOU SO I CAN DO THAT!
I KNOW! CAN YOU PLAY THE PIANO?
I WANT TO HEAR YOU PLAY!
GUI (PUSH)
GUI
GUI

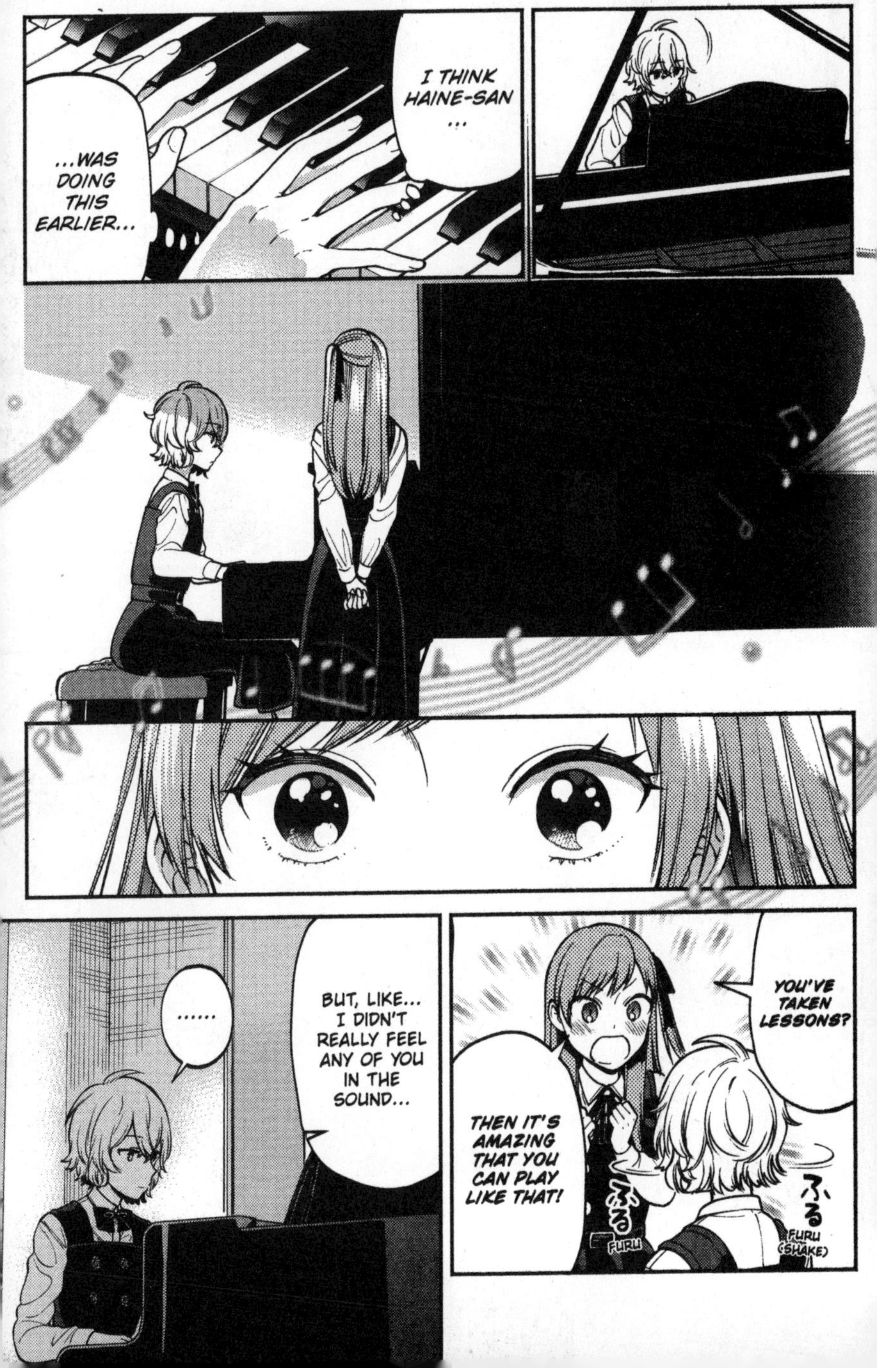
I THINK HAINE-SAN ...
...WAS DOING THIS EARLIER...
YOU'VE TAKEN LESSONS?
ふる
FURU (SHAKE)
THEN IT'S AMAZING THAT YOU CAN PLAY LIKE THAT!
ふる
FURU
BUT, LIKE... I DIDN'T REALLY FEEL ANY OF YOU IN THE SOUND...
......

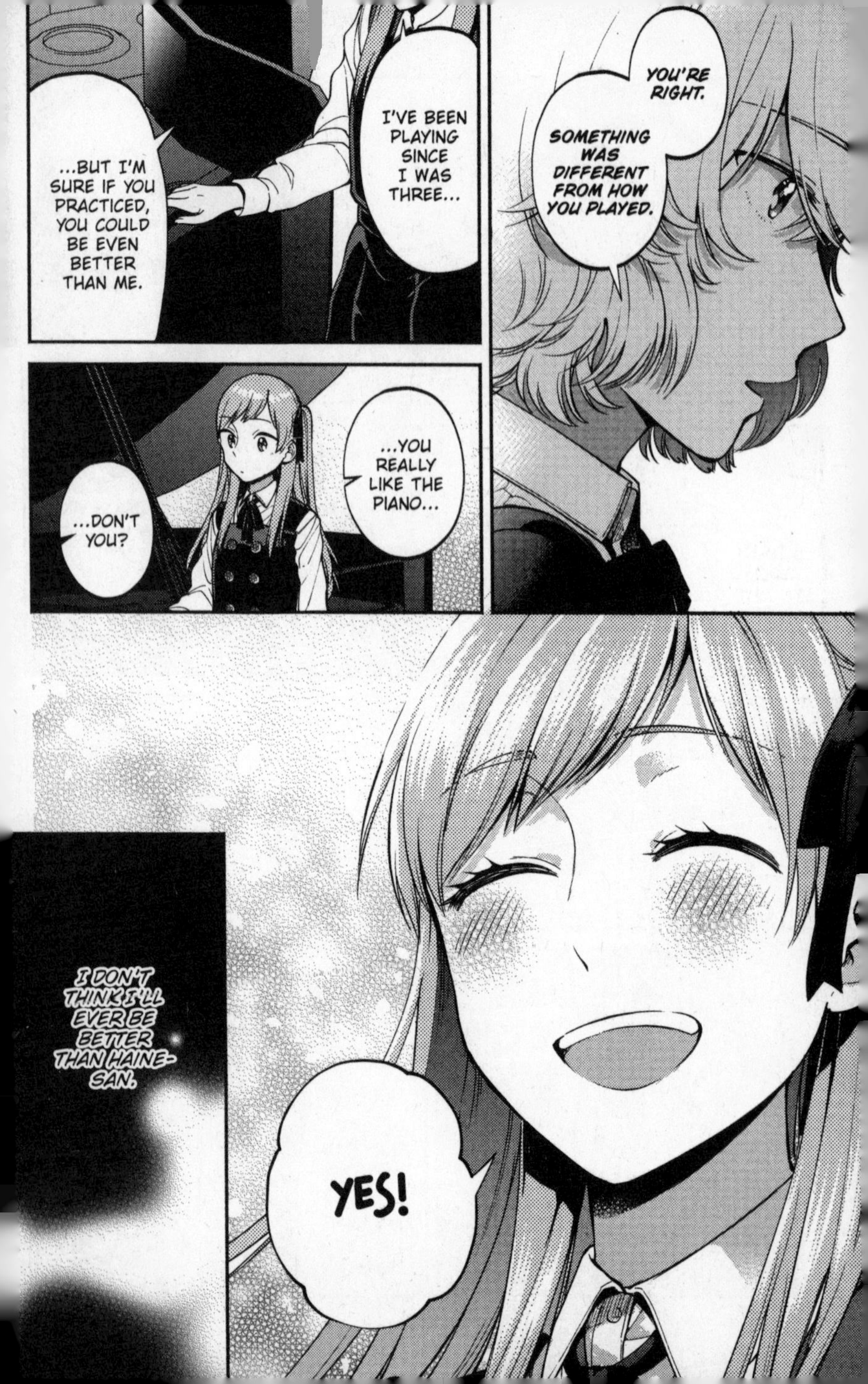
YOU'RE RIGHT.
SOMETHING WAS DIFFERENT FROM HOW YOU PLAYED.
I'VE BEEN PLAYING SINCE I WAS THREE...
...BUT I'M SURE IF YOU PRACTICED, YOU COULD BE EVEN BETTER THAN ME.
...YOU REALLY LIKE THE PIANO...
...DON'T YOU?
YES!
I DON'T THINK I'LL EVER BE BETTER THAN HAINE-SAN.

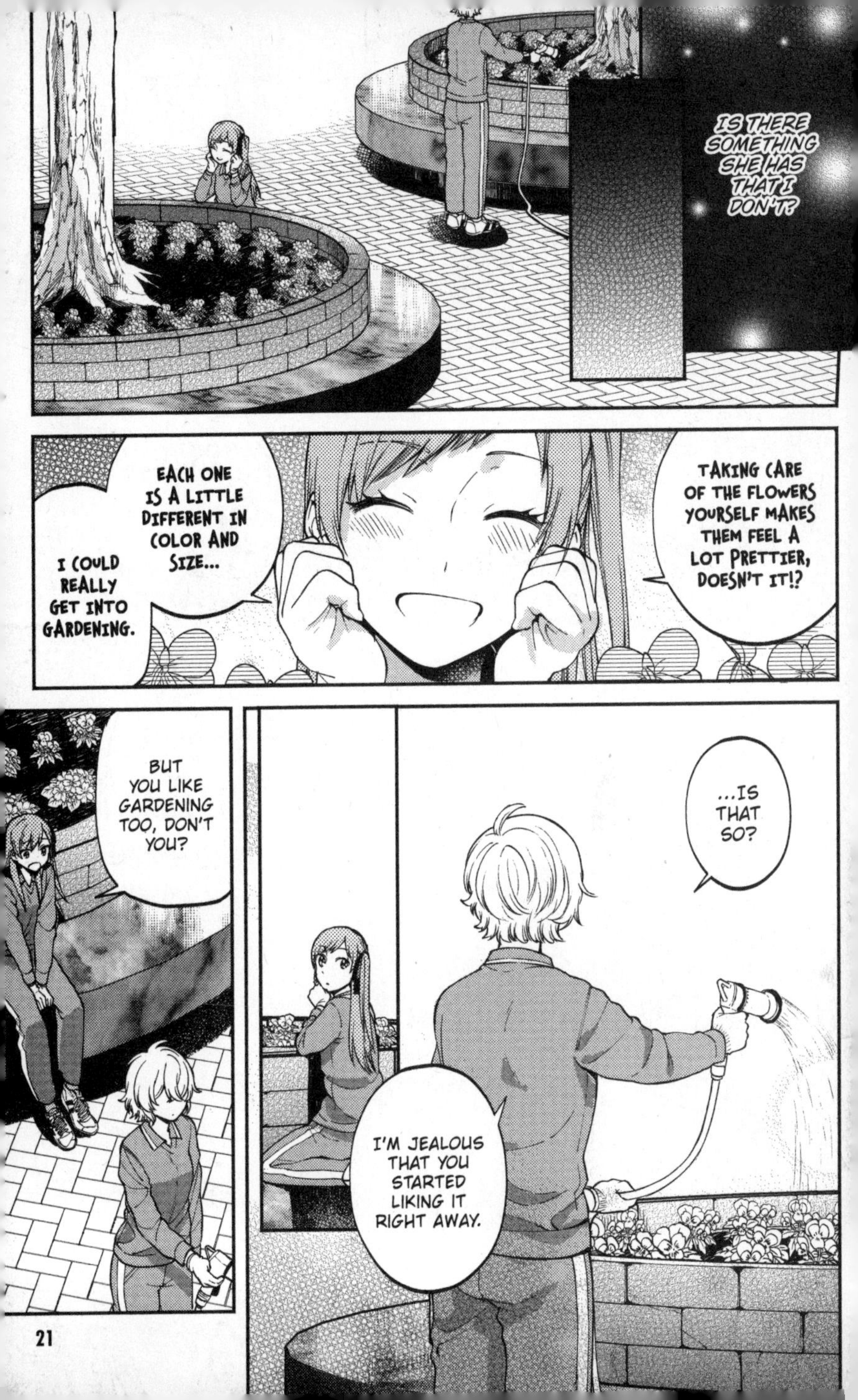
IS THERE SOMETHING SHE HAS THAT I DON'T?
TAKING CARE OF THE FLOWERS YOURSELF MAKES THEM FEEL A LOT PRETTIER, DOESN'T IT!?
EACH ONE IS A LITTLE DIFFERENT IN COLOR AND SIZE...
I COULD REALLY GET INTO GARDENING.
...IS THAT SO?
I'M JEALOUS THAT YOU STARTED LIKING IT RIGHT AWAY.
BUT YOU LIKE GARDENING TOO, DON'T YOU?

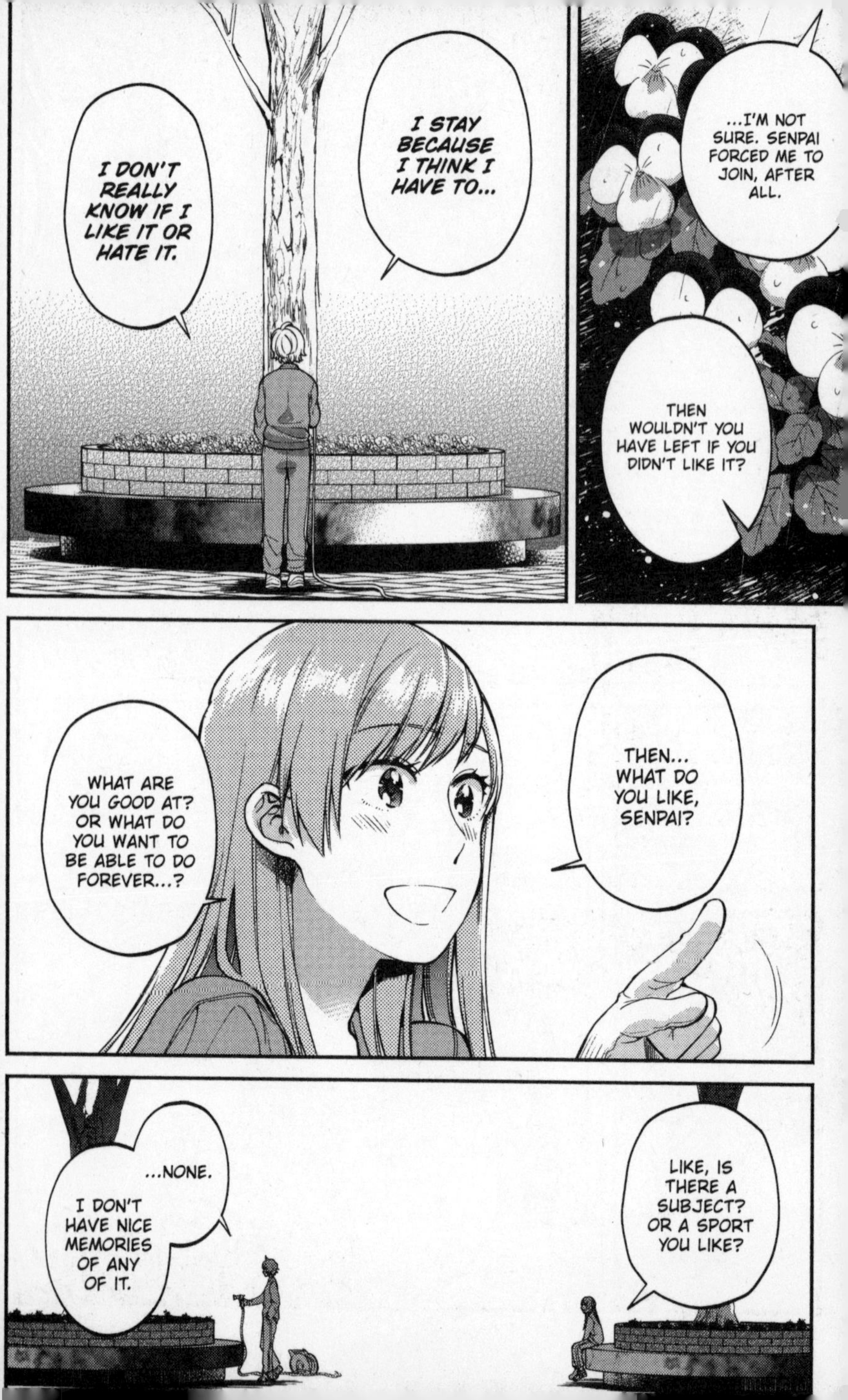
...I'M NOT SURE. SENPAI FORCED ME TO JOIN, AFTER ALL.
THEN WOULDN'T YOU HAVE LEFT IF YOU DIDN'T LIKE IT?
I STAY BECAUSE I THINK I HAVE TO...
I DON'T REALLY KNOW IF I LIKE IT OR HATE IT.
THEN... WHAT DO YOU LIKE, SENPAI?
WHAT ARE YOU GOOD AT? OR WHAT DO YOU WANT TO BE ABLE TO DO FOREVER...?
LIKE, IS THERE A SUBJECT? OR A SPORT YOU LIKE?
...NONE. I DON'T HAVE NICE MEMORIES OF ANY OF IT.

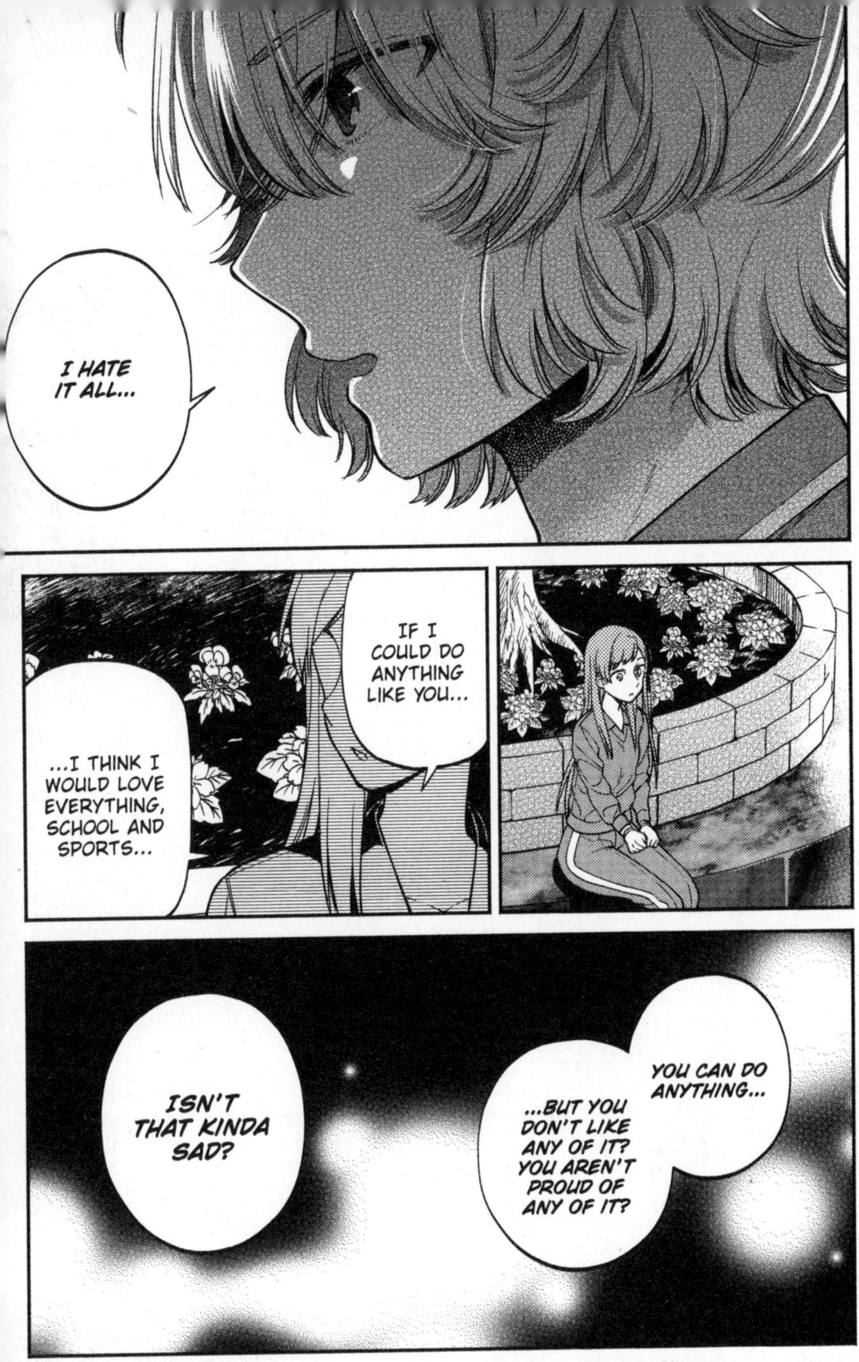
I HATE IT ALL...
IF I COULD DO ANYTHING LIKE YOU...
...I THINK I WOULD LOVE EVERYTHING, SCHOOL AND SPORTS...
YOU CAN DO ANYTHING...
...BUT YOU DON'T LIKE ANY OF IT? YOU AREN'T PROUD OF ANY OF IT?
ISN'T THAT KINDA SAD?

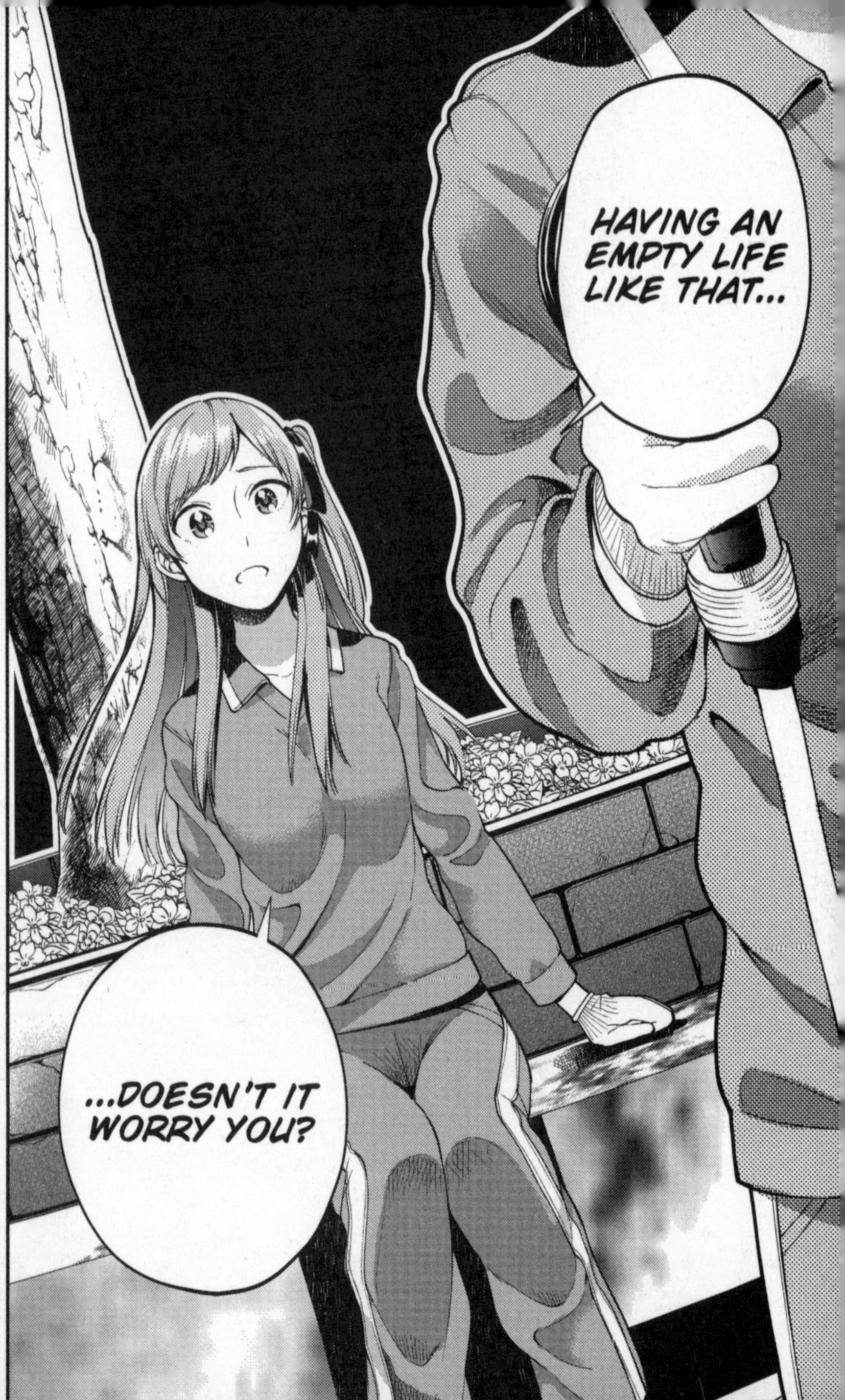
HAVING AN EMPTY LIFE LIKE THAT...
...DOESN'T IT WORRY YOU?

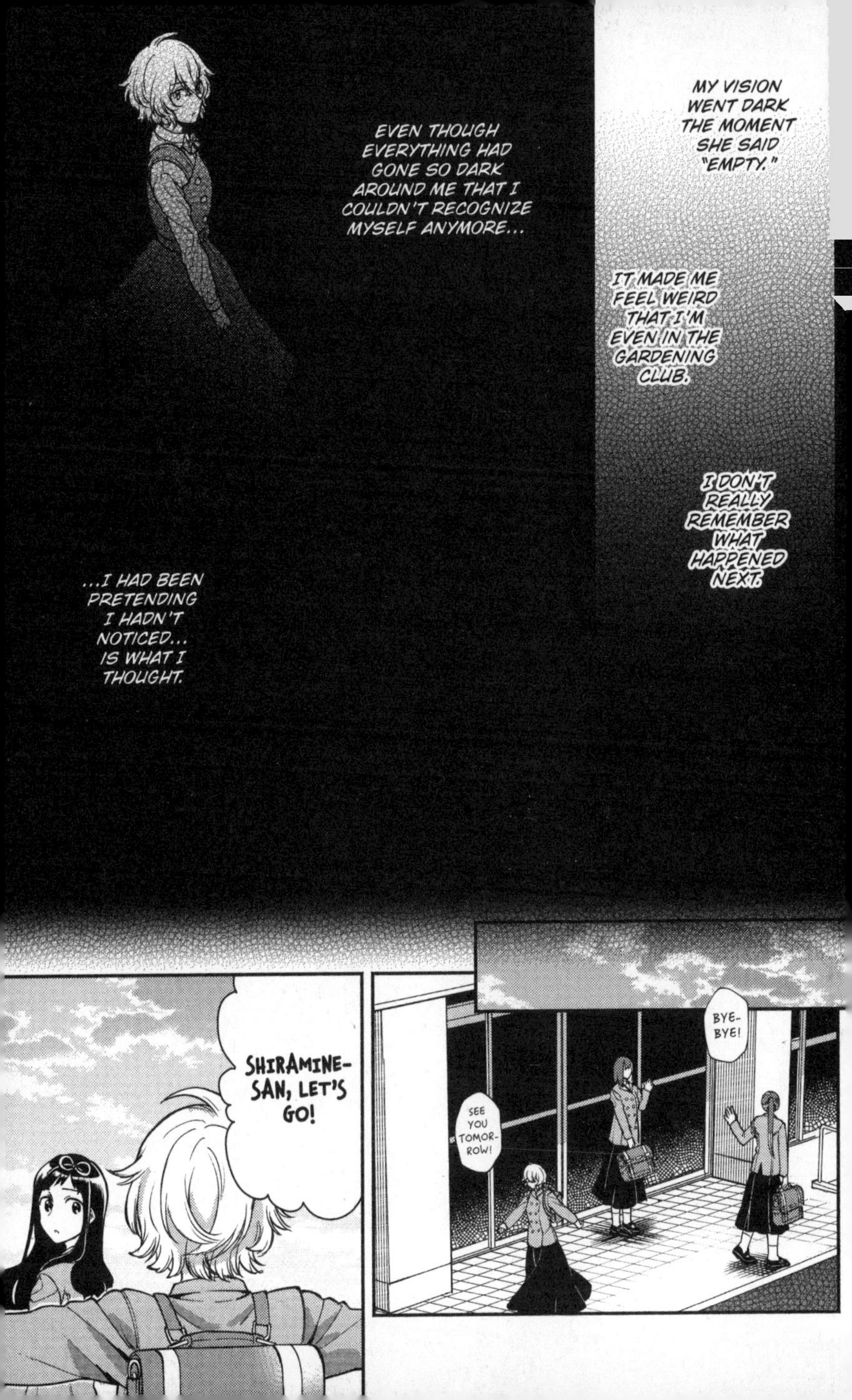
MY VISION WENT DARK THE MOMENT SHE SAID "EMPTY."
IT MADE ME FEEL WEIRD THAT I'M EVEN IN THE GARDENING CLUB.
I DON'T REALLY REMEMBER WHAT HAPPENED NEXT.
EVEN THOUGH EVERYTHING HAD GONE SO DARK AROUND ME THAT I COULDN'T RECOGNIZE MYSELF ANYMORE...
...I HAD BEEN PRETENDING I HADN'T NOTICED... IS WHAT I THOUGHT.
BYE-BYE!
SEE YOU TOMORROW!
SHIRAMINE-SAN, LET'S GO!

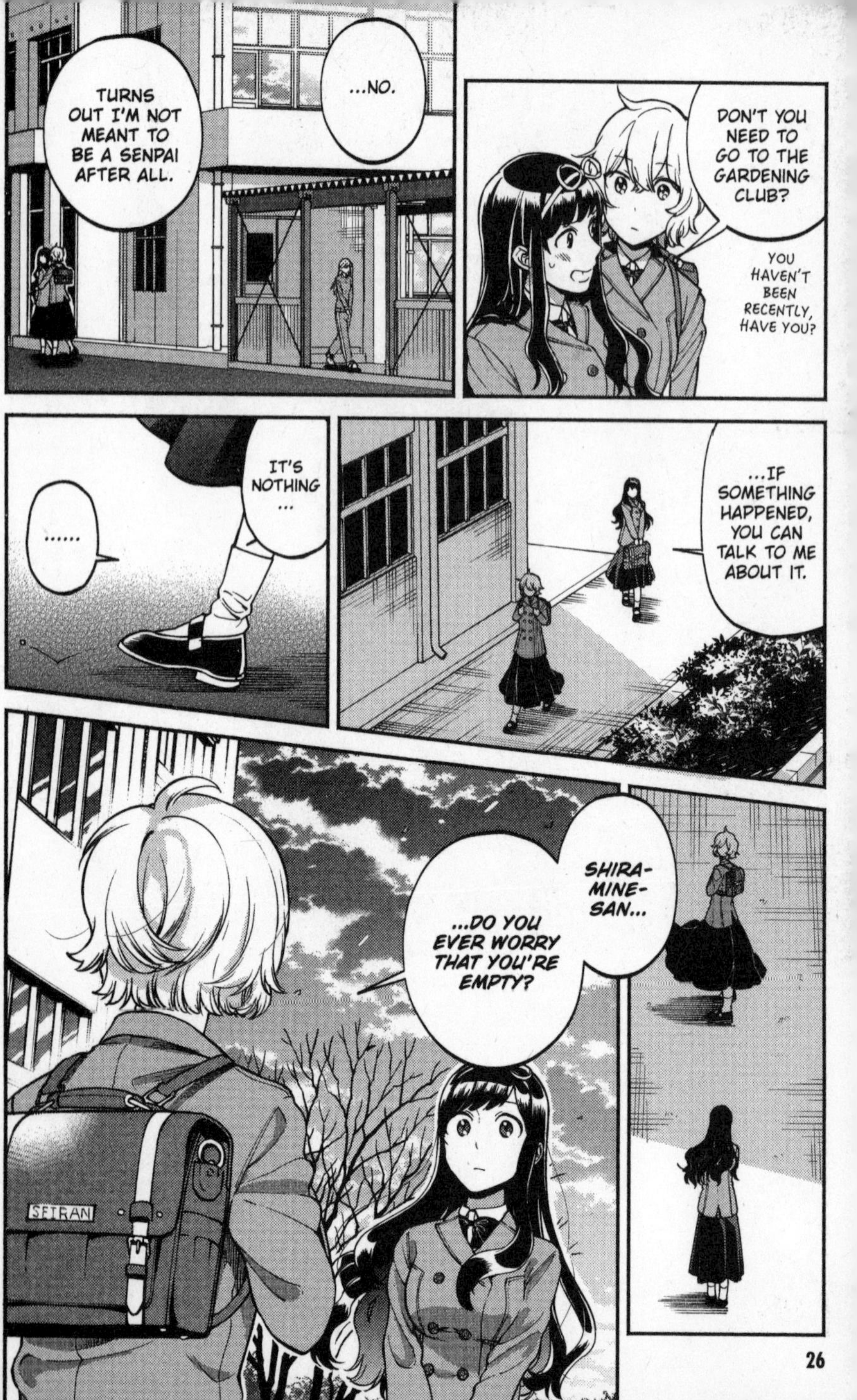
DON'T YOU NEED TO GO TO THE GARDENING CLUB?
YOU HAVEN'T BEEN RECENTLY, HAVE YOU?
...NO.
TURNS OUT I'M NOT MEANT TO BE A SENPAI AFTER ALL.
...IF SOMETHING HAPPENED, YOU CAN TALK TO ME ABOUT IT.
IT'S NOTHING ...
......
SHIRA-MINE-SAN...
...DO YOU EVER WORRY THAT YOU'RE EMPTY?
SEIRAN

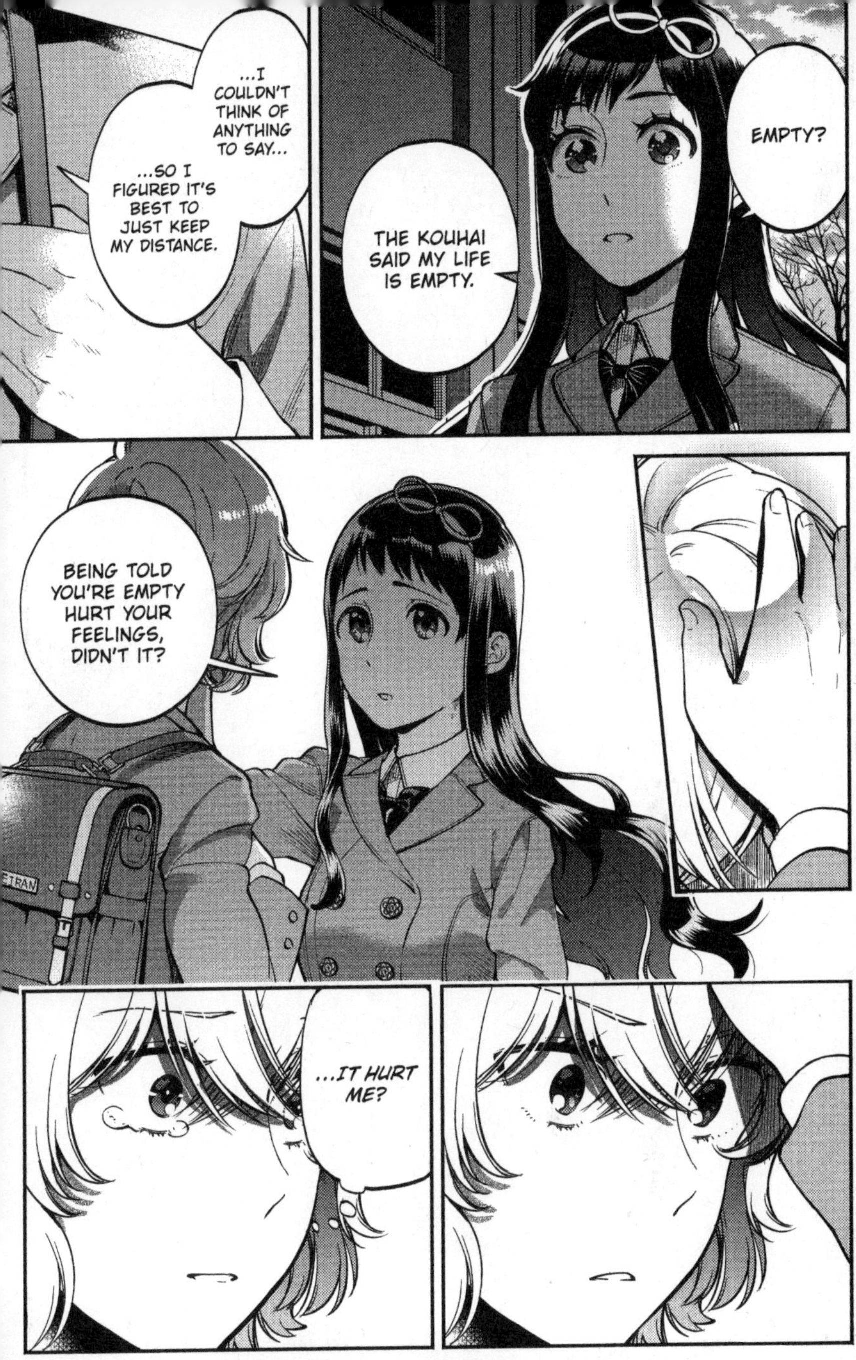
EMPTY?
THE KOUHAI SAID MY LIFE IS EMPTY.
...I COULDN'T THINK OF ANYTHING TO SAY...
...SO I FIGURED IT'S BEST TO JUST KEEP MY DISTANCE.
BEING TOLD YOU'RE EMPTY HURT YOUR FEELINGS, DIDN'T IT?
...IT HURT ME?

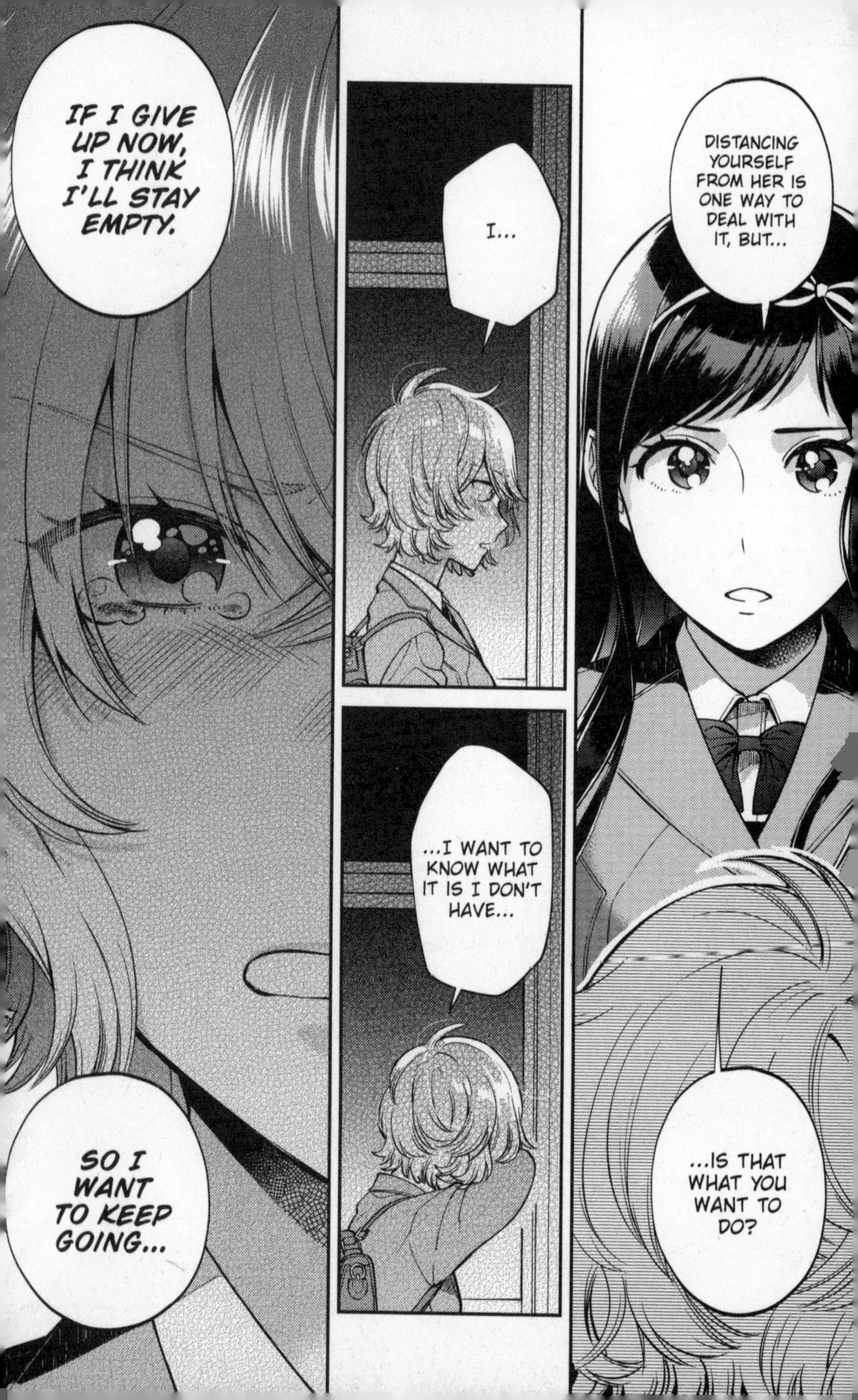
DISTANCING YOURSELF FROM HER IS ONE WAY TO DEAL WITH IT, BUT...
...IS THAT WHAT YOU WANT TO DO?
I...
...I WANT TO KNOW WHAT IT IS I DON'T HAVE...
IF I GIVE UP NOW, I THINK I'LL STAY EMPTY.
SO I WANT TO KEEP GOING...

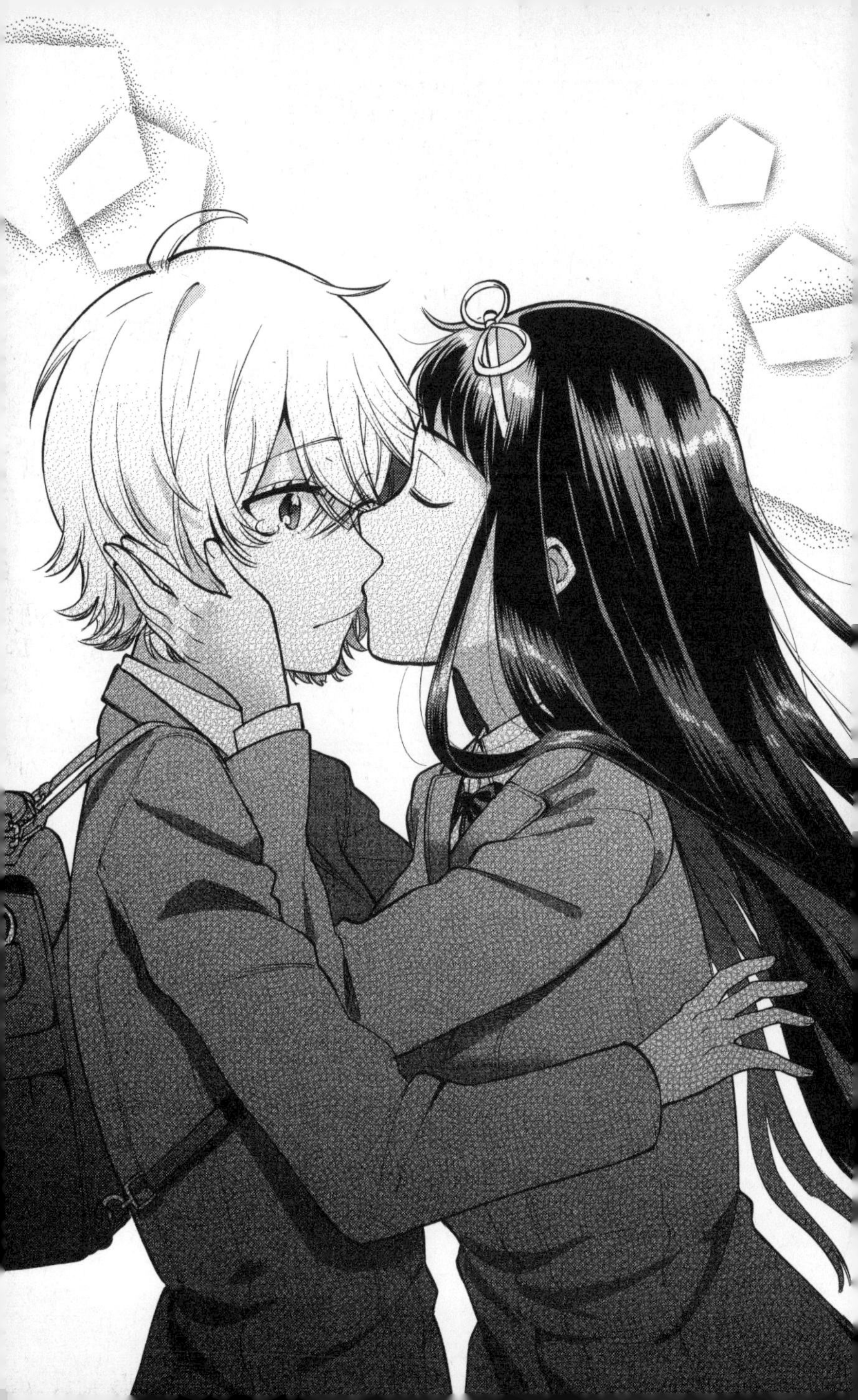

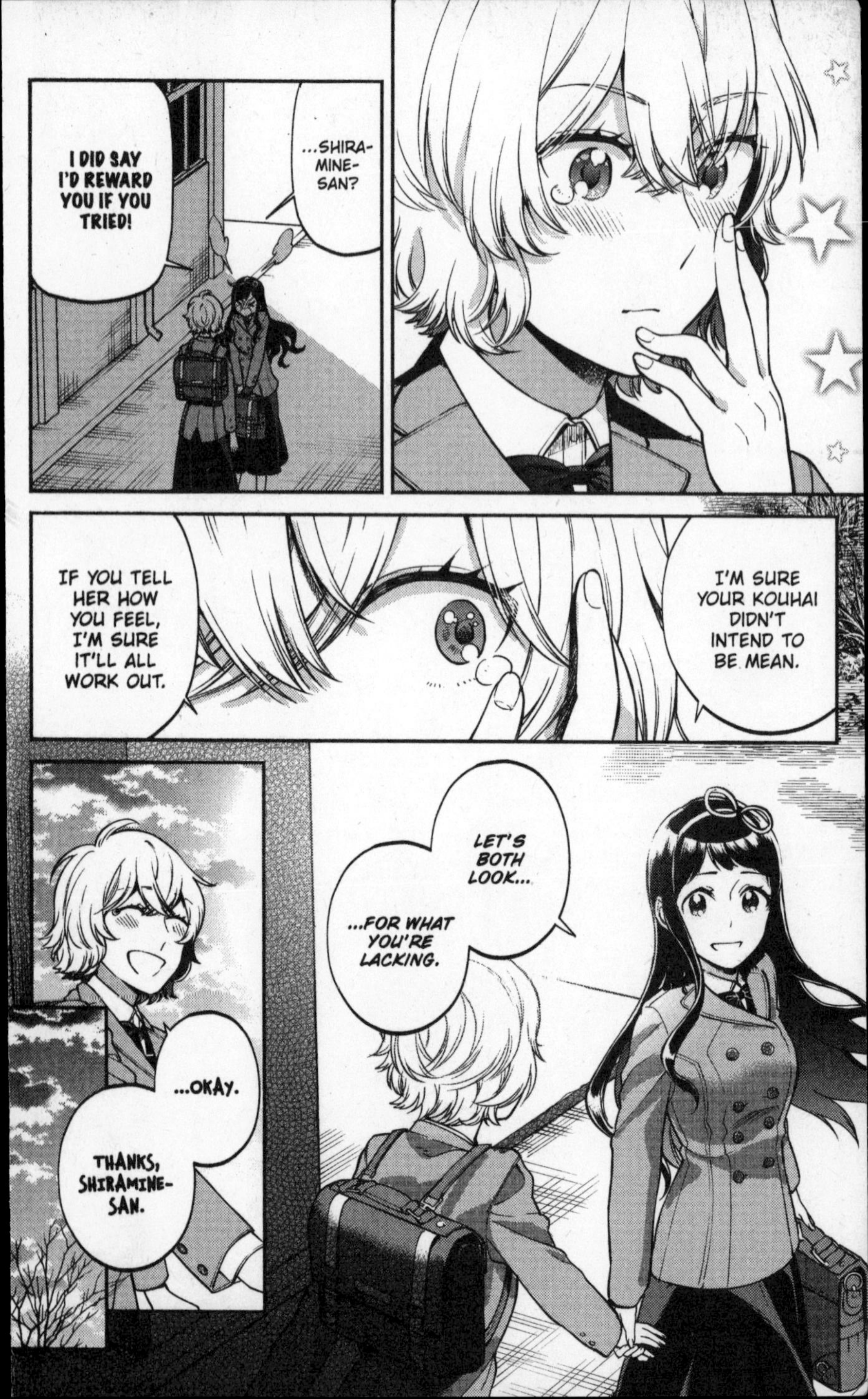
...SHIRA-MINE-SAN?
I DID SAY I'D REWARD YOU IF YOU TRIED!
I'M SURE YOUR KOUHAI DIDN'T INTEND TO BE MEAN.
IF YOU TELL HER HOW YOU FEEL, I'M SURE IT'LL ALL WORK OUT.
LET'S BOTH LOOK...
...FOR WHAT YOU'RE LACKING.
...OKAY.
THANKS, SHIRAMINE-SAN.

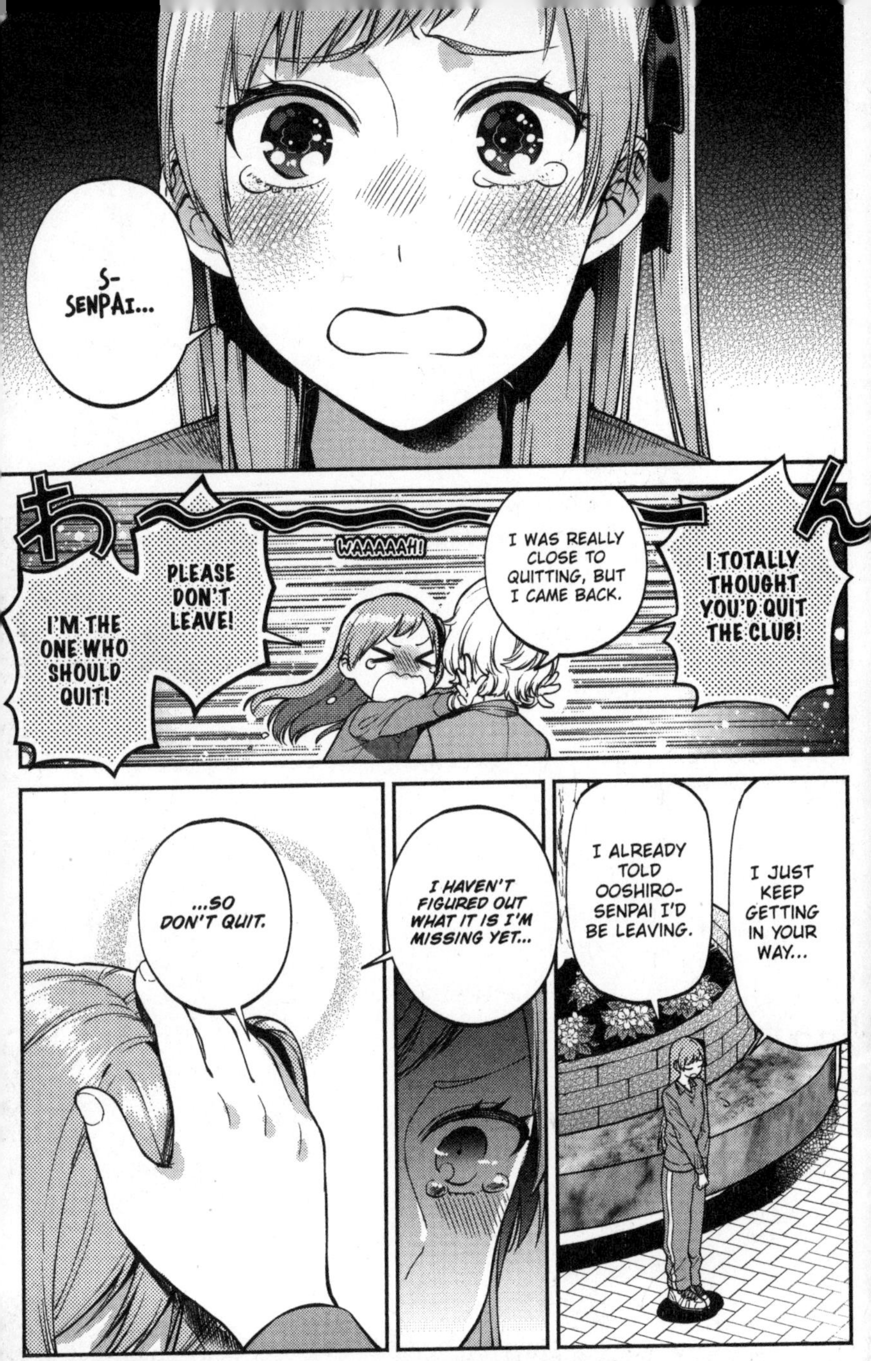
S-SENPAI...
わ〜〜〜ん
I TOTALLY THOUGHT YOU'D QUIT THE CLUB!
I WAS REALLY CLOSE TO QUITTING, BUT I CAME BACK.
WAAAAAH!
PLEASE DON'T LEAVE!
I'M THE ONE WHO SHOULD QUIT!
I JUST KEEP GETTING IN YOUR WAY...
I ALREADY TOLD OOSHIRO-SENPAI I'D BE LEAVING.
I HAVEN'T FIGURED OUT WHAT IT IS I'M MISSING YET...
...SO DON'T QUIT.

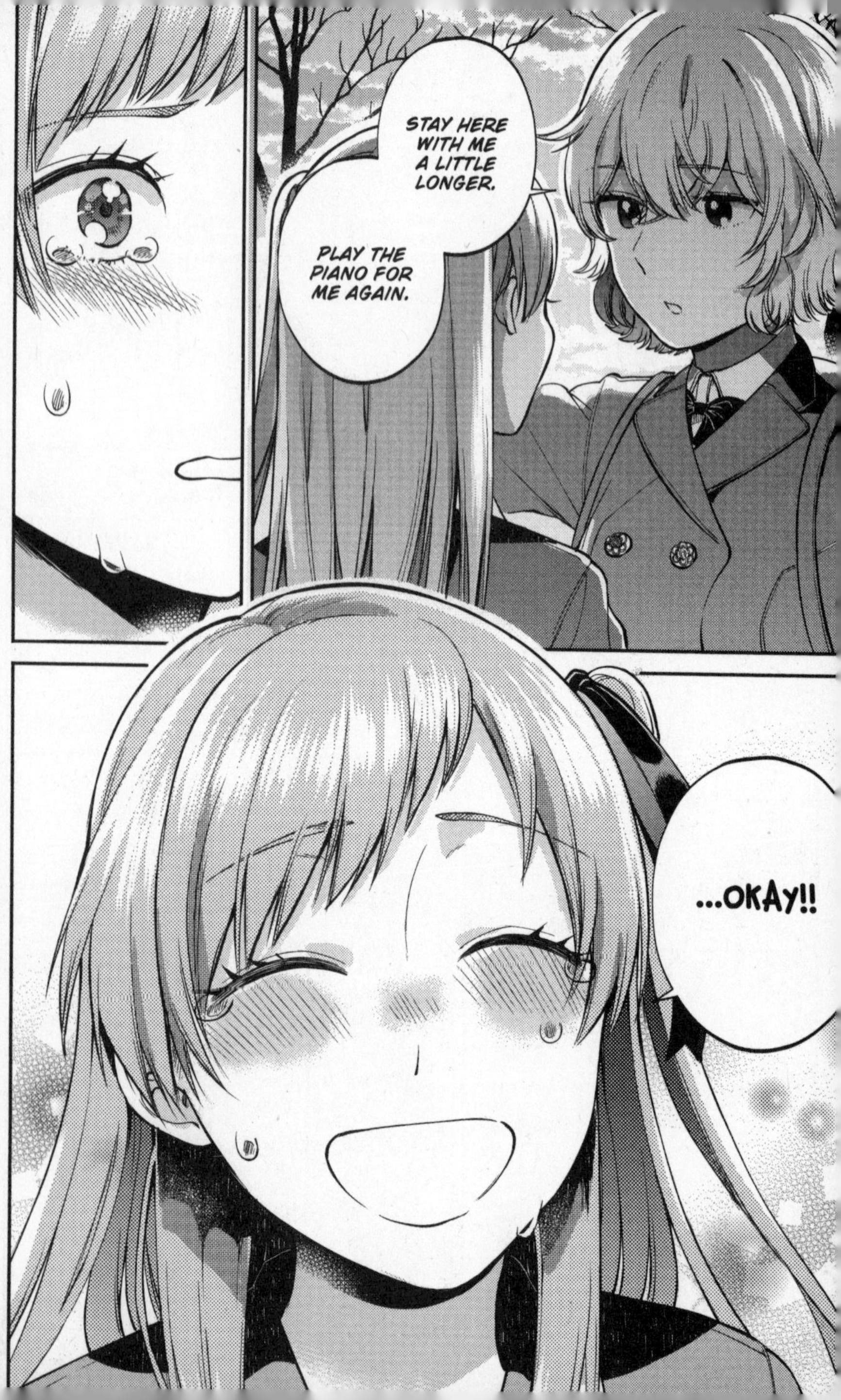
STAY HERE WITH ME A LITTLE LONGER.
PLAY THE PIANO FOR ME AGAIN.
...OKAY!!

The Phantom Person

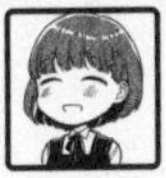

SAORI
MIDDLE SCHOOL SECOND-YEAR. MEMBER OF THE LITERATURE CLUB.

KISS THEATER: WHAT'S BEHIND THE STORY!? ✷ PEOPLE OTHER THAN THE MAIN CHARACTERS HAVE STORIES TOO. HERE, WE PRESENT THE "LITTLE LOVE" STORIES HAPPENING BEHIND THE SCENES.

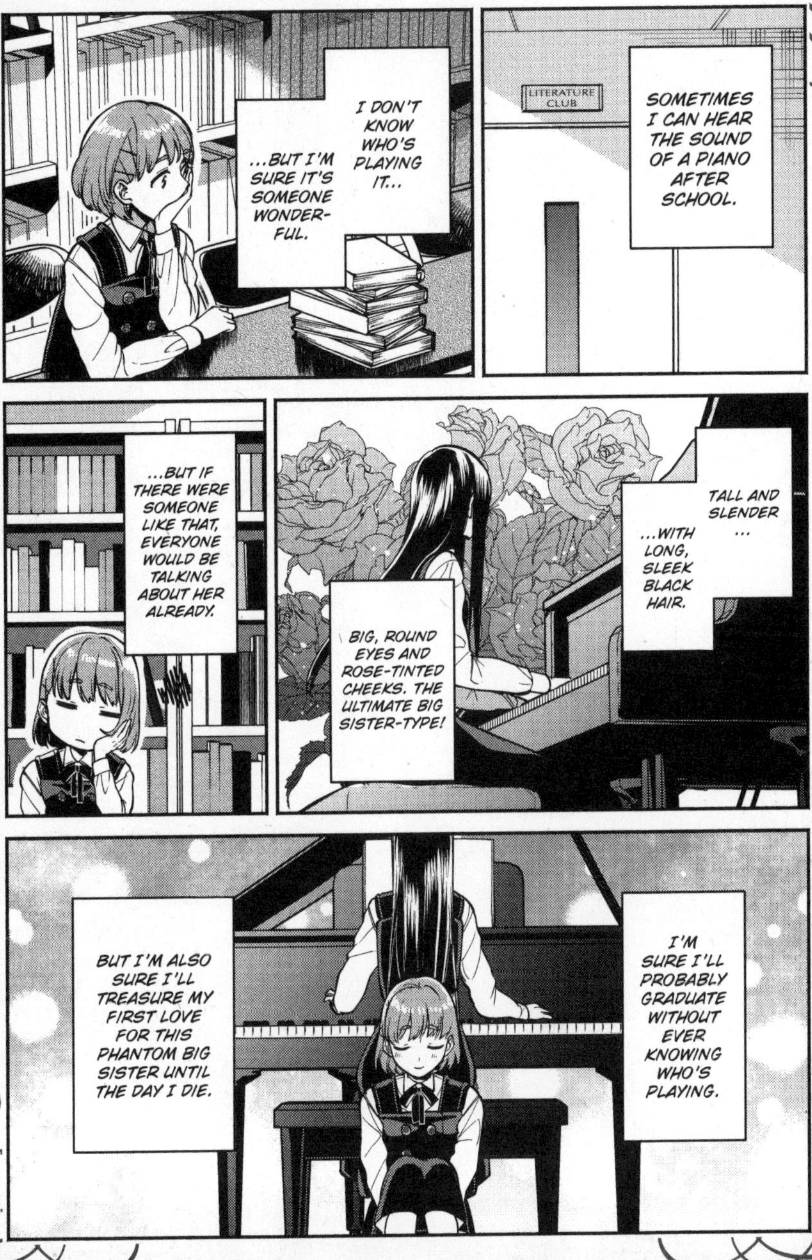
LITERATURE CLUB
SOMETIMES I CAN HEAR THE SOUND OF A PIANO AFTER SCHOOL.
I DON'T KNOW WHO'S PLAYING IT...
...BUT I'M SURE IT'S SOMEONE WONDERFUL.
TALL AND SLENDER...
...WITH LONG, SLEEK BLACK HAIR.
BIG, ROUND EYES AND ROSE-TINTED CHEEKS. THE ULTIMATE BIG SISTER-TYPE!
...BUT IF THERE WERE SOMEONE LIKE THAT, EVERYONE WOULD BE TALKING ABOUT HER ALREADY.
I'M SURE I'LL PROBABLY GRADUATE WITHOUT EVER KNOWING WHO'S PLAYING.
BUT I'M ALSO SURE I'LL TREASURE MY FIRST LOVE FOR THIS PHANTOM BIG SISTER UNTIL THE DAY I DIE.

Haine Aoi

Haine Aoi

Second-year student in the Seiran Academy Middle School. Member of the gardening club. She's a limited prodigy who is exceptional at the piano but hopeless at school and sports. Her family, especially her aunt Aika, cares for her very much, but she wants to be independent. Her skill at the piano is truly outstanding, and she has a history of winning prizes in competitions against people older than her.

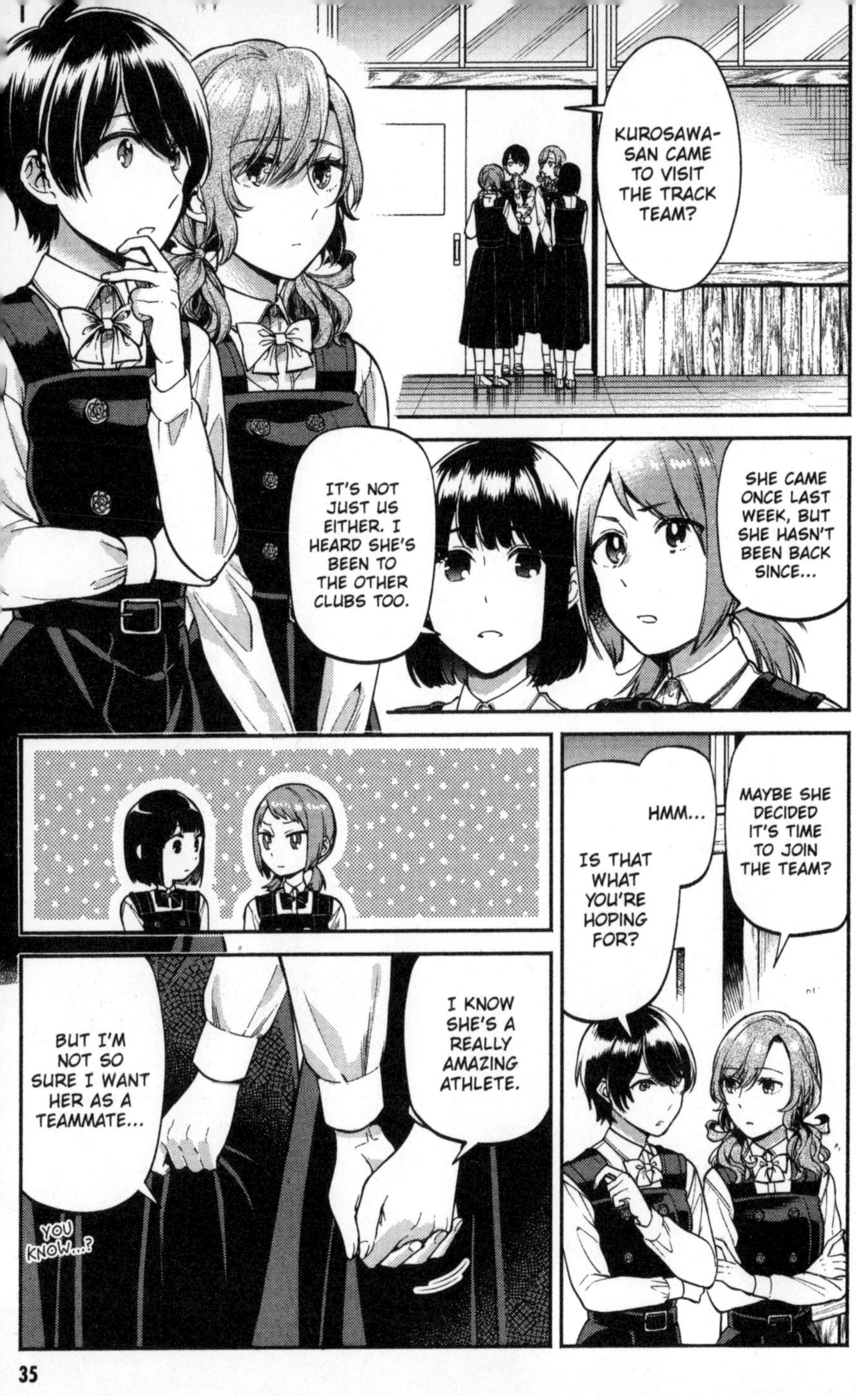
KUROSAWA-SAN CAME TO VISIT THE TRACK TEAM?
SHE CAME ONCE LAST WEEK, BUT SHE HASN'T BEEN BACK SINCE...
IT'S NOT JUST US EITHER. I HEARD SHE'S BEEN TO THE OTHER CLUBS TOO.
MAYBE SHE DECIDED IT'S TIME TO JOIN THE TEAM?
HMM...
IS THAT WHAT YOU'RE HOPING FOR?
I KNOW SHE'S A REALLY AMAZING ATHLETE.
BUT I'M NOT SO SURE I WANT HER AS A TEAMMATE...
YOU KNOW...?

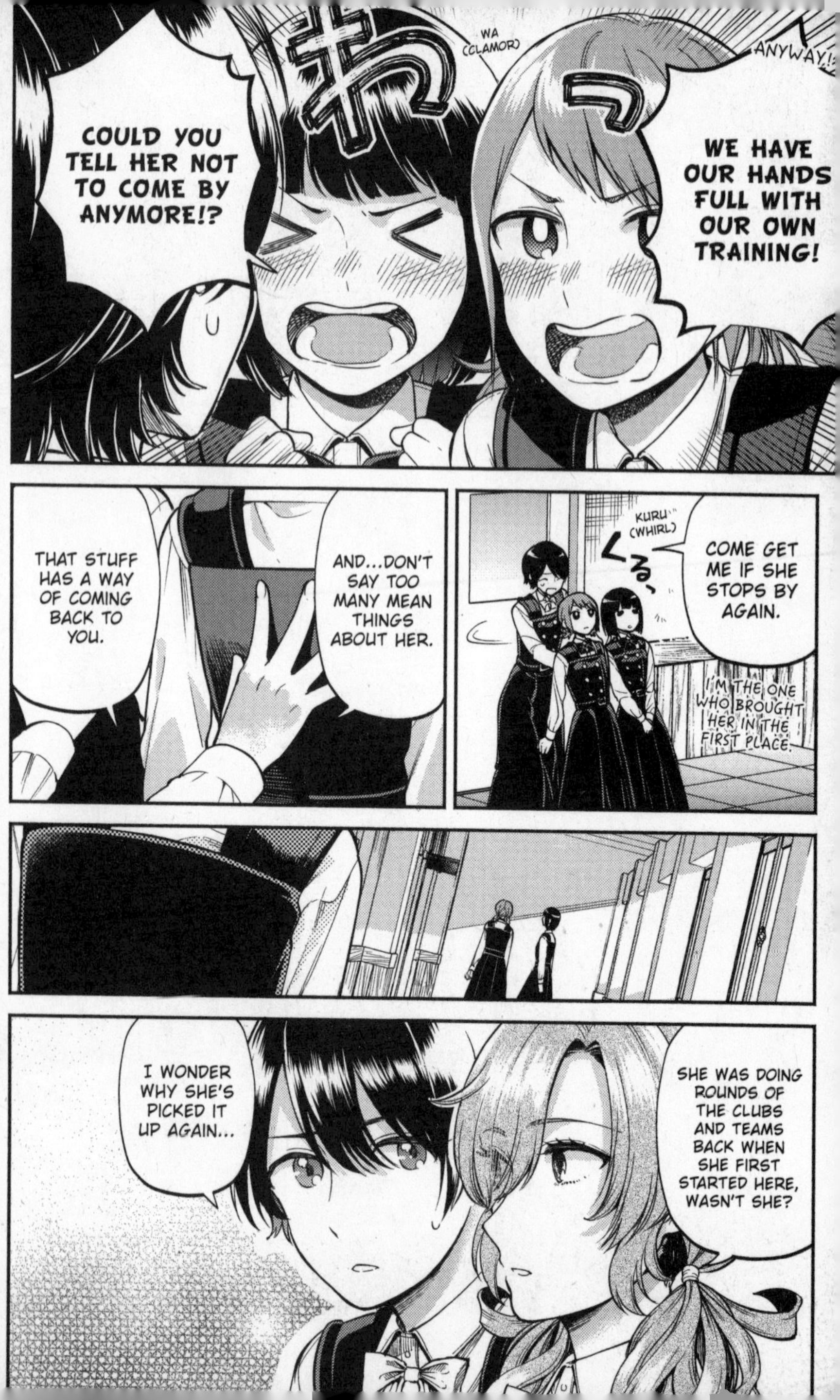
ANYWAY!!
WE HAVE OUR HANDS FULL WITH OUR OWN TRAINING!
WA (CLAMOR)
わっ
COULD YOU TELL HER NOT TO COME BY ANYMORE!?
KURU (WHIRL)
くる
COME GET ME IF SHE STOPS BY AGAIN.
I'M THE ONE WHO BROUGHT HER IN THE FIRST PLACE.
AND...DON'T SAY TOO MANY MEAN THINGS ABOUT HER.
THAT STUFF HAS A WAY OF COMING BACK TO YOU.
SHE WAS DOING ROUNDS OF THE CLUBS AND TEAMS BACK WHEN SHE FIRST STARTED HERE, WASN'T SHE?
I WONDER WHY SHE'S PICKED IT UP AGAIN...

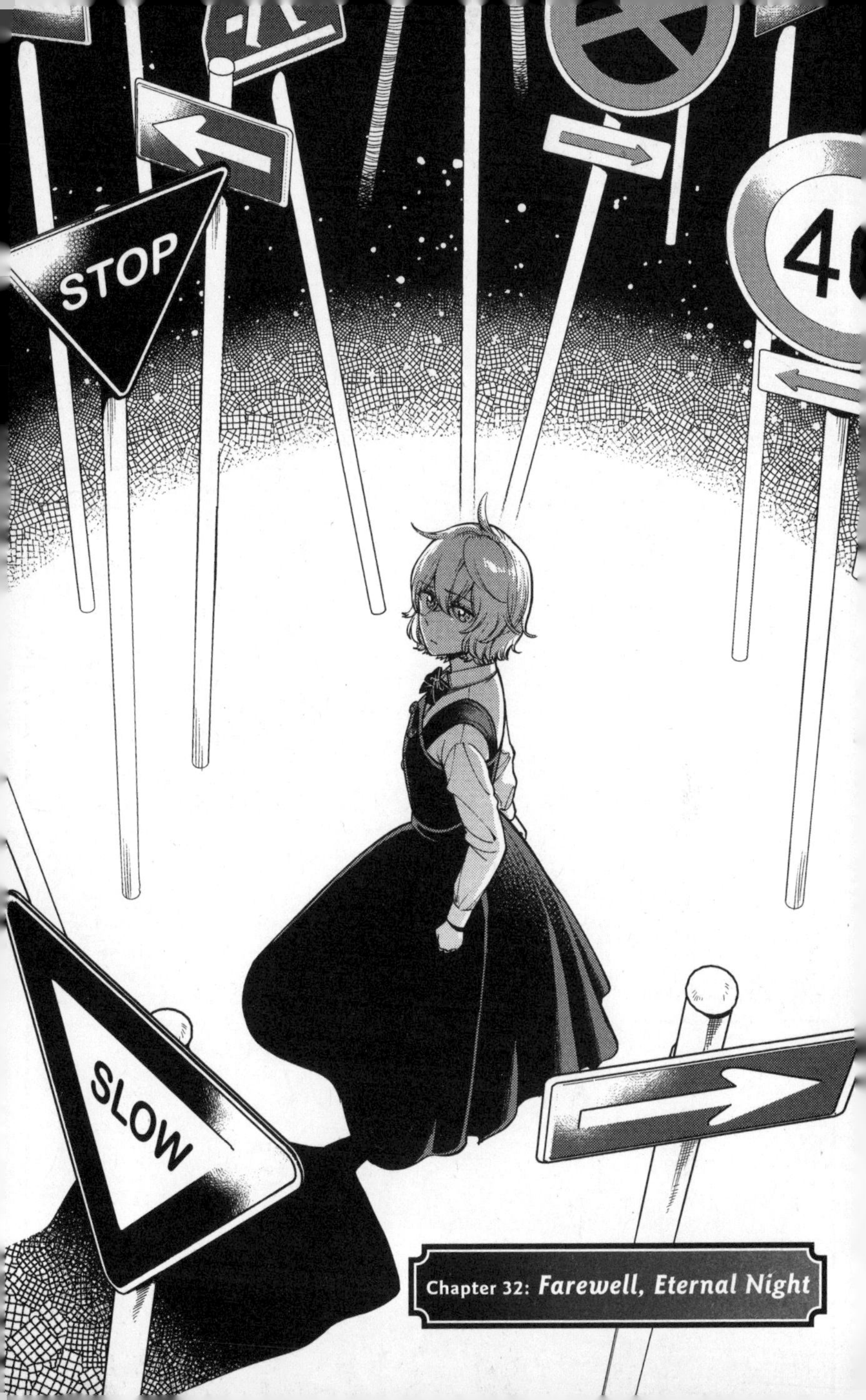
STOP
40
SLOW

Chapter 32: *Farewell, Eternal Night*

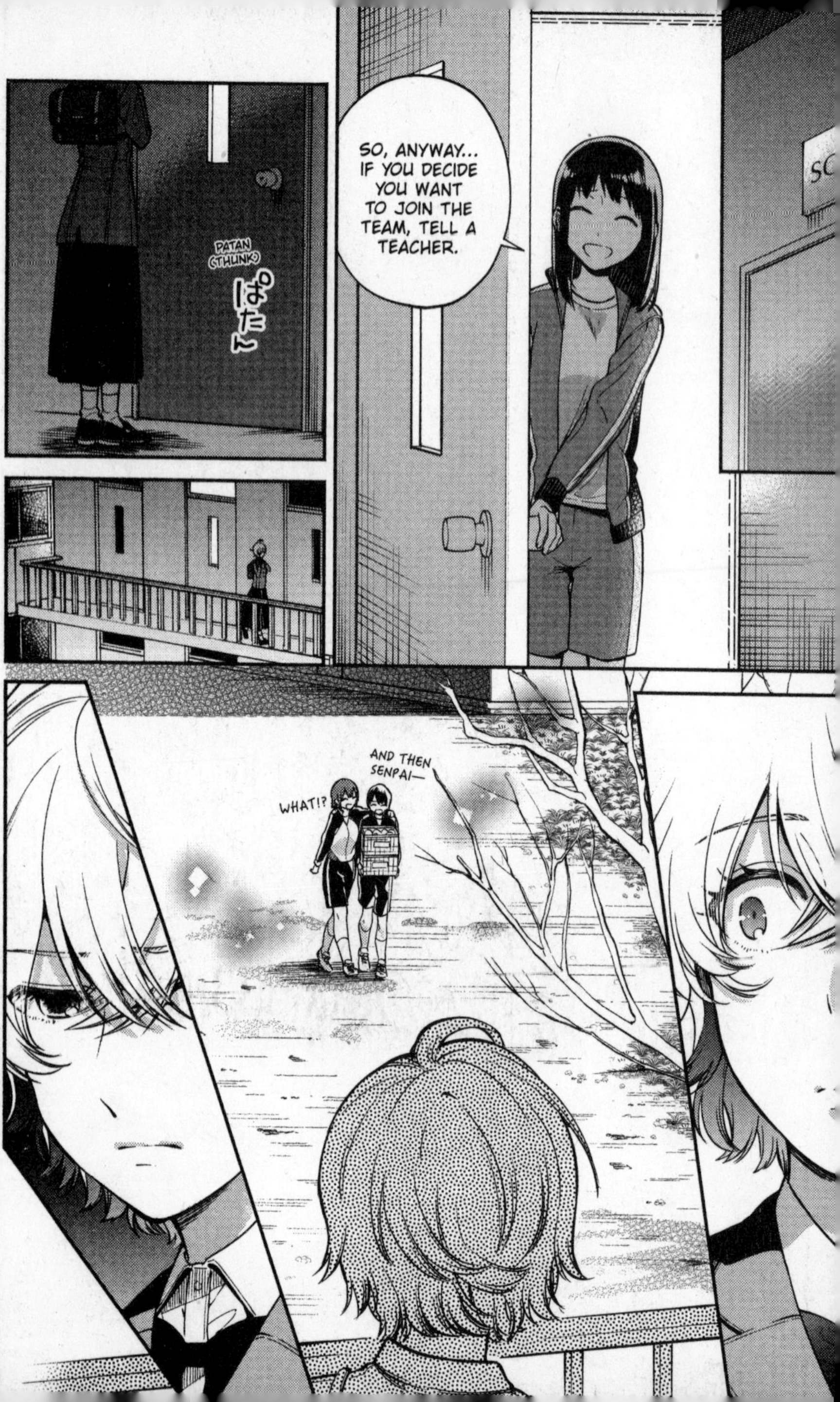

SO, ANYWAY... IF YOU DECIDE YOU WANT TO JOIN THE TEAM, TELL A TEACHER.
PATAN (THUNK)
ぱたん
AND THEN SENPAI—
WHAT!?

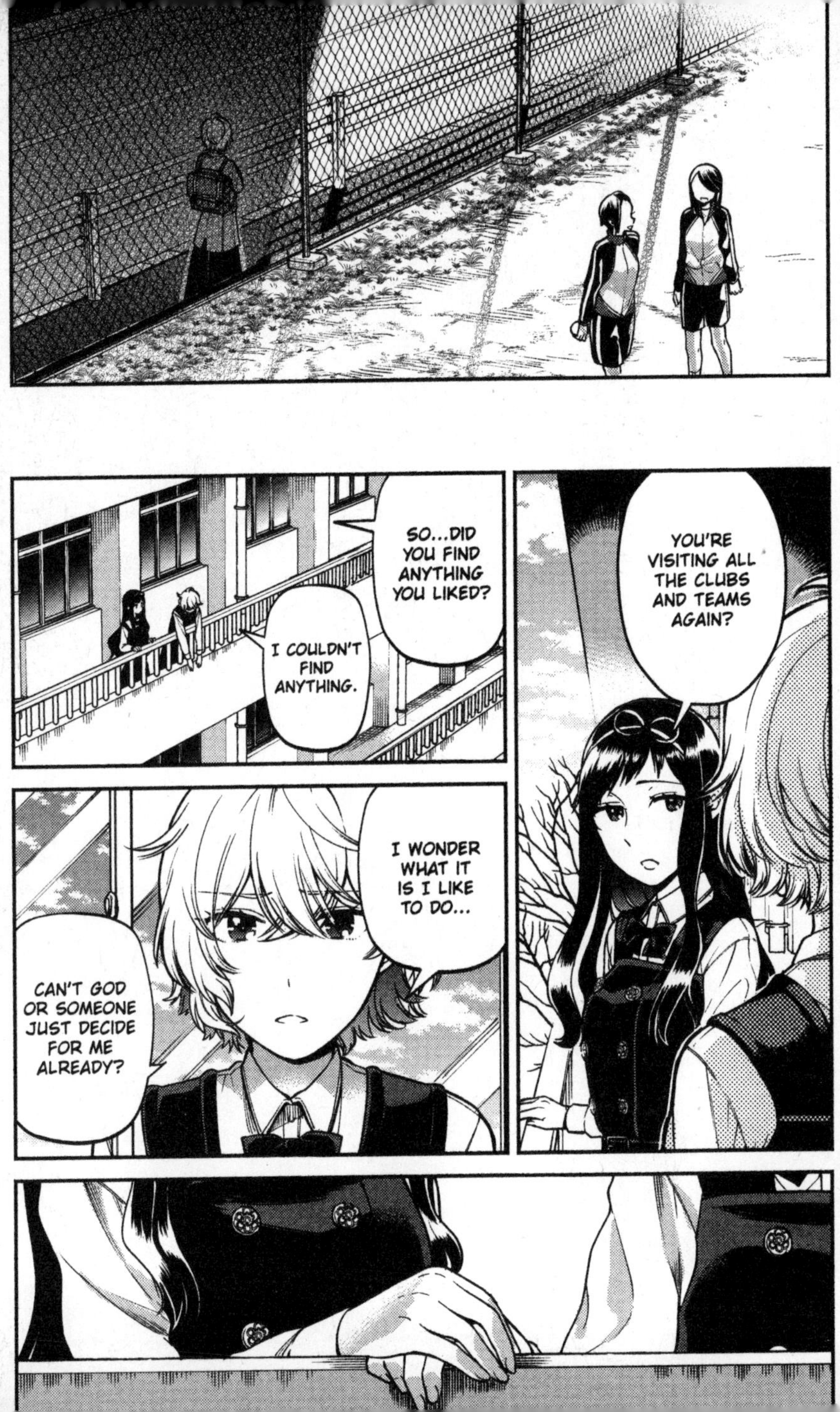
YOU'RE VISITING ALL THE CLUBS AND TEAMS AGAIN?
SO...DID YOU FIND ANYTHING YOU LIKED?
I COULDN'T FIND ANYTHING.
I WONDER WHAT IT IS I LIKE TO DO...
CAN'T GOD OR SOMEONE JUST DECIDE FOR ME ALREADY?

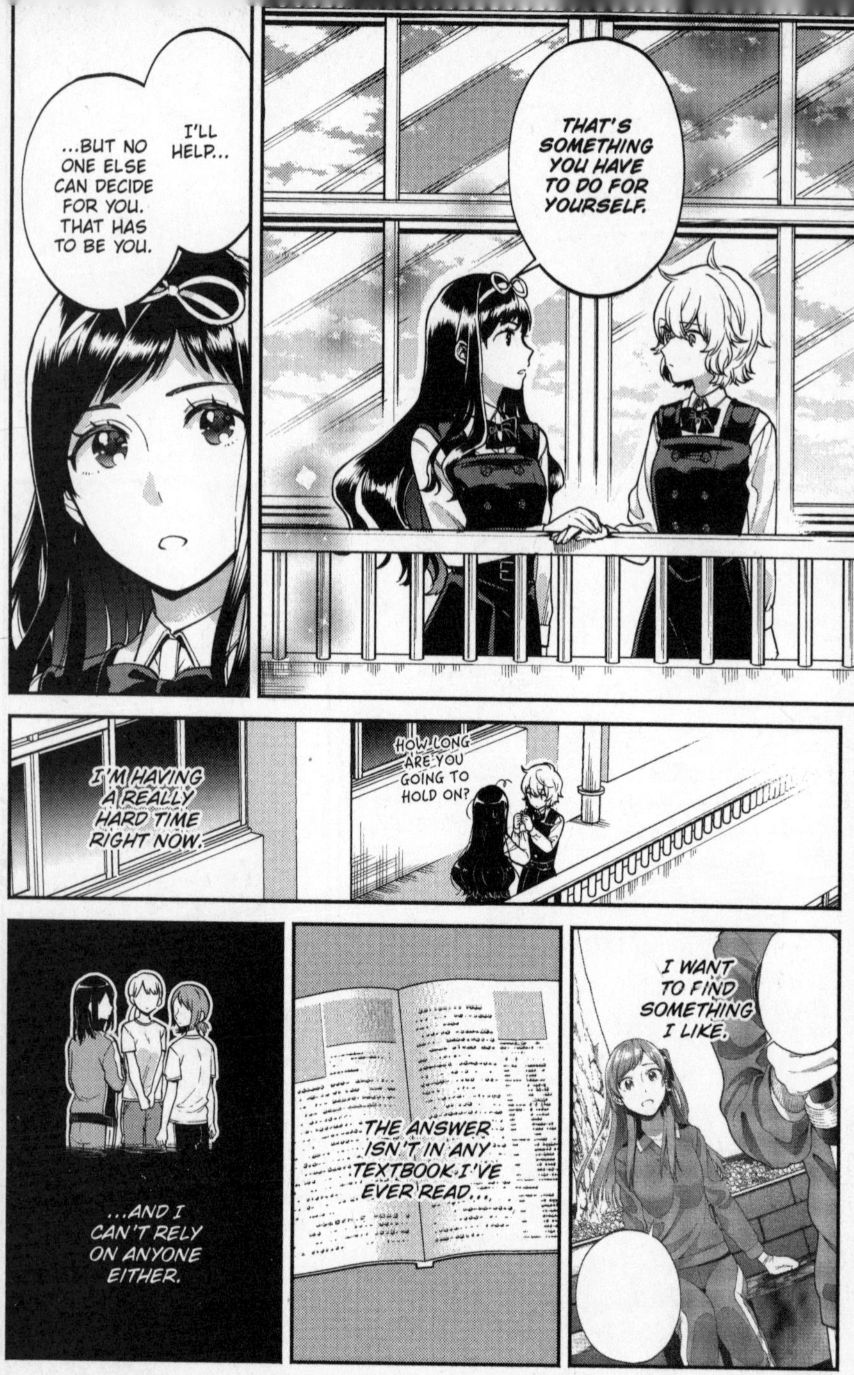
THAT'S SOMETHING YOU HAVE TO DO FOR YOURSELF.
I'LL HELP...
...BUT NO ONE ELSE CAN DECIDE FOR YOU. THAT HAS TO BE YOU.
HOW LONG ARE YOU GOING TO HOLD ON?
I'M HAVING A REALLY HARD TIME RIGHT NOW.
I WANT TO FIND SOMETHING I LIKE.
THE ANSWER ISN'T IN ANY TEXTBOOK I'VE EVER READ...
...AND I CAN'T RELY ON ANYONE EITHER.

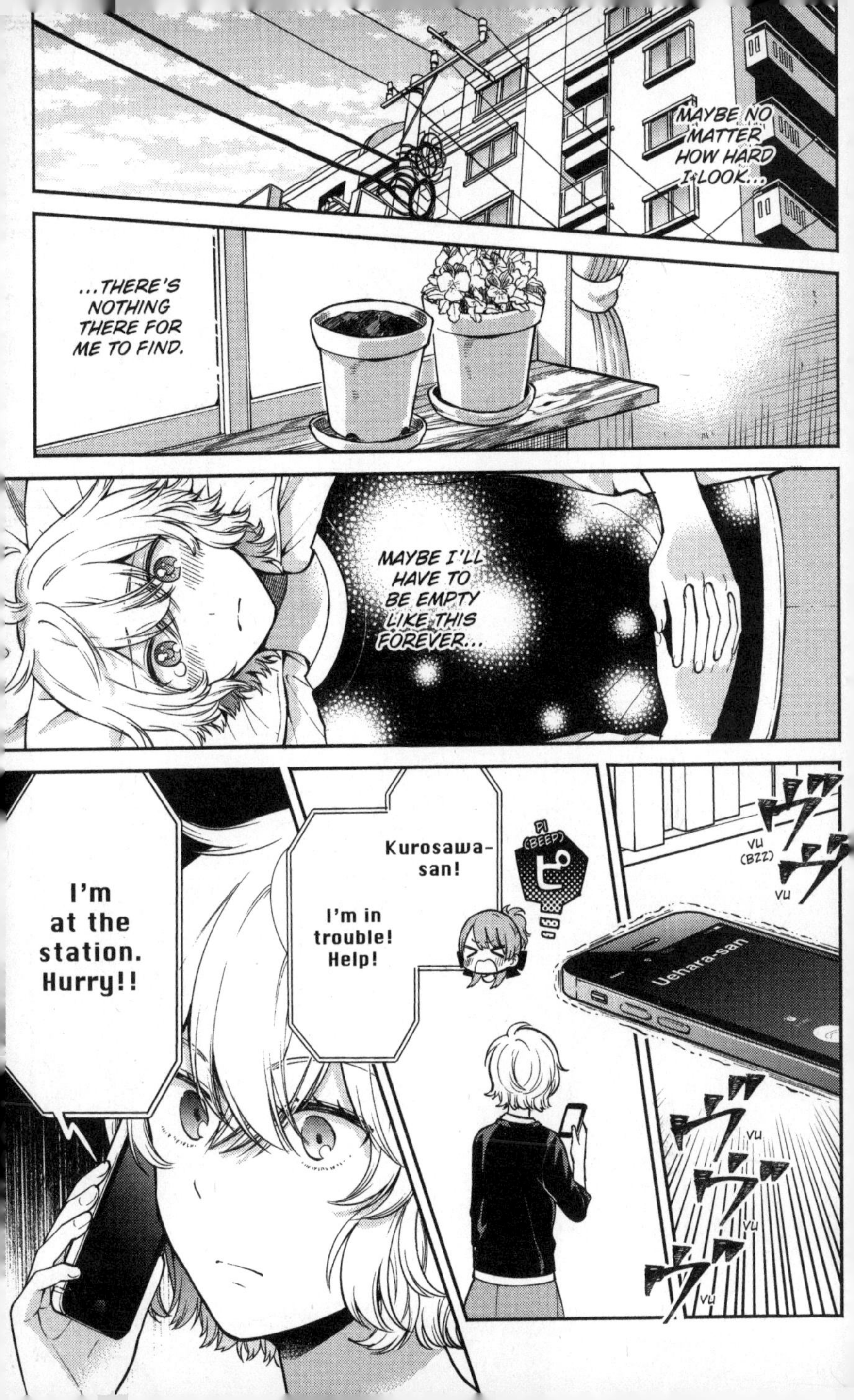
MAYBE NO MATTER HOW HARD I LOOK...
...THERE'S NOTHING THERE FOR ME TO FIND.
MAYBE I'LL HAVE TO BE EMPTY LIKE THIS FOREVER...
VU (BZZ)
VU
Uehara-San
VU
VU
VU
PI (BEEP)
Kurosawa-san!
I'm in trouble! Help!
I'm at the station. Hurry!!

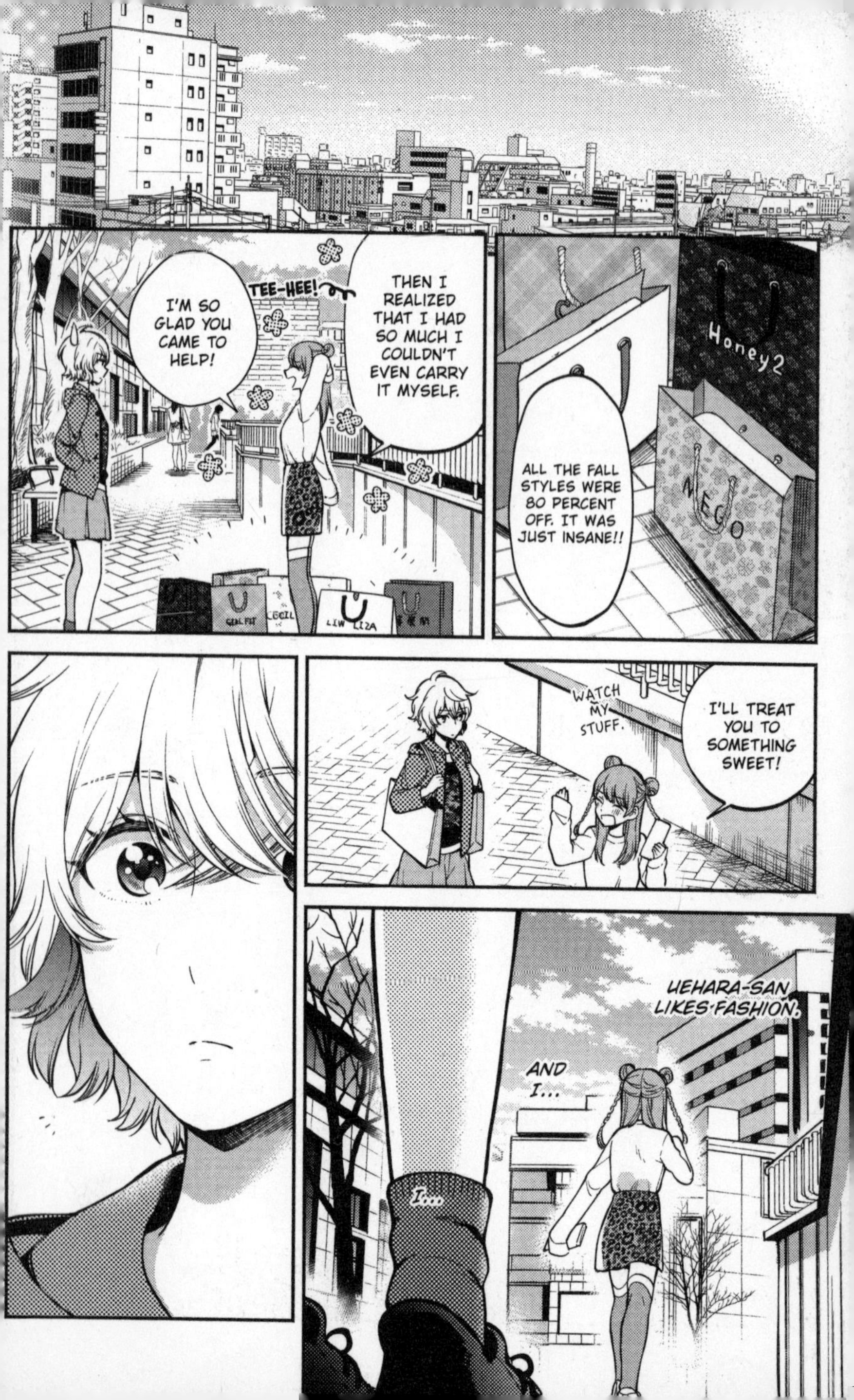
ALL THE FALL STYLES WERE 80 PERCENT OFF. IT WAS JUST INSANE!!
Honey2
NEGO
THEN I REALIZED THAT I HAD SO MUCH I COULDN'T EVEN CARRY IT MYSELF.
TEE-HEE!
I'M SO GLAD YOU CAME TO HELP!
I'LL TREAT YOU TO SOMETHING SWEET!
WATCH MY STUFF.
UEHARA-SAN LIKES FASHION.
AND I...

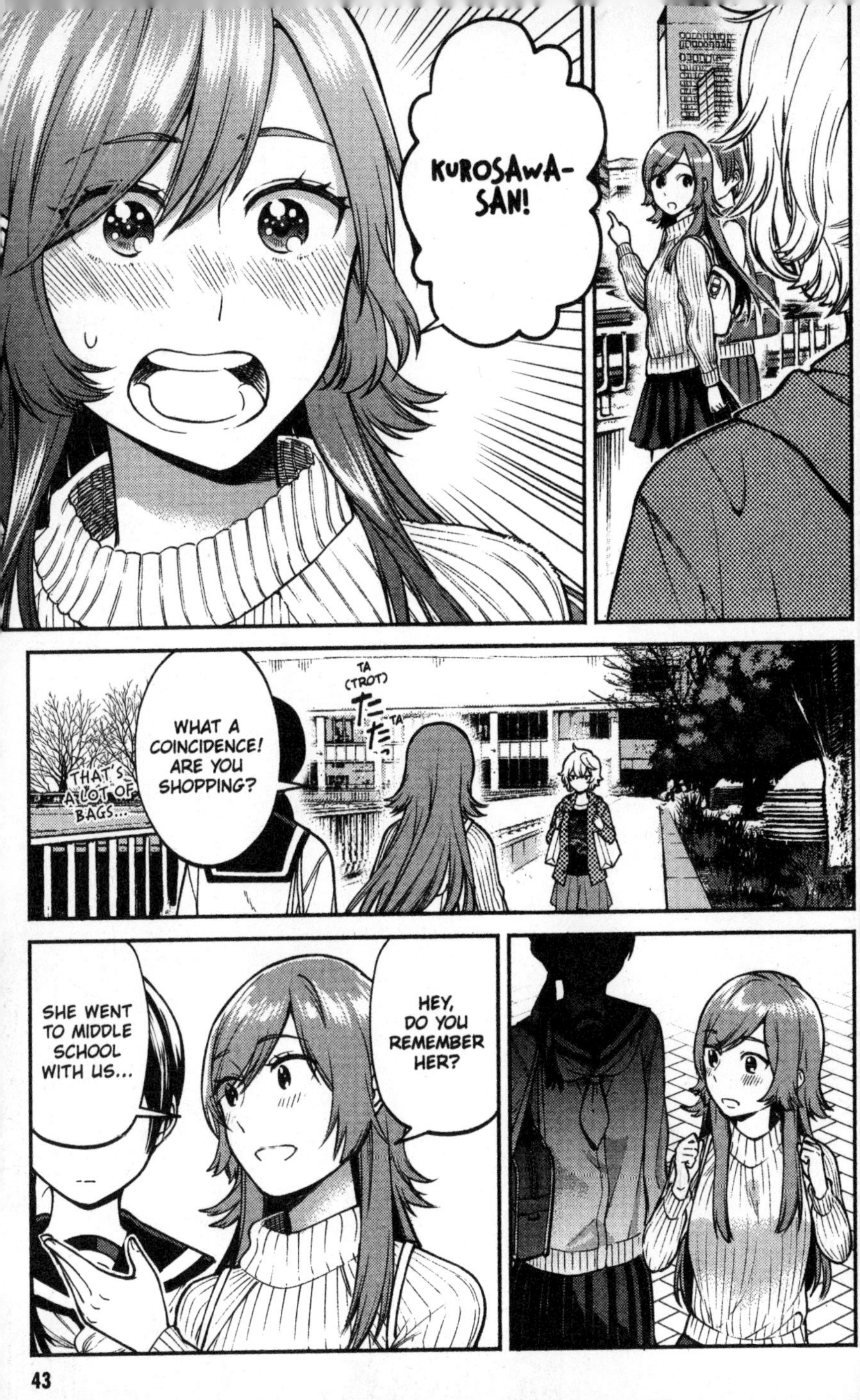
KUROSAWA-SAN!
TA (TROT) TA
WHAT A COINCIDENCE! ARE YOU SHOPPING?
THAT'S A LOT OF BAGS...
HEY, DO YOU REMEMBER HER?
SHE WENT TO MIDDLE SCHOOL WITH US...

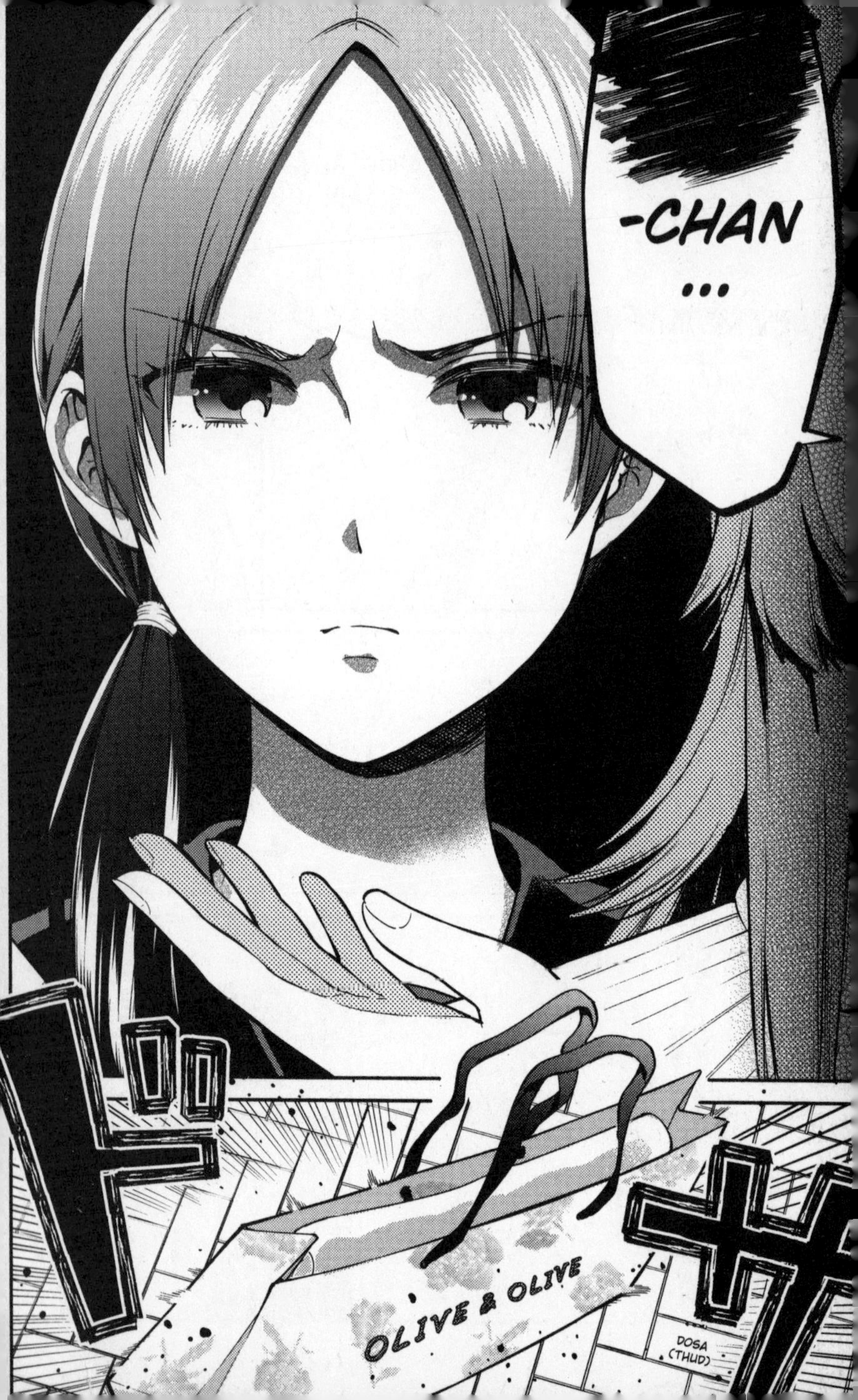
[redacted]
-CHAN
...
OLIVE & OLIVE
DOSA
(THUD)

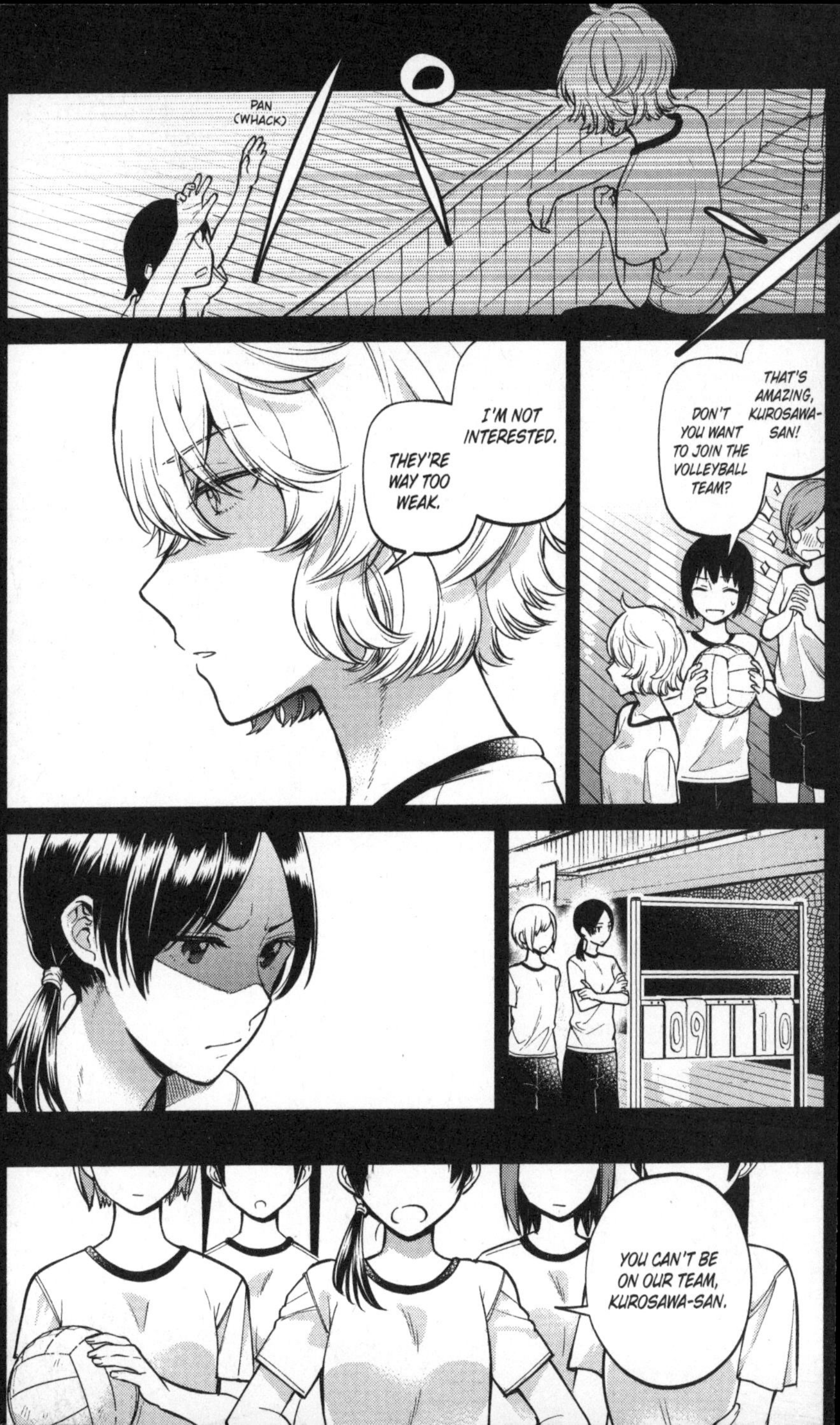
PAN (WHACK)
THAT'S AMAZING, KUROSAWA-SAN!
DON'T YOU WANT TO JOIN THE VOLLEYBALL TEAM?
I'M NOT INTERESTED.
THEY'RE WAY TOO WEAK.
YOU CAN'T BE ON OUR TEAM, KUROSAWA-SAN.

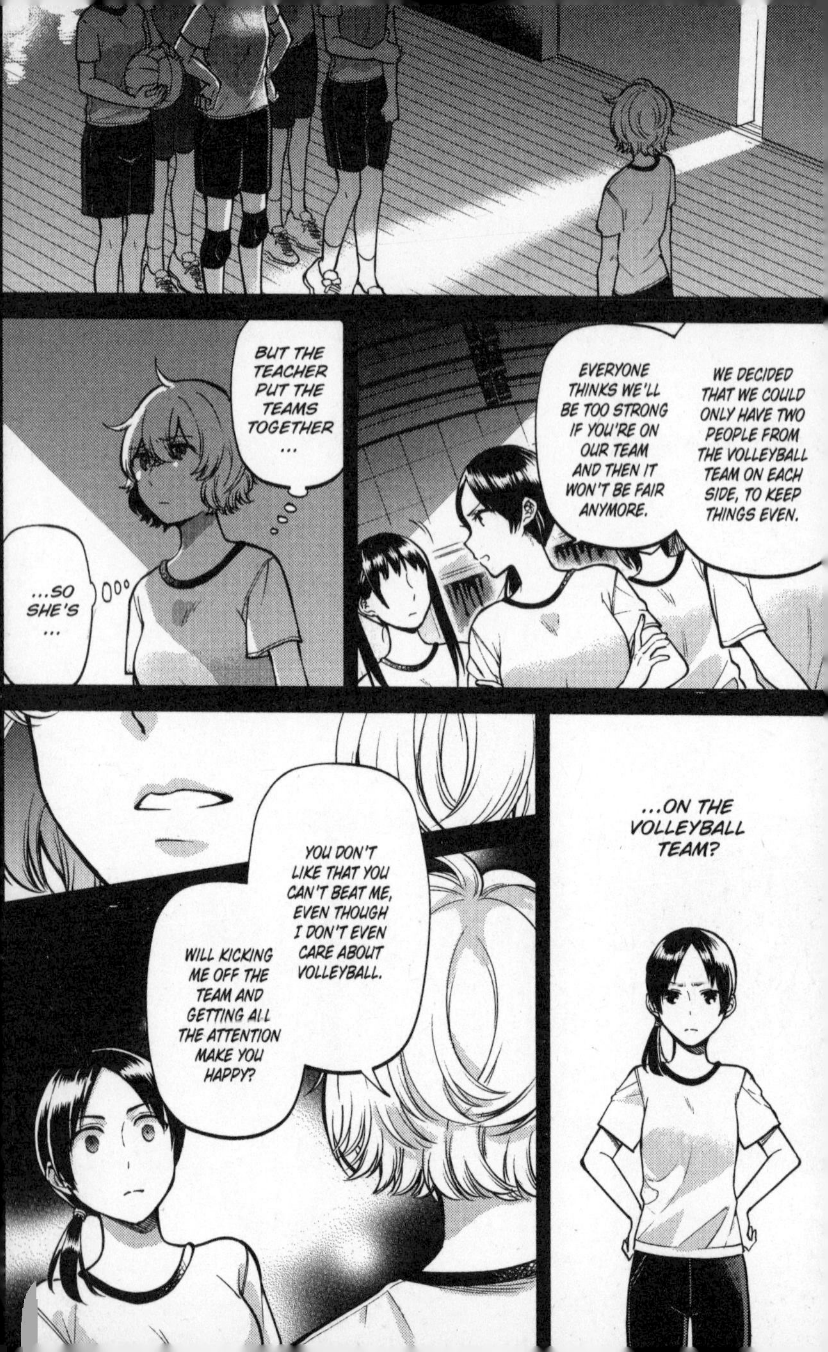
WE DECIDED THAT WE COULD ONLY HAVE TWO PEOPLE FROM THE VOLLEYBALL TEAM ON EACH SIDE, TO KEEP THINGS EVEN.
EVERYONE THINKS WE'LL BE TOO STRONG IF YOU'RE ON OUR TEAM AND THEN IT WON'T BE FAIR ANYMORE.
BUT THE TEACHER PUT THE TEAMS TOGETHER ...
...SO SHE'S ...
...ON THE VOLLEYBALL TEAM?
YOU DON'T LIKE THAT YOU CAN'T BEAT ME, EVEN THOUGH I DON'T EVEN CARE ABOUT VOLLEYBALL.
WILL KICKING ME OFF THE TEAM AND GETTING ALL THE ATTENTION MAKE YOU HAPPY?

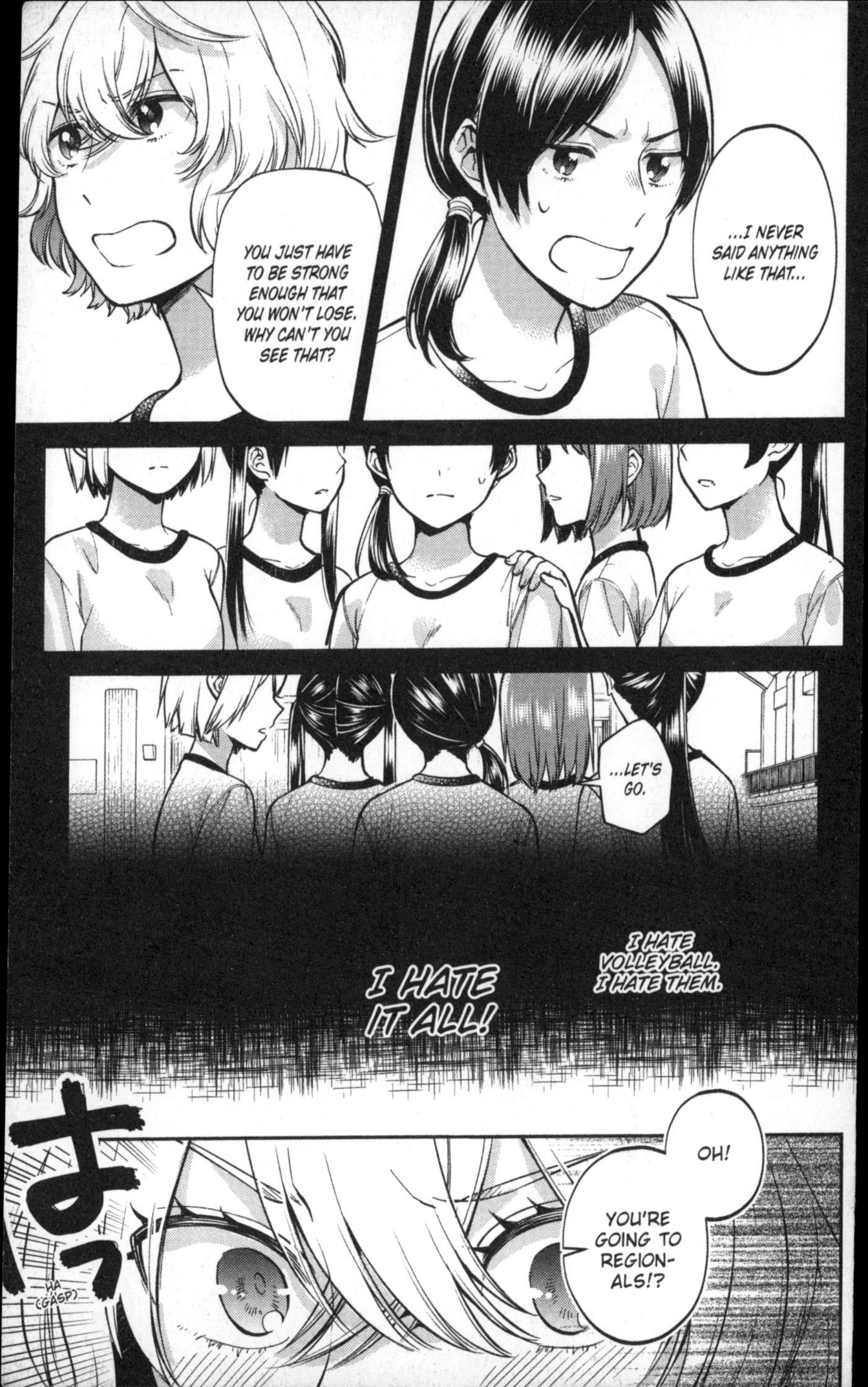
...I NEVER SAID ANYTHING LIKE THAT...
YOU JUST HAVE TO BE STRONG ENOUGH THAT YOU WON'T LOSE. WHY CAN'T YOU SEE THAT?
...LET'S GO.
I HATE VOLLEYBALL. I HATE THEM.
I HATE IT ALL!
OH!
YOU'RE GOING TO REGION-ALS!?
HA (GASP)

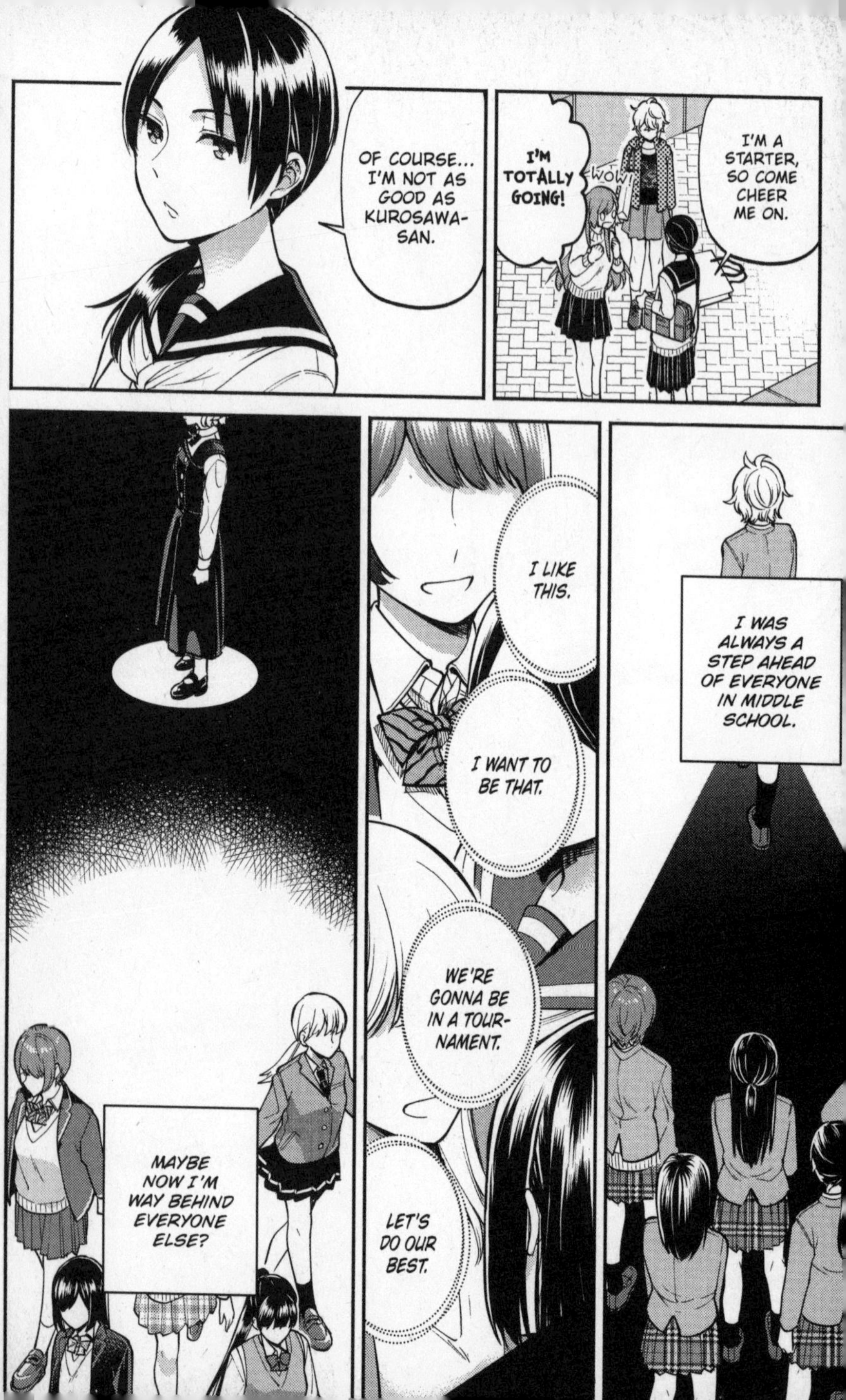
I'M A STARTER, SO COME CHEER ME ON.
I'M TOTALLY GOING!
WOW!
OF COURSE... I'M NOT AS GOOD AS KUROSAWA-SAN.
I WAS ALWAYS A STEP AHEAD OF EVERYONE IN MIDDLE SCHOOL.
I LIKE THIS.
I WANT TO BE THAT.
WE'RE GONNA BE IN A TOUR-NAMENT.
LET'S DO OUR BEST.
MAYBE NOW I'M WAY BEHIND EVERYONE ELSE?

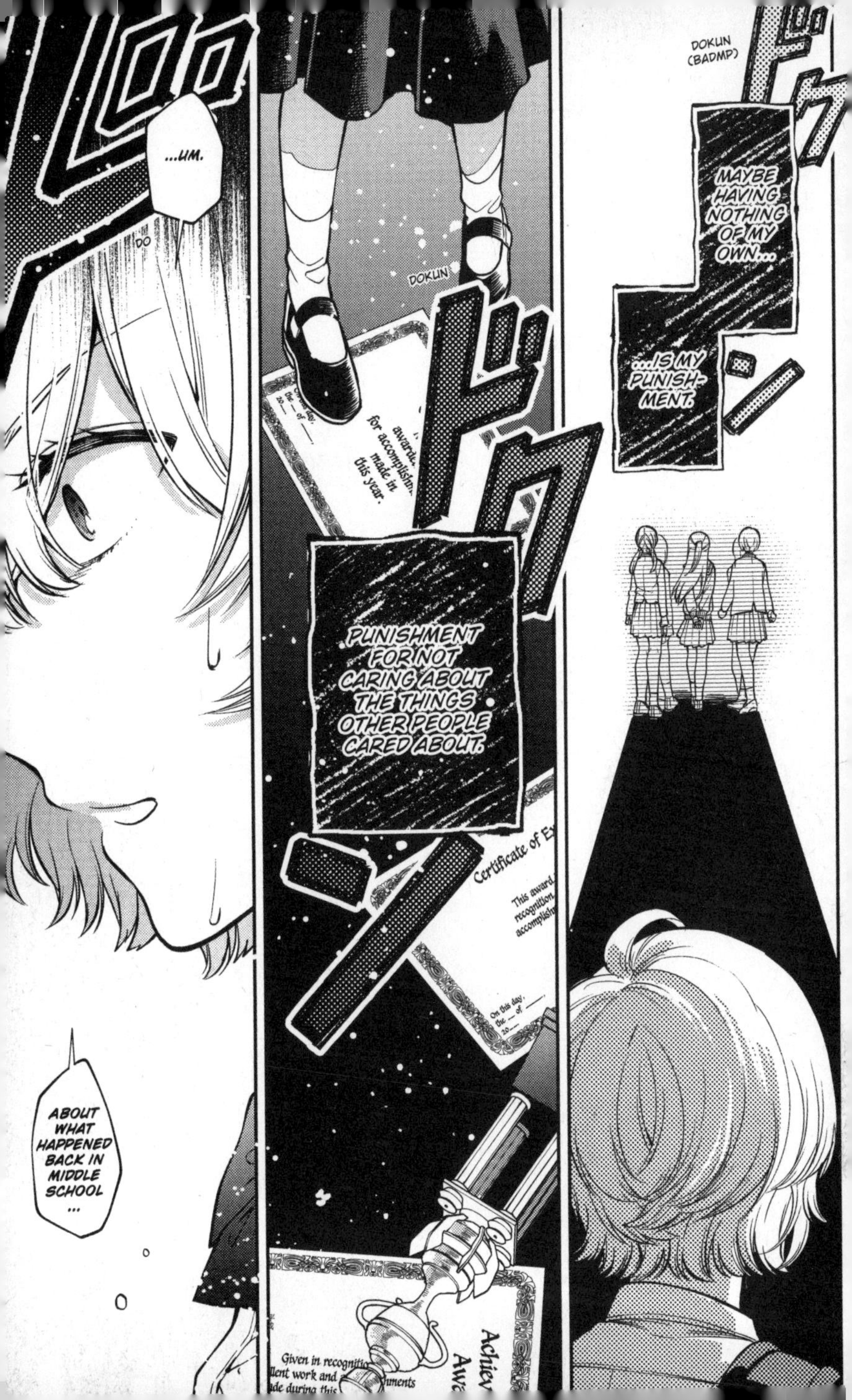
DOKUN (BADMP)
MAYBE HAVING NOTHING OF MY OWN...
...IS MY PUNISHMENT.
DOKUN
PUNISHMENT FOR NOT CARING ABOUT THE THINGS OTHER PEOPLE CARED ABOUT.
made in this year.
Certificate of
On this day, the __ of ____, 20__
Given in recognitio
...UM.
DO
ABOUT WHAT HAPPENED BACK IN MIDDLE SCHOOL ...

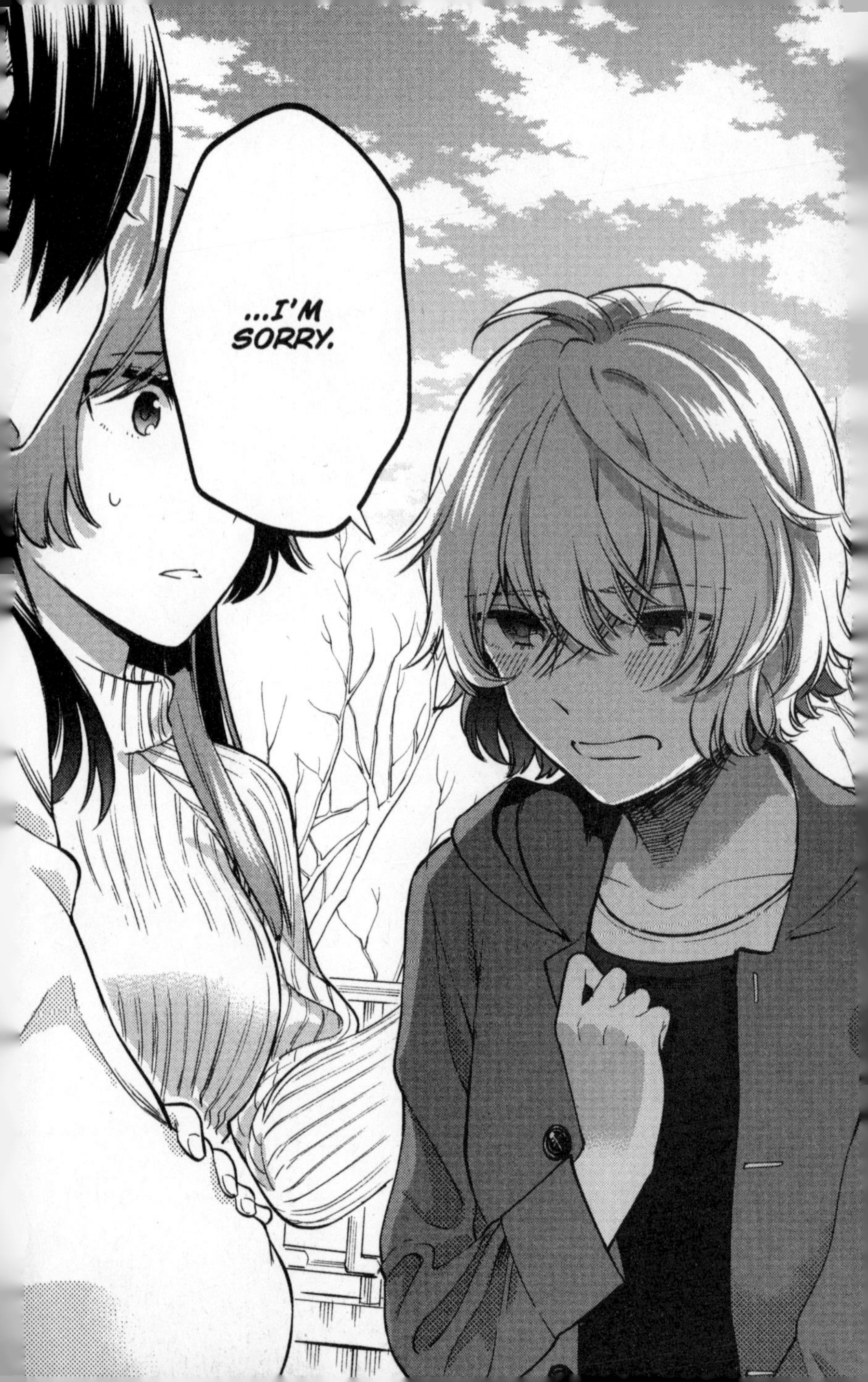
...I'M SORRY.

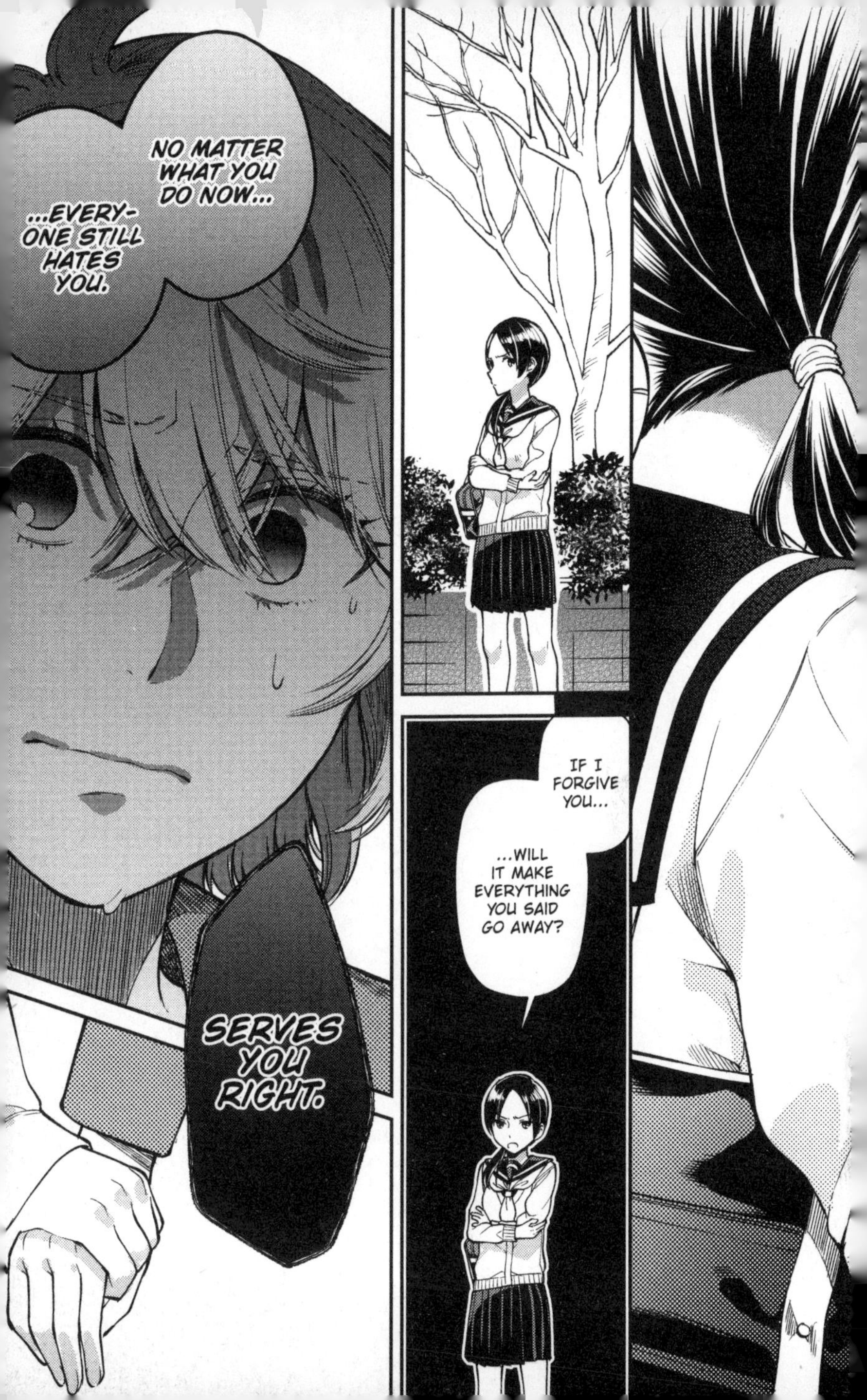
IF I FORGIVE YOU...
...WILL IT MAKE EVERYTHING YOU SAID GO AWAY?
NO MATTER WHAT YOU DO NOW...
...EVERY-ONE STILL HATES YOU.
SERVES YOU RIGHT.

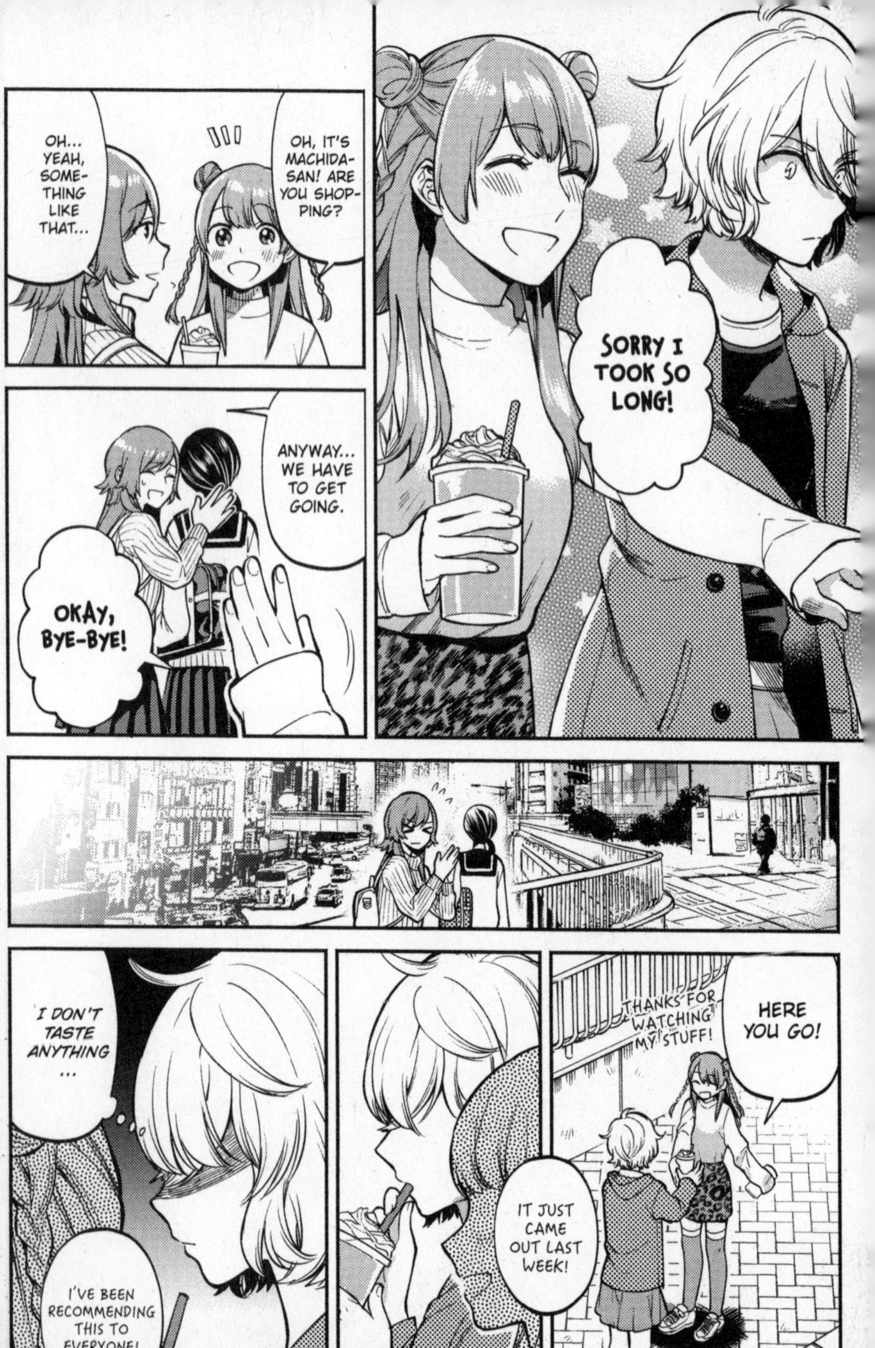
SORRY I TOOK SO LONG!
OH, IT'S MACHIDA-SAN! ARE YOU SHOPPING?
OH... YEAH, SOMETHING LIKE THAT...
ANYWAY... WE HAVE TO GET GOING.
OKAY, BYE-BYE!
HERE YOU GO!
THANKS FOR WATCHING MY STUFF!
IT JUST CAME OUT LAST WEEK!
I DON'T TASTE ANYTHING ...
I'VE BEEN RECOMMENDING THIS TO EVERYONE!

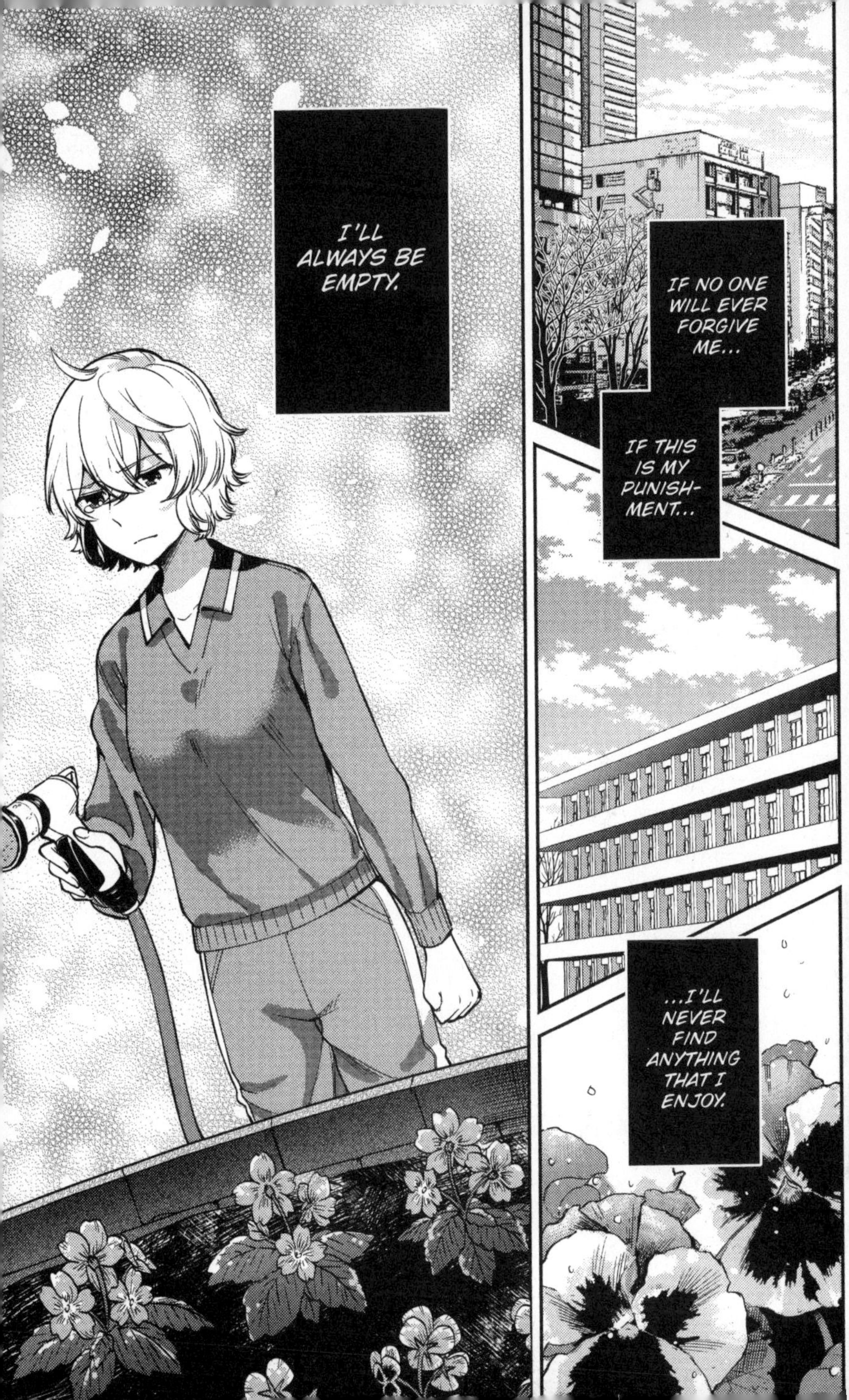
IF NO ONE WILL EVER FORGIVE ME...
IF THIS IS MY PUNISHMENT...
...I'LL NEVER FIND ANYTHING THAT I ENJOY.
I'LL ALWAYS BE EMPTY.

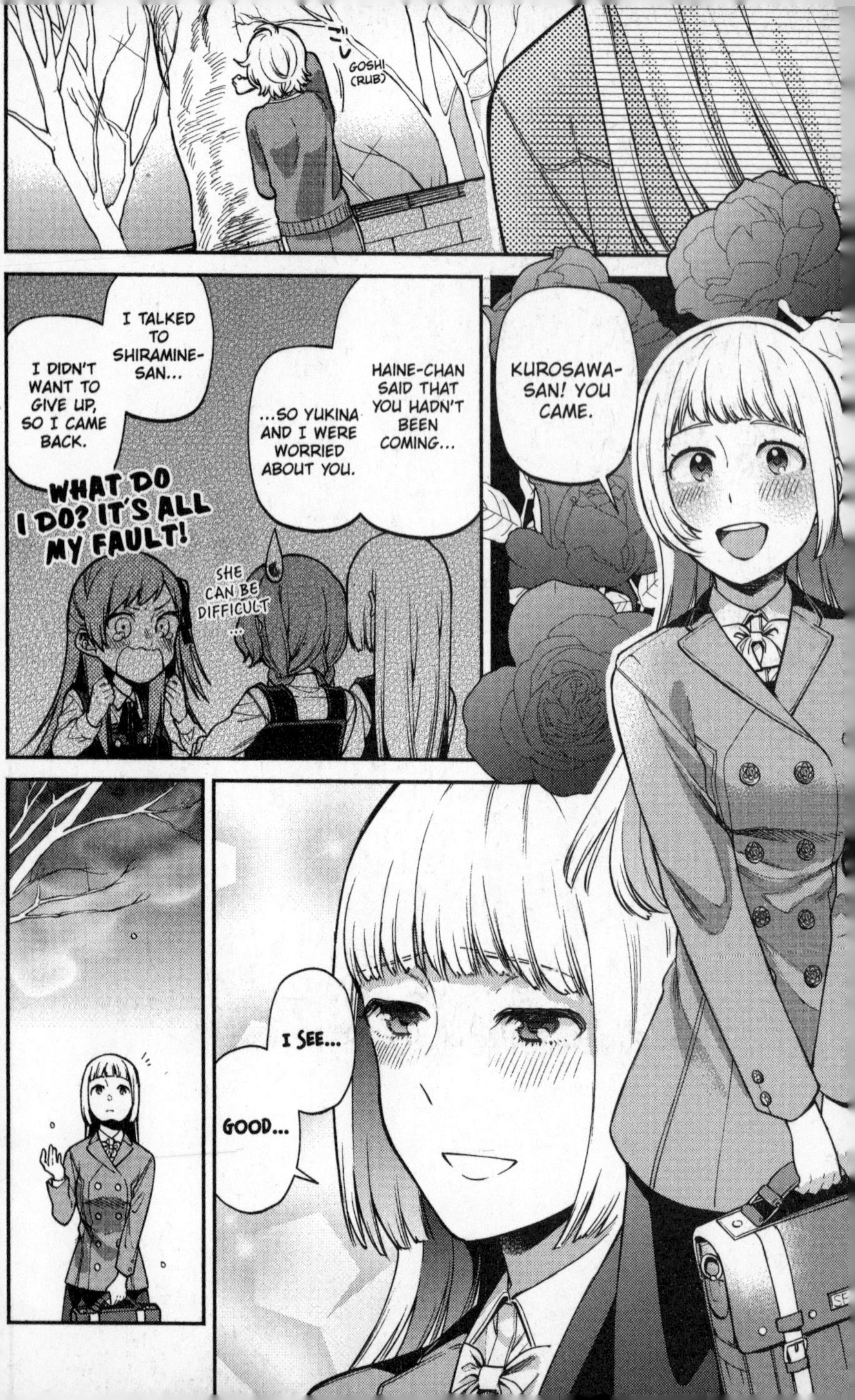
ゴシ
GOSHI (RUB)
KUROSAWA-SAN! YOU CAME.
HAINE-CHAN SAID THAT YOU HADN'T BEEN COMING...
...SO YUKINA AND I WERE WORRIED ABOUT YOU.
I TALKED TO SHIRAMINE-SAN...
I DIDN'T WANT TO GIVE UP, SO I CAME BACK.
WHAT DO I DO? IT'S ALL MY FAULT!
SHE CAN BE DIFFICULT...
I SEE...
GOOD...

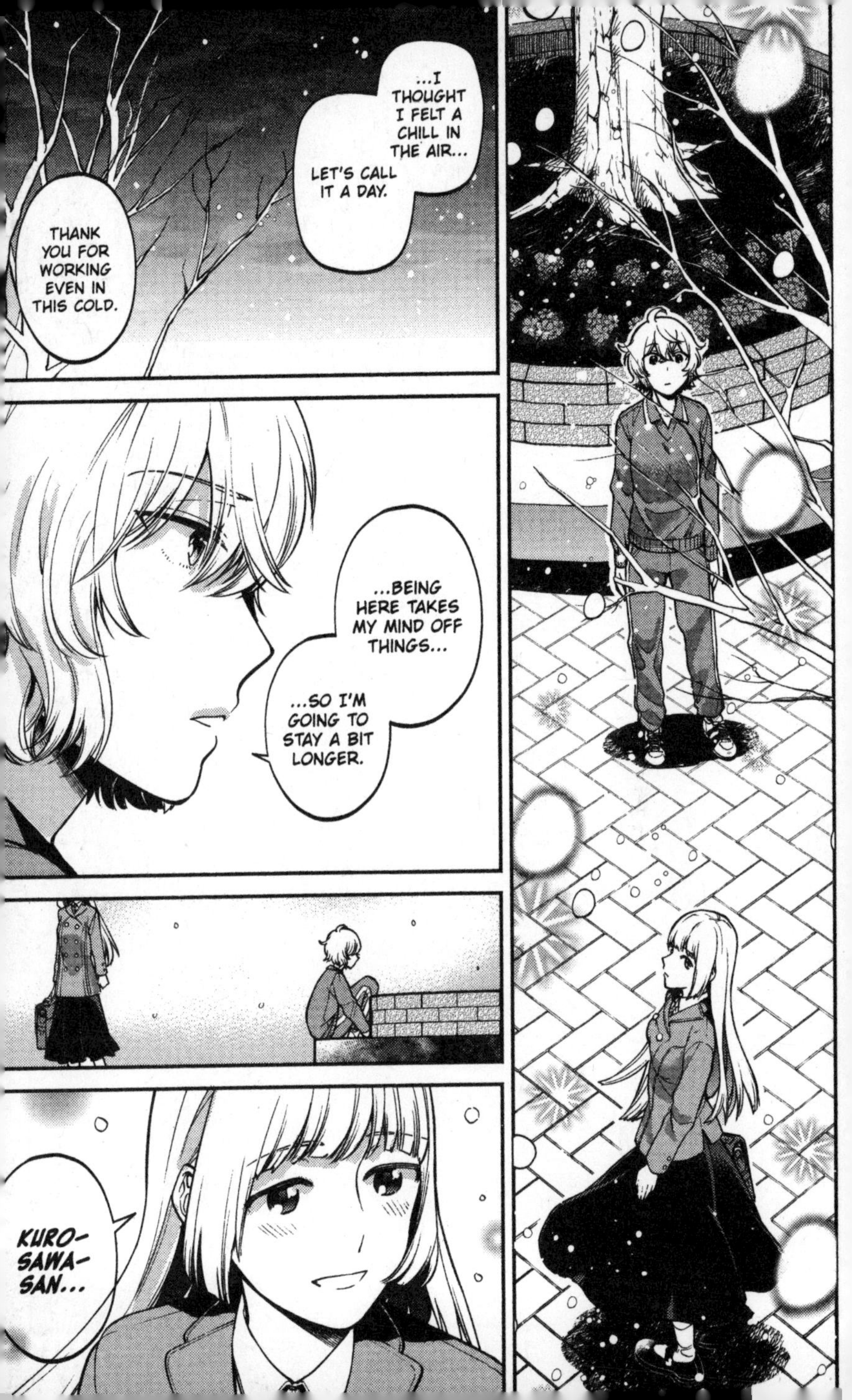
...I THOUGHT I FELT A CHILL IN THE AIR...
LET'S CALL IT A DAY.
THANK YOU FOR WORKING EVEN IN THIS COLD.
...BEING HERE TAKES MY MIND OFF THINGS...
...SO I'M GOING TO STAY A BIT LONGER.
KURO-SAWA-SAN...

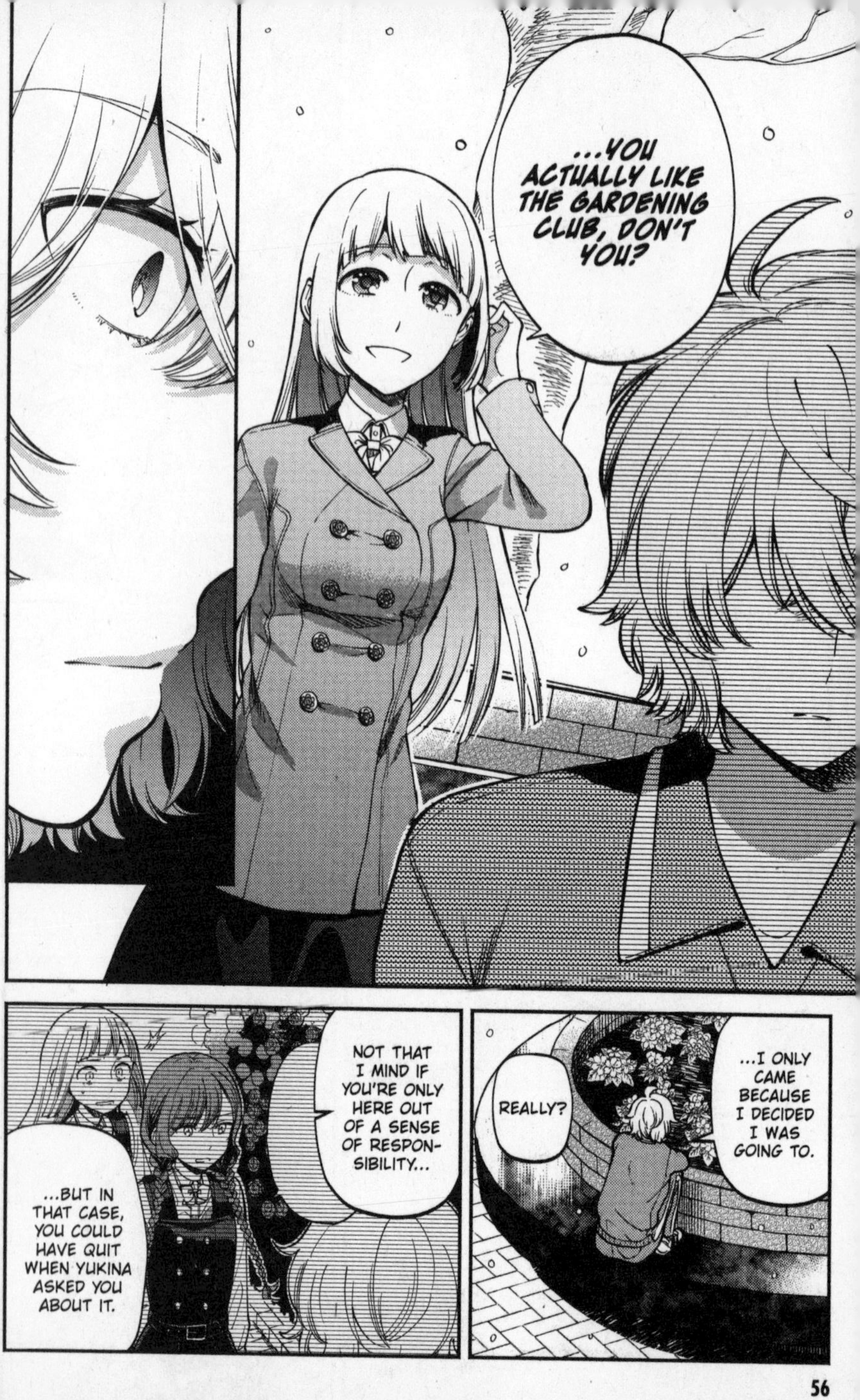

...YOU ACTUALLY LIKE THE GARDENING CLUB, DON'T YOU?
...I ONLY CAME BECAUSE I DECIDED I WAS GOING TO.
REALLY?
NOT THAT I MIND IF YOU'RE ONLY HERE OUT OF A SENSE OF RESPON-SIBILITY...
...BUT IN THAT CASE, YOU COULD HAVE QUIT WHEN YUKINA ASKED YOU ABOUT IT.

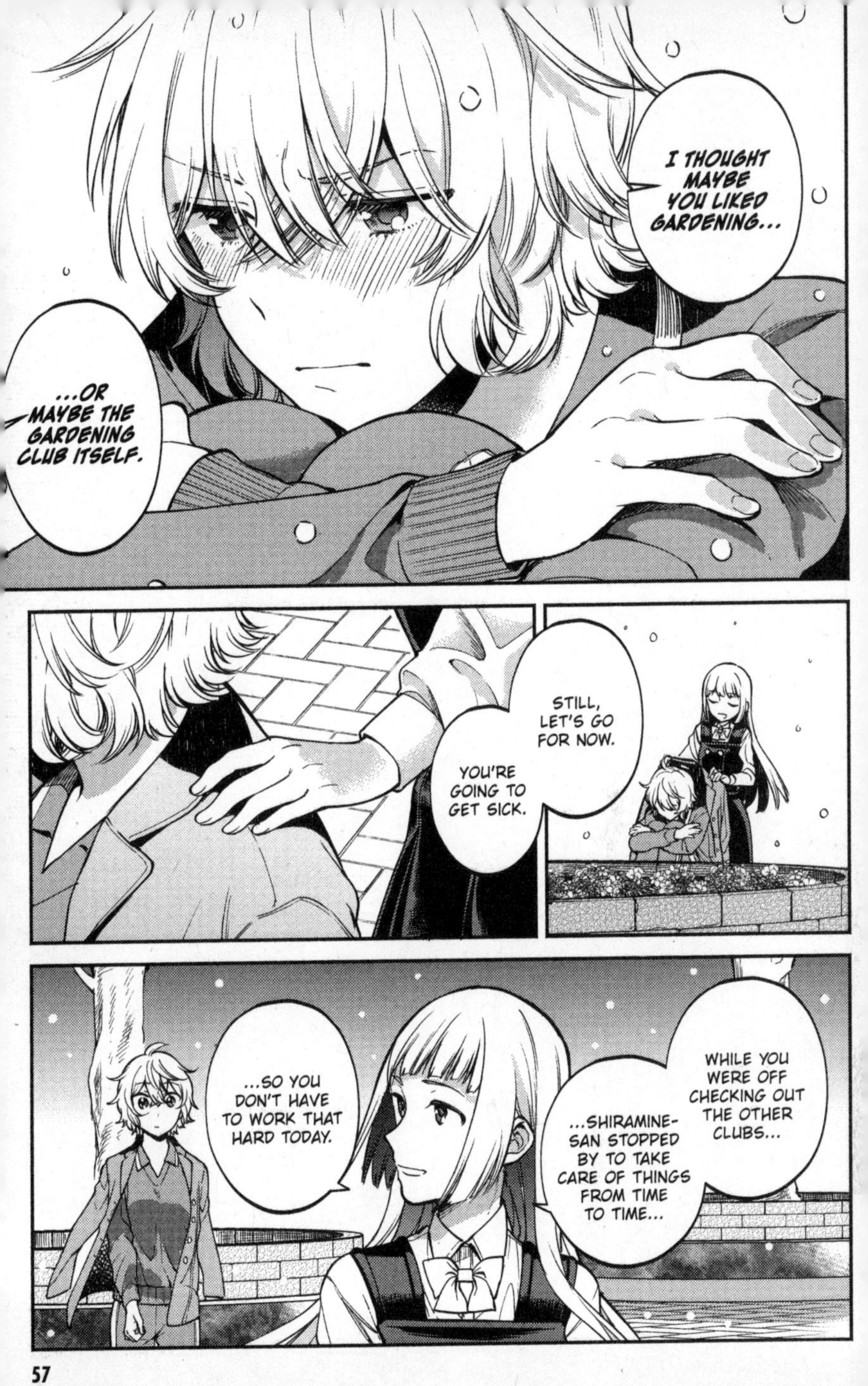
I THOUGHT MAYBE YOU LIKED GARDENING...
...OR MAYBE THE GARDENING CLUB ITSELF.
STILL, LET'S GO FOR NOW.
YOU'RE GOING TO GET SICK.
WHILE YOU WERE OFF CHECKING OUT THE OTHER CLUBS...
...SHIRAMINE-SAN STOPPED BY TO TAKE CARE OF THINGS FROM TIME TO TIME...
...SO YOU DON'T HAVE TO WORK THAT HARD TODAY.

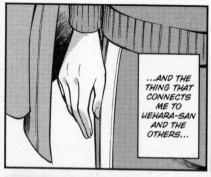

...AND THE THING THAT CONNECTS ME TO UEHARA-SAN AND THE OTHERS...

THE THING THAT BROUGHT ME BACK TO THE GARDENING CLUB...

...IS SHIRAMINE-SAN.

...EVERYONE I'VE MET IN HIGH SCHOOL...

...UEHARA-SAN...

THE GARDENING CLUB...

SHIRAMINE-SAN GAVE ME ALL OF IT.

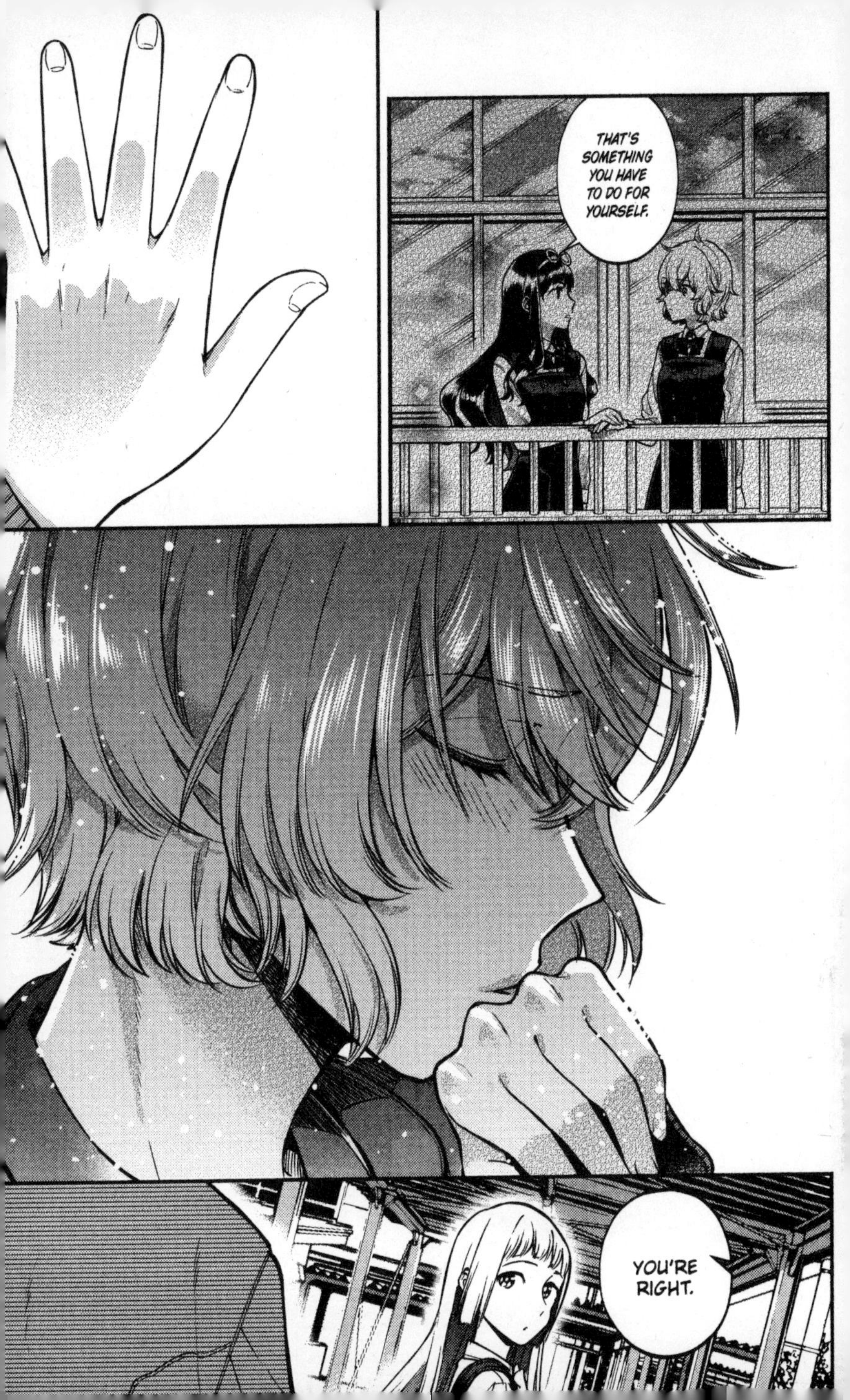
THAT'S SOMETHING YOU HAVE TO DO FOR YOURSELF.
YOU'RE RIGHT.

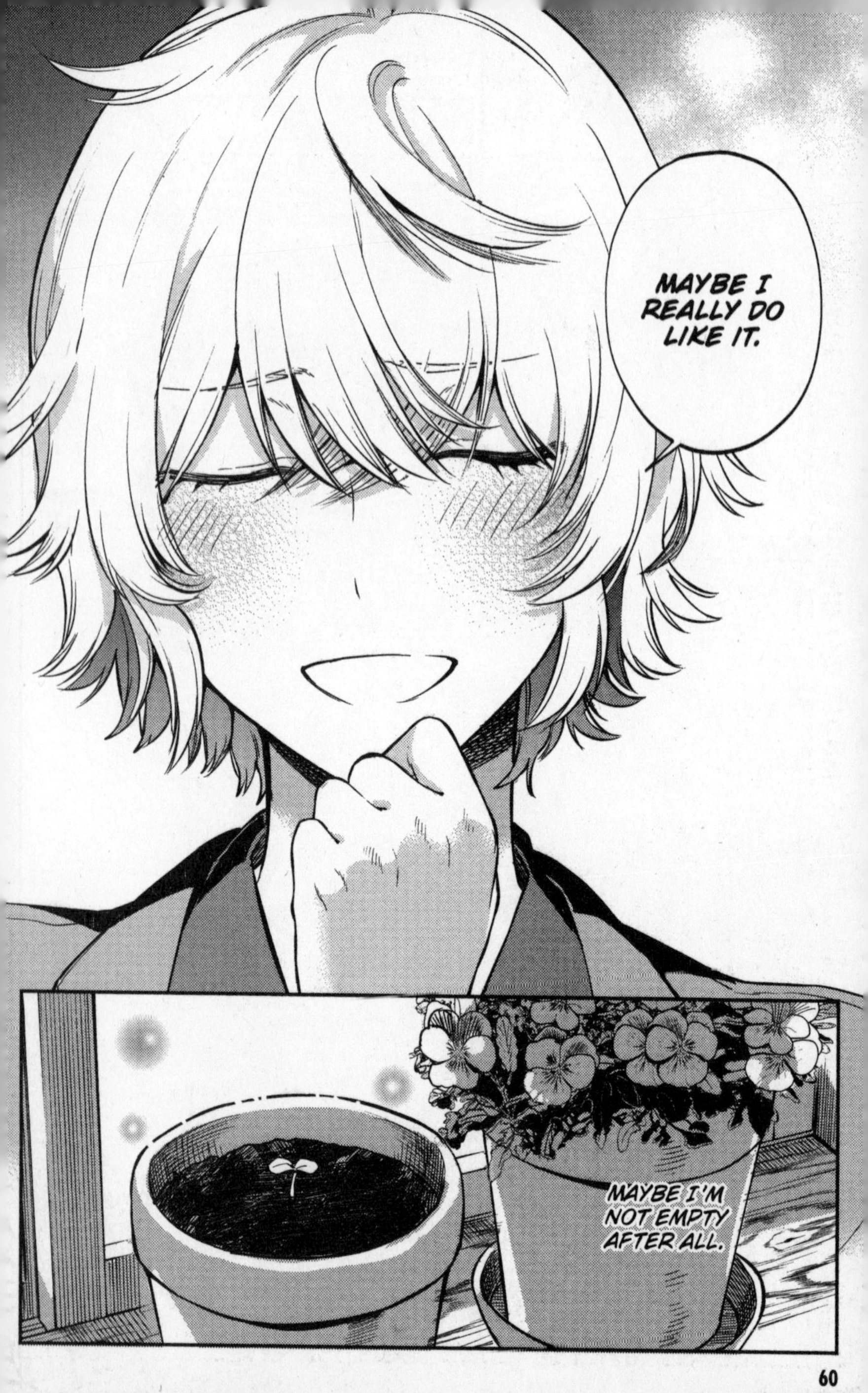
MAYBE I REALLY DO LIKE IT.
MAYBE I'M NOT EMPTY AFTER ALL.

Machida-san the Next Day

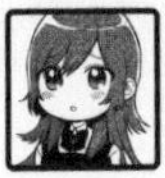

KAORU
HIGH SCHOOL SECOND-YEAR. A BIT RESERVED AT TIMES.

KISS THEATER: WHAT'S BEHIND THE STORY!? ✷ PEOPLE OTHER THAN THE MAIN CHARACTERS HAVE STORIES TOO. HERE, WE PRESENT THE "LITTLE LOVE" STORIES HAPPENING BEHIND THE SCENES!

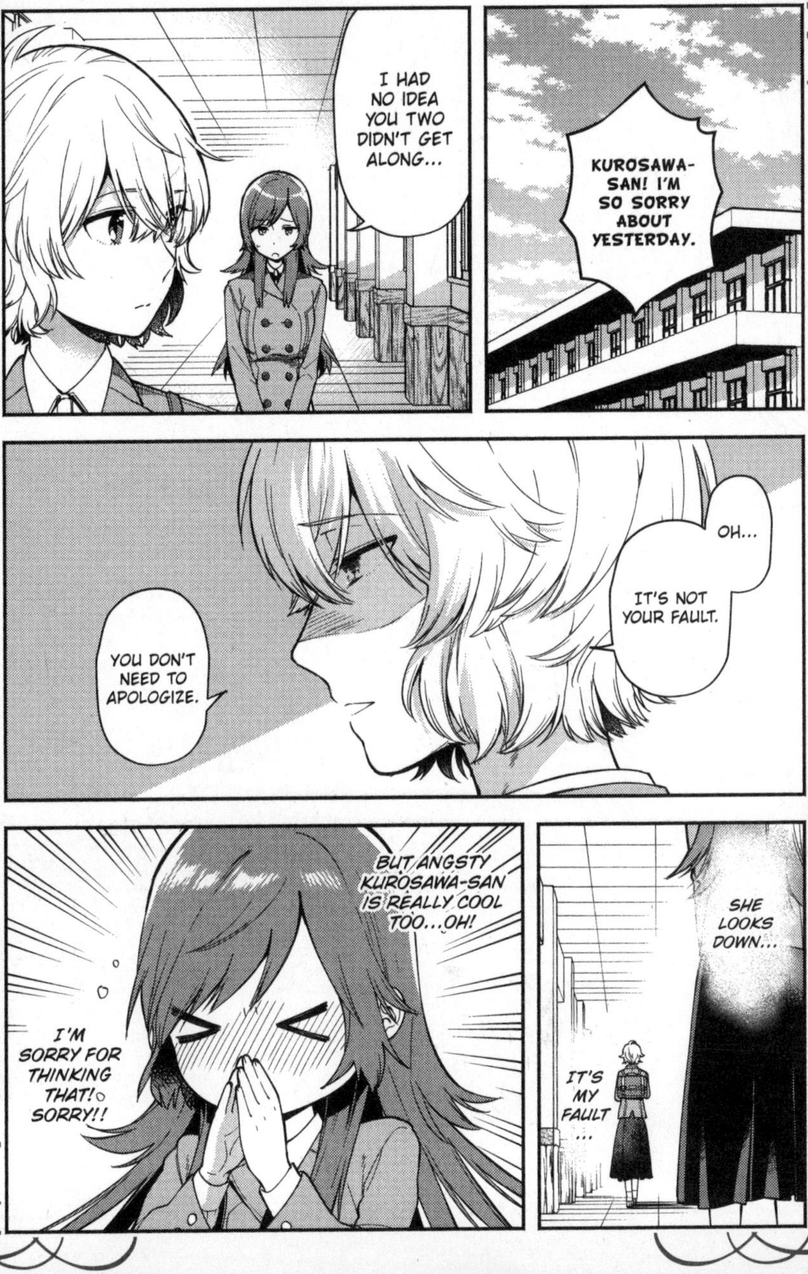
KUROSAWA-SAN! I'M SO SORRY ABOUT YESTERDAY.
I HAD NO IDEA YOU TWO DIDN'T GET ALONG...
OH...
IT'S NOT YOUR FAULT.
YOU DON'T NEED TO APOLOGIZE.
SHE LOOKS DOWN...
IT'S MY FAULT...
BUT ANGSTY KUROSAWA-SAN IS REALLY COOL TOO...OH!
I'M SORRY FOR THINKING THAT! SORRY!!

✳ *Yurine Kurosawa* ✳

Yurine Kurosawa

Second-year student in the Seiran Academy High School. Member of the gardening club. An apparent genius, she gets above-average results even when she's not trying. She's had some hang-ups about people ever since middle school. She tried to just ignore them, but as she grows in high school, she's finding she has to face them head-on more often.

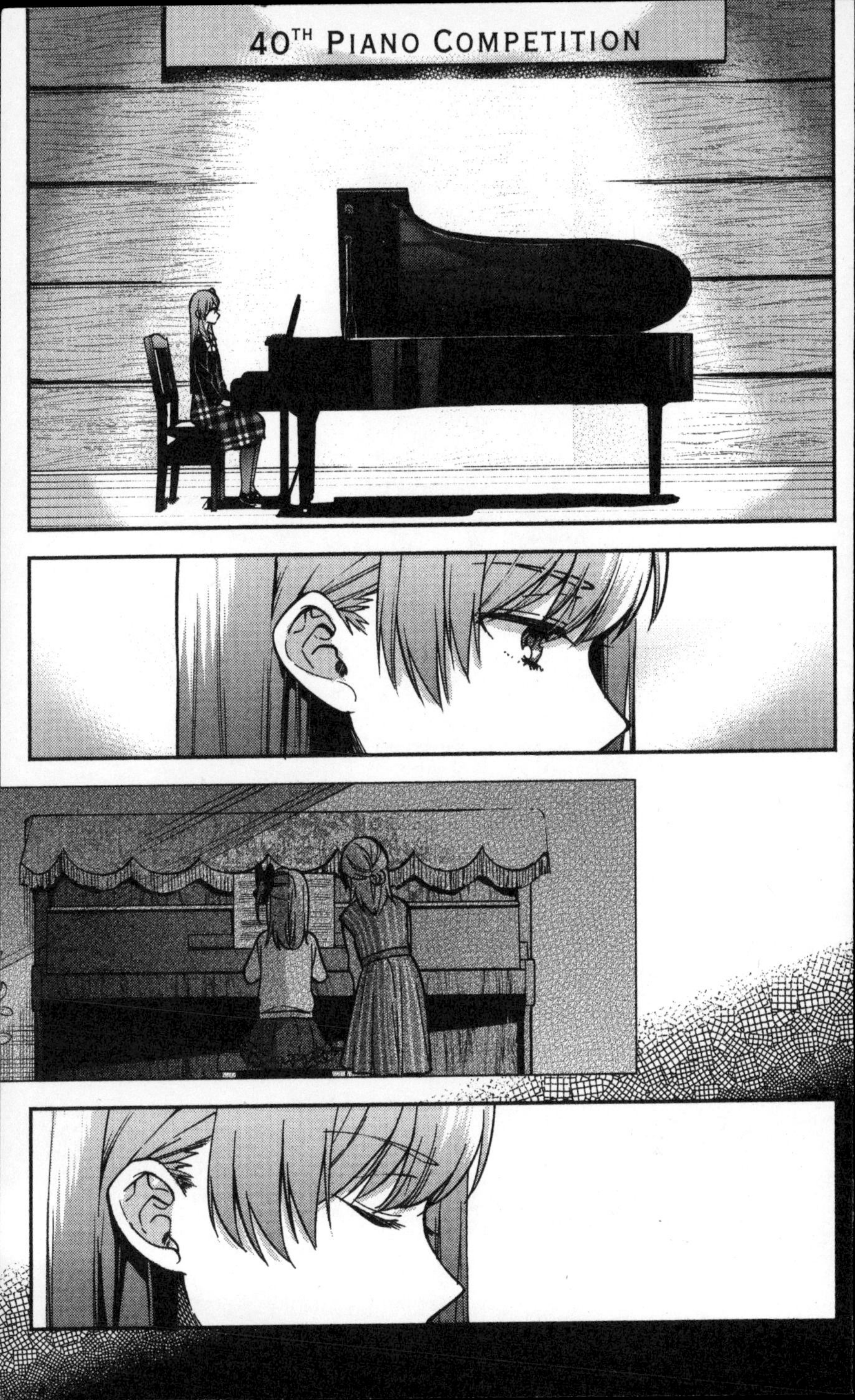
40TH PIANO COMPETITION

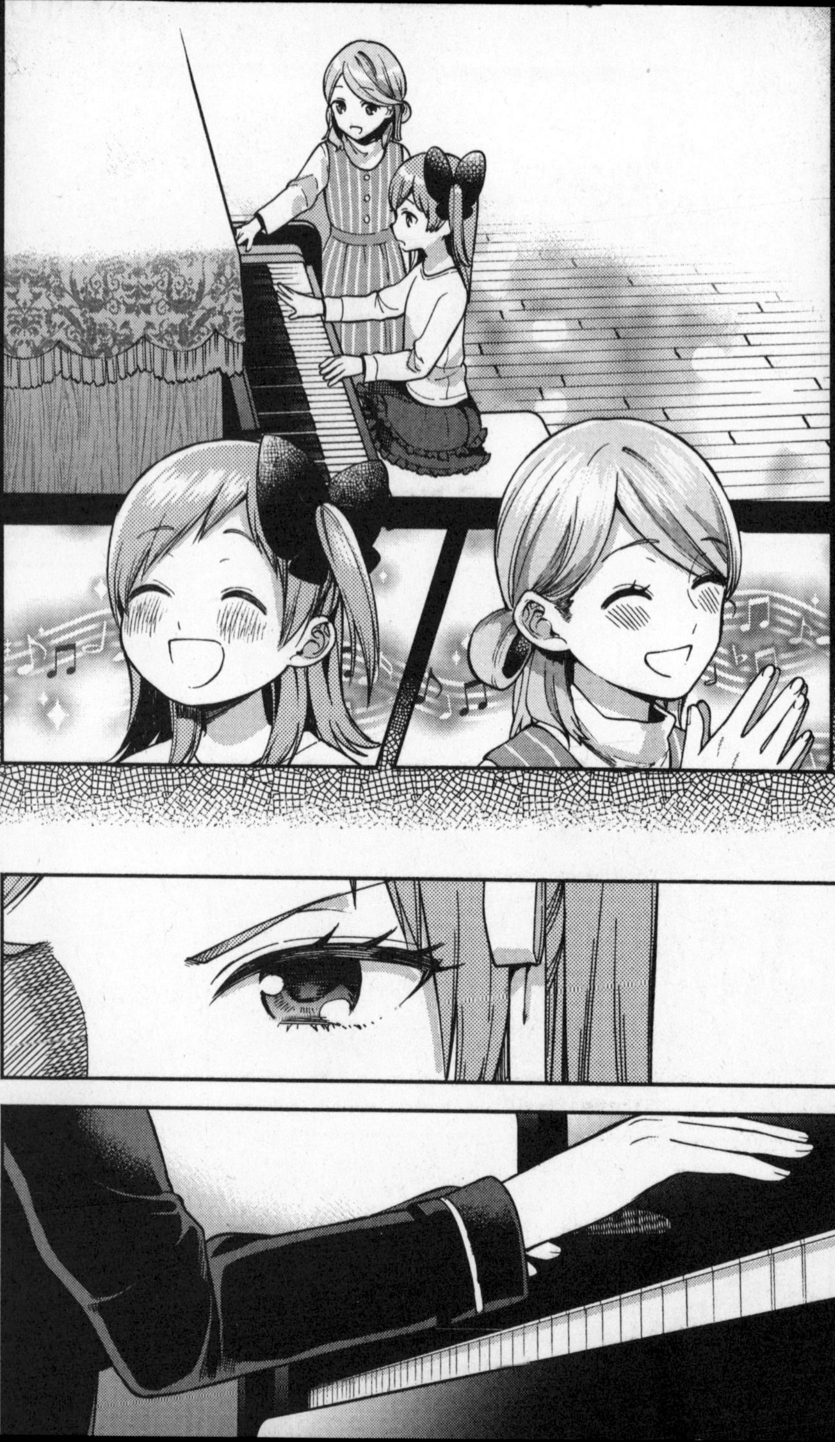

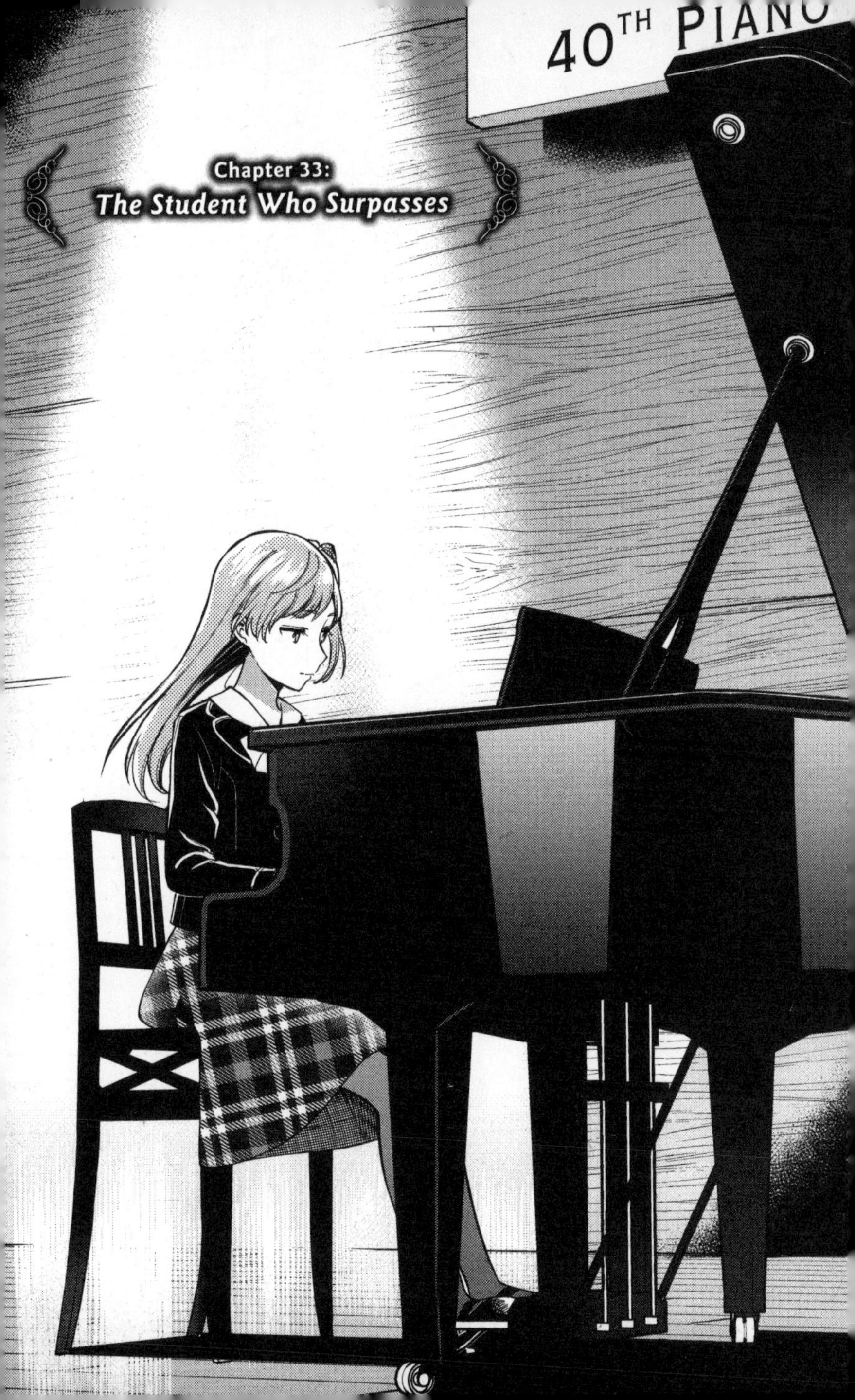
40TH PIANO
Chapter 33:
The Student Who Surpasses

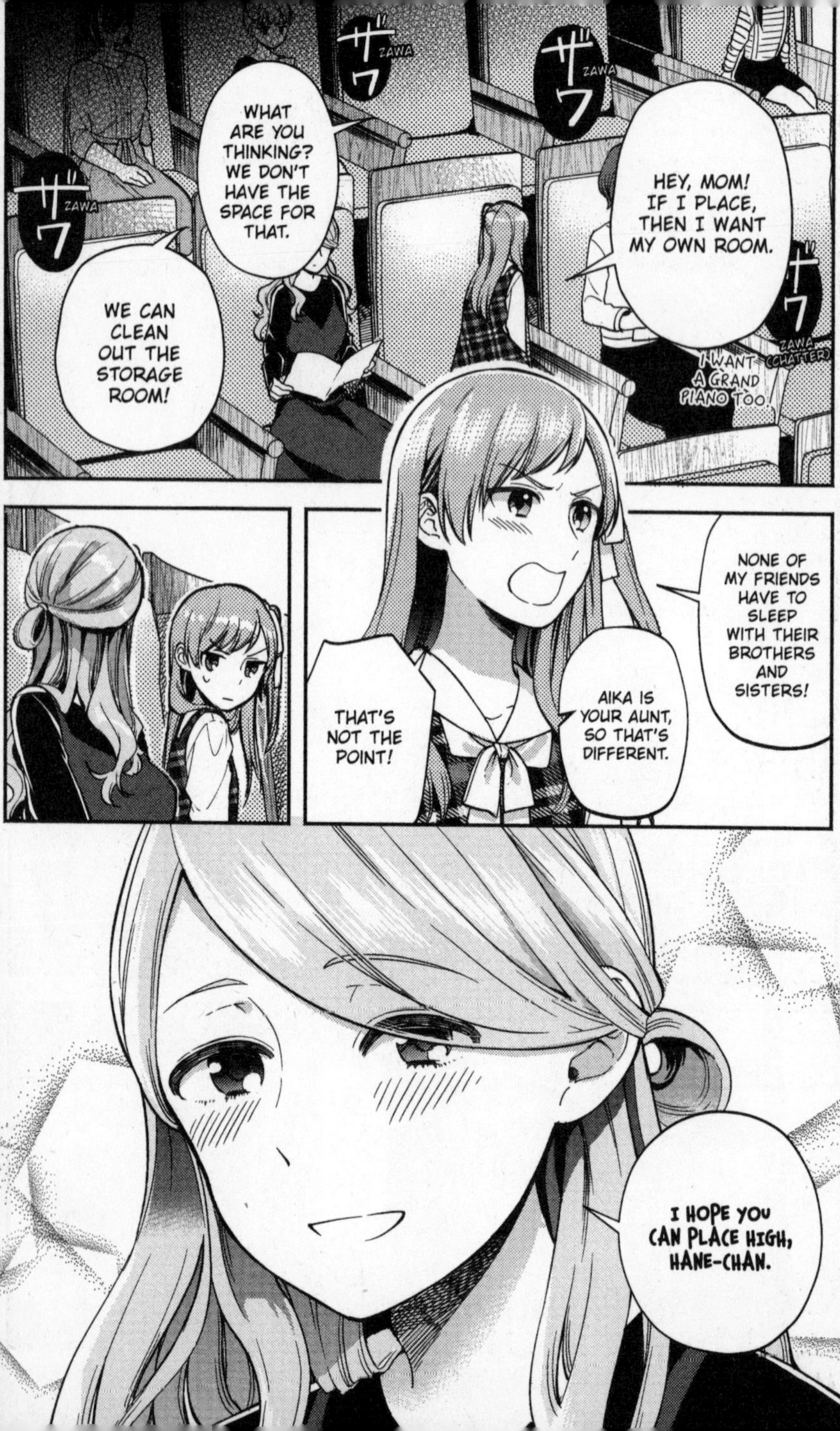
ザワ ZAWA
ザワ ZAWA
HEY, MOM! IF I PLACE, THEN I WANT MY OWN ROOM.
ザワ ZAWA (CHATTER)
I WANT A GRAND PIANO TOO.
WHAT ARE YOU THINKING? WE DON'T HAVE THE SPACE FOR THAT.
ザワ ZAWA
WE CAN CLEAN OUT THE STORAGE ROOM!
NONE OF MY FRIENDS HAVE TO SLEEP WITH THEIR BROTHERS AND SISTERS!
AIKA IS YOUR AUNT, SO THAT'S DIFFERENT.
THAT'S NOT THE POINT!
I HOPE YOU CAN PLACE HIGH, HANE-CHAN.

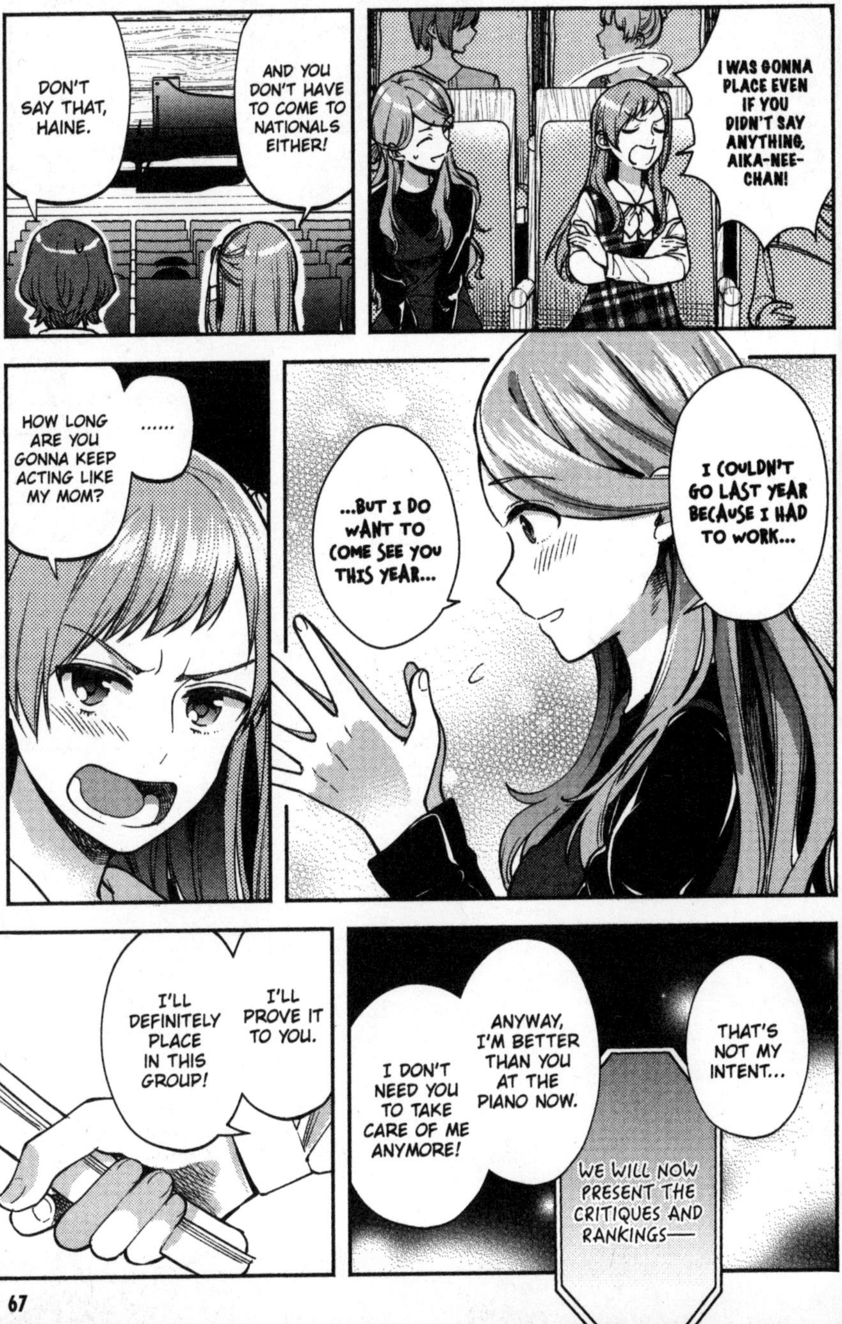
I WAS GONNA PLACE EVEN IF YOU DIDN'T SAY ANYTHING, AIKA-NEE-CHAN!
AND YOU DON'T HAVE TO COME TO NATIONALS EITHER!
DON'T SAY THAT, HAINE.
I COULDN'T GO LAST YEAR BECAUSE I HAD TO WORK...
...BUT I DO WANT TO COME SEE YOU THIS YEAR...
......
HOW LONG ARE YOU GONNA KEEP ACTING LIKE MY MOM?
THAT'S NOT MY INTENT...
ANYWAY, I'M BETTER THAN YOU AT THE PIANO NOW.
I DON'T NEED YOU TO TAKE CARE OF ME ANYMORE!
WE WILL NOW PRESENT THE CRITIQUES AND RANKINGS—
I'LL PROVE IT TO YOU.
I'LL DEFINITELY PLACE IN THIS GROUP!

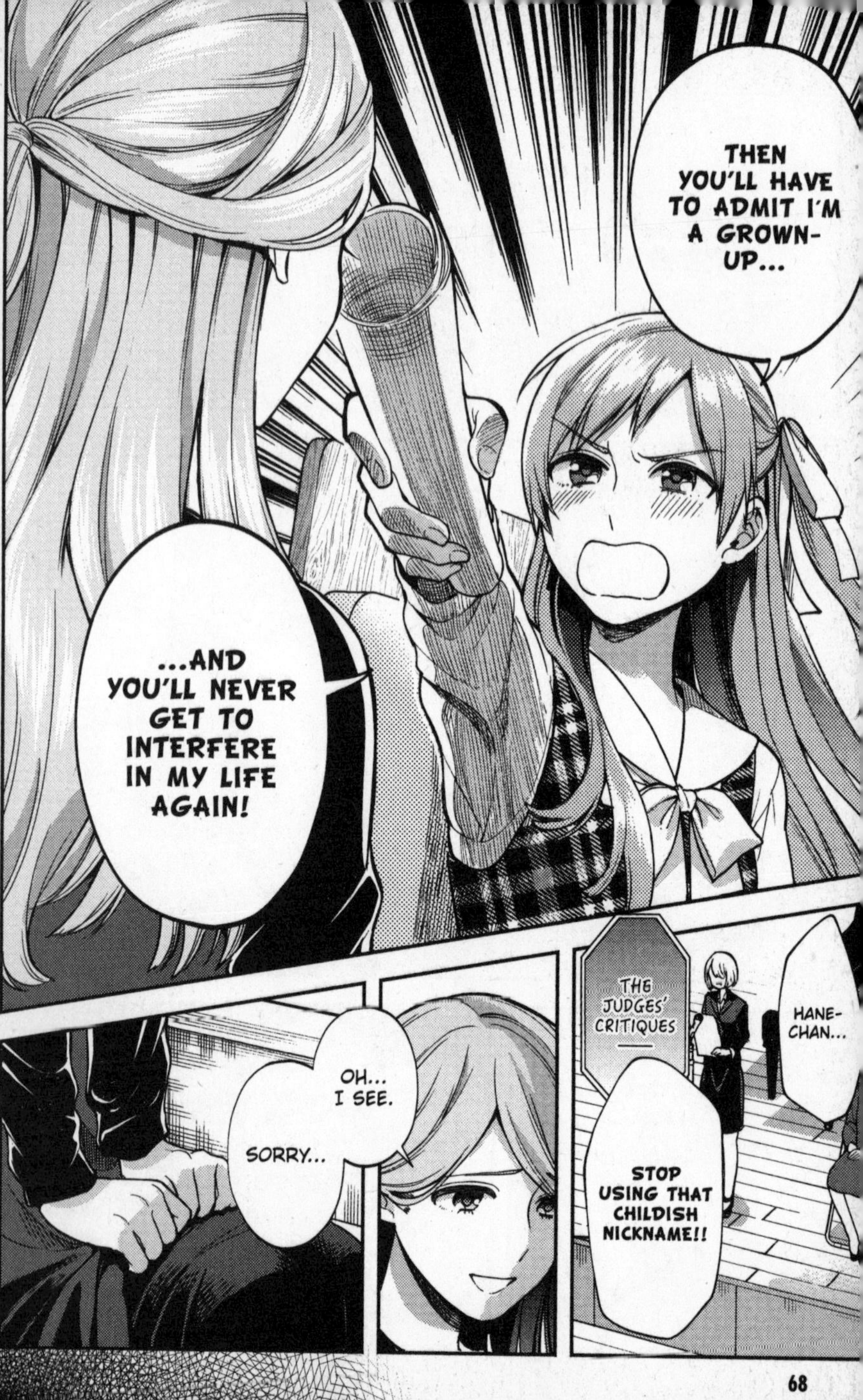
THEN YOU'LL HAVE TO ADMIT I'M A GROWN-UP...
...AND YOU'LL NEVER GET TO INTERFERE IN MY LIFE AGAIN!
THE JUDGES' CRITIQUES
HANE-CHAN...
STOP USING THAT CHILDISH NICKNAME!!
OH... I SEE.
SORRY...

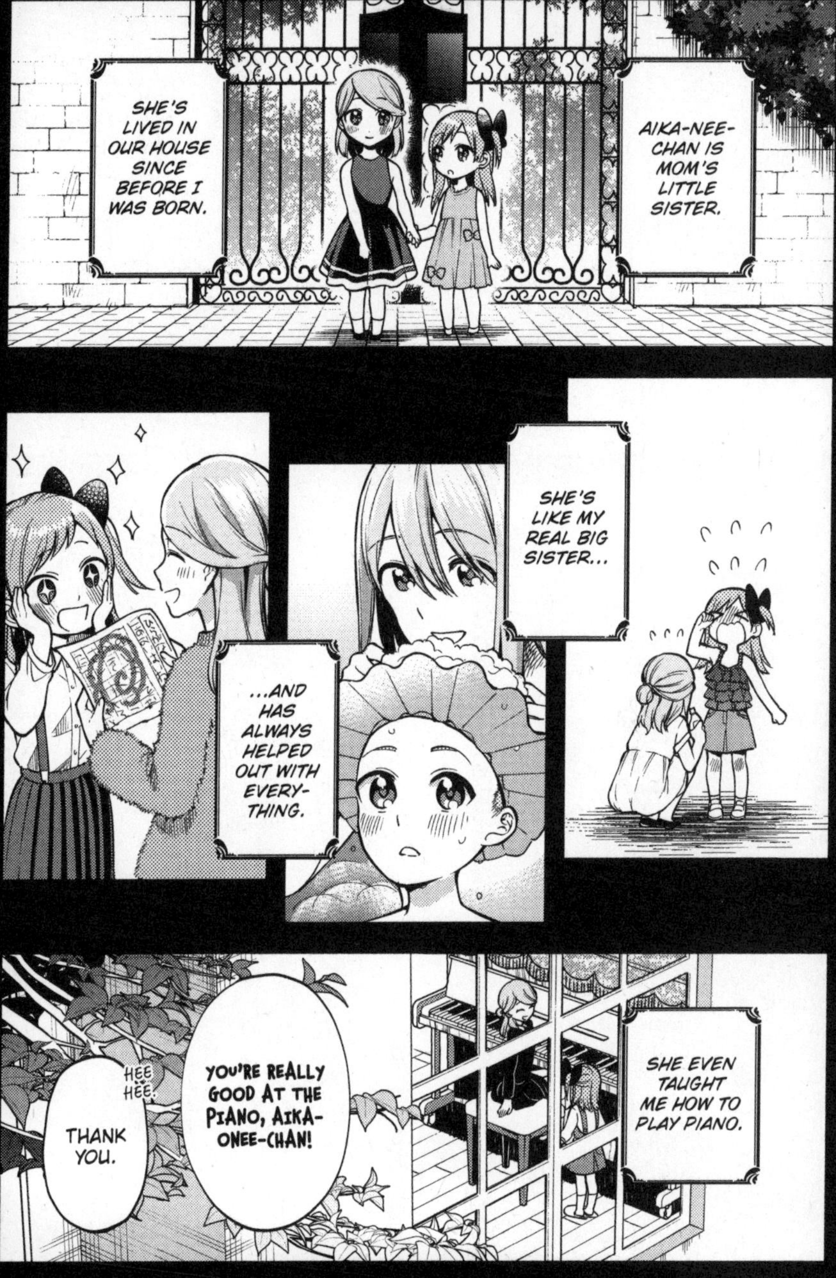
AIKA-NEE-CHAN IS MOM'S LITTLE SISTER.
SHE'S LIVED IN OUR HOUSE SINCE BEFORE I WAS BORN.
SHE'S LIKE MY REAL BIG SISTER...
...AND HAS ALWAYS HELPED OUT WITH EVERY-THING.
SHE EVEN TAUGHT ME HOW TO PLAY PIANO.
YOU'RE REALLY GOOD AT THE PIANO, AIKA-ONEE-CHAN!
HEE HEE.
THANK YOU.

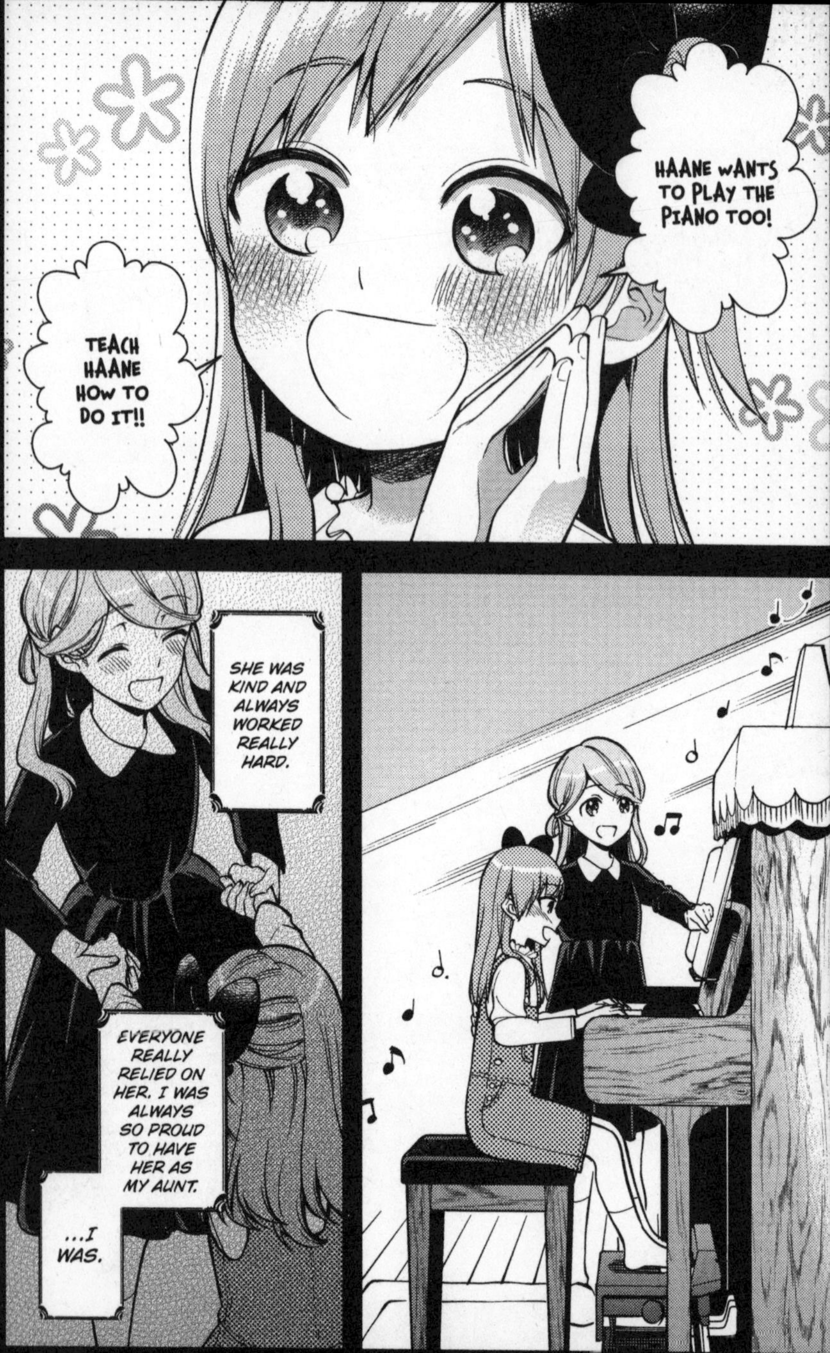
HAANE WANTS TO PLAY THE PIANO TOO!
TEACH HAANE HOW TO DO IT!!
SHE WAS KIND AND ALWAYS WORKED REALLY HARD.
EVERYONE REALLY RELIED ON HER. I WAS ALWAYS SO PROUD TO HAVE HER AS MY AUNT.
...I WAS.

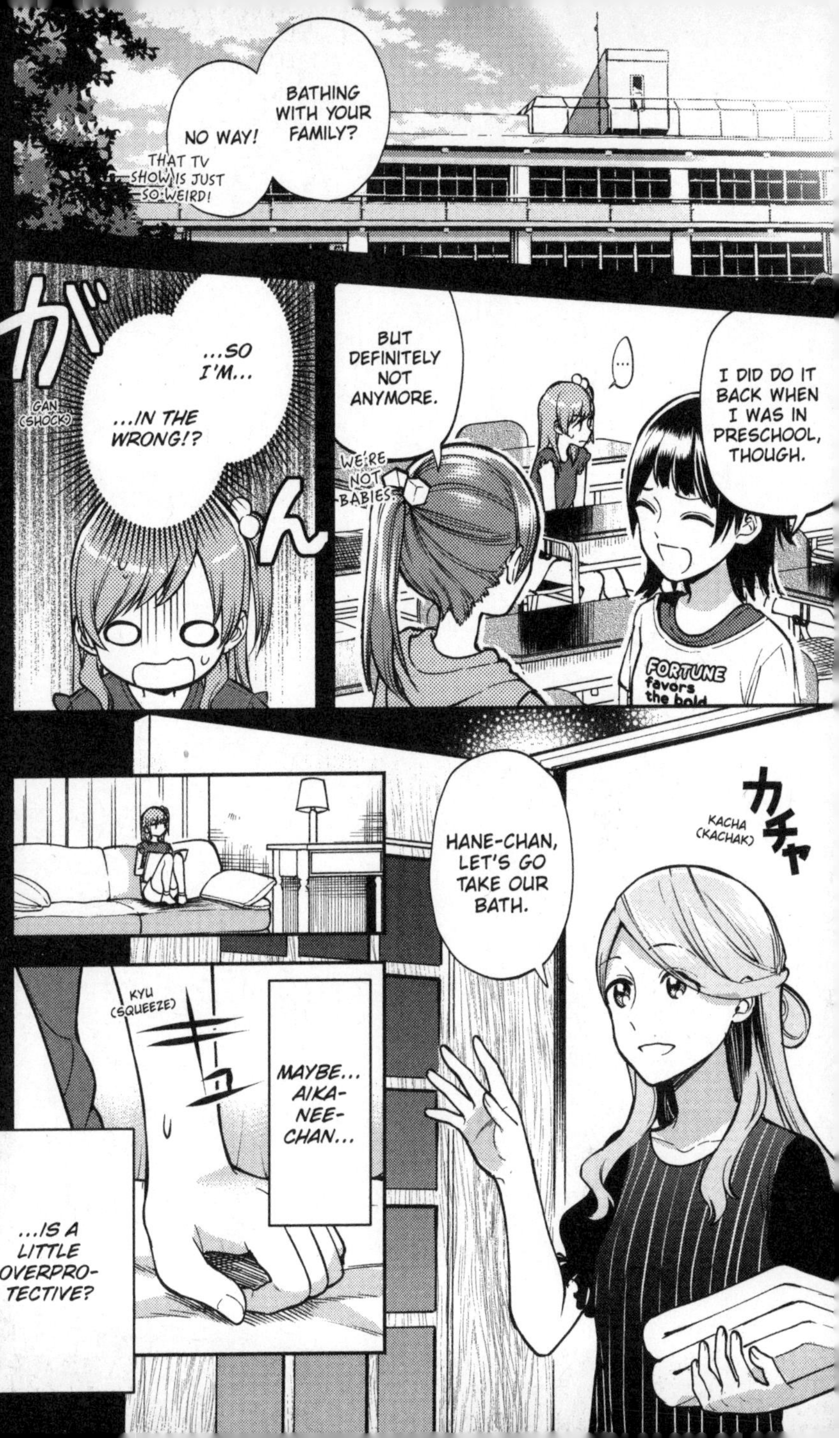
BATHING WITH YOUR FAMILY?
NO WAY!
THAT TV SHOW IS JUST SO WEIRD!
I DID DO IT BACK WHEN I WAS IN PRESCHOOL, THOUGH.
...
BUT DEFINITELY NOT ANYMORE.
WE'RE NOT BABIES.
FORTUNE favors the bold
...SO I'M...
...IN THE WRONG!?
がーん
GAN (SHOCK)
カチャ
KACHA (KACHAK)
HANE-CHAN, LET'S GO TAKE OUR BATH.
キュ
KYU (SQUEEZE)
MAYBE... AIKA-NEE-CHAN...
...IS A LITTLE OVERPROTECTIVE?

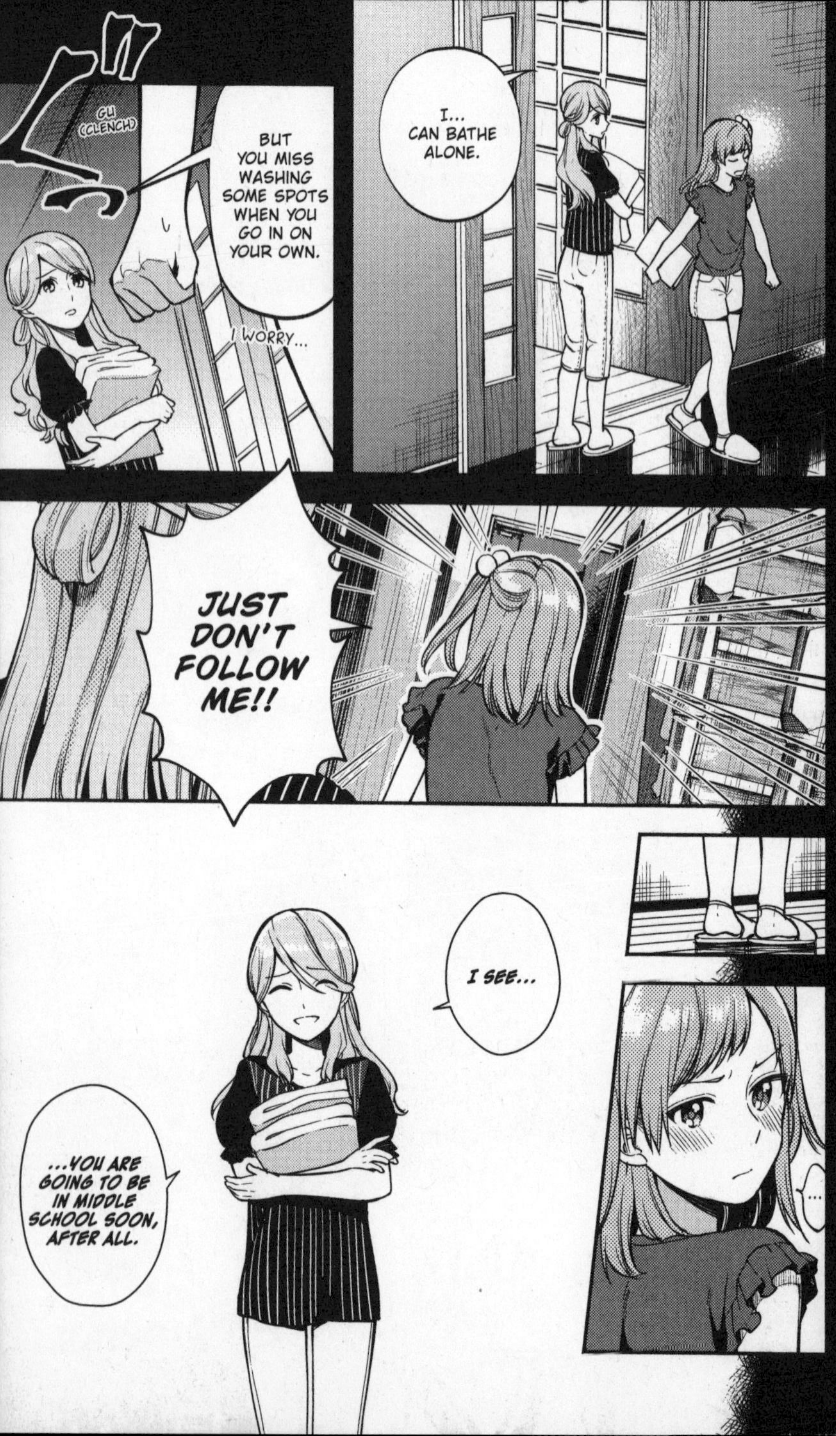
I... CAN BATHE ALONE.
GU (CLENCH)
BUT YOU MISS WASHING SOME SPOTS WHEN YOU GO IN ON YOUR OWN.
I WORRY...
JUST DON'T FOLLOW ME!!
...
I SEE...
...YOU ARE GOING TO BE IN MIDDLE SCHOOL SOON, AFTER ALL.

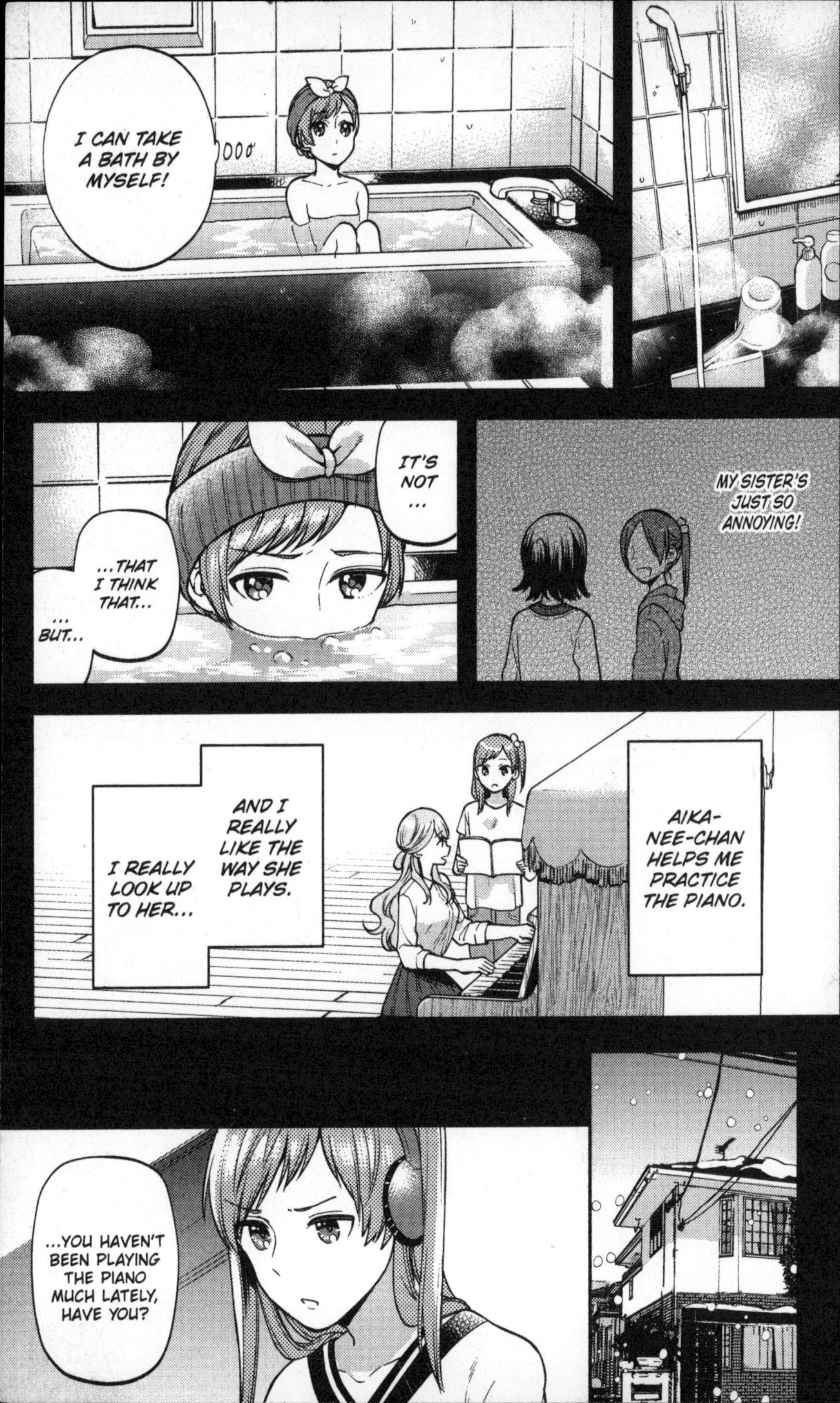
I CAN TAKE A BATH BY MYSELF!
MY SISTER'S JUST SO ANNOYING!
IT'S NOT ...
...THAT I THINK THAT...
... BUT...
AIKA-NEE-CHAN HELPS ME PRACTICE THE PIANO.
AND I REALLY LIKE THE WAY SHE PLAYS.
I REALLY LOOK UP TO HER...
...YOU HAVEN'T BEEN PLAYING THE PIANO MUCH LATELY, HAVE YOU?

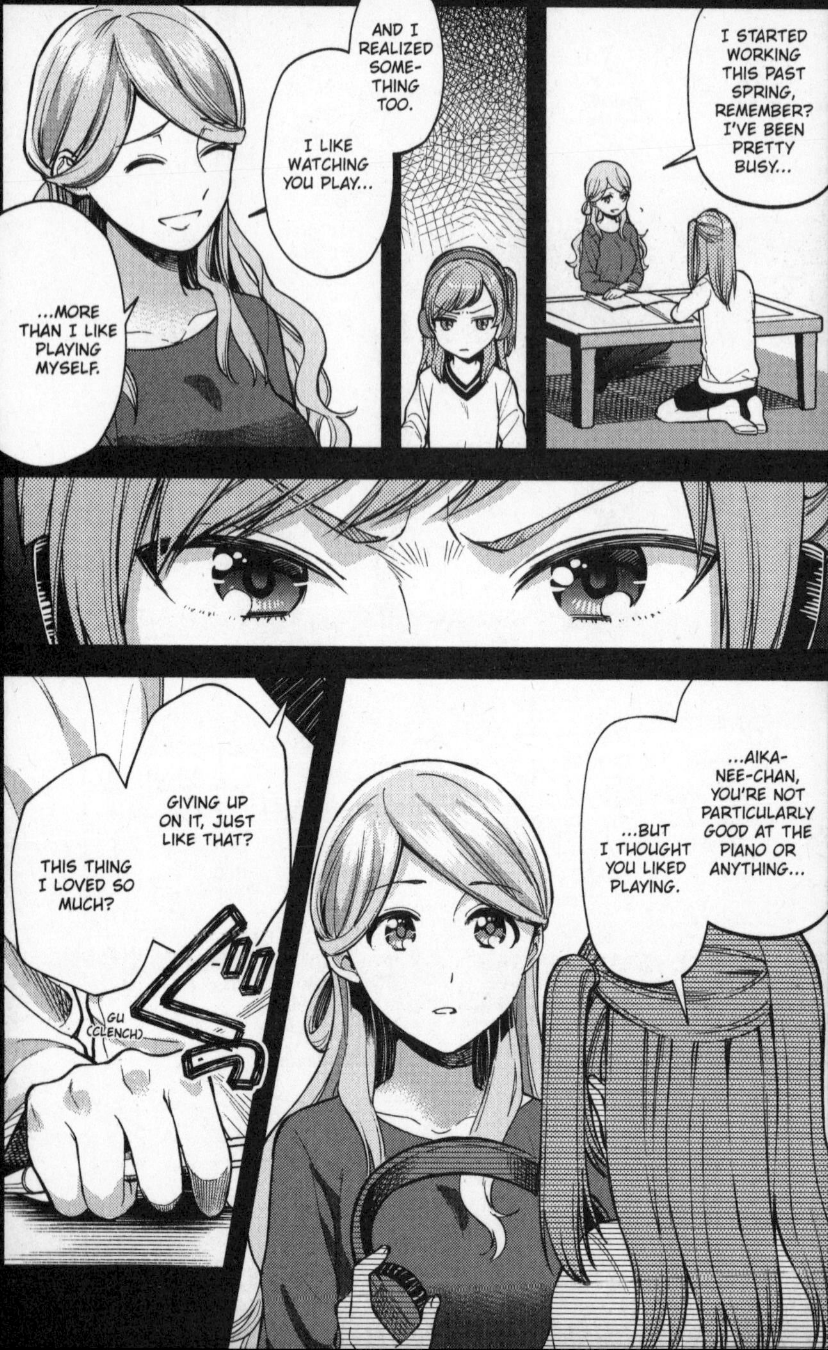
I STARTED WORKING THIS PAST SPRING, REMEMBER? I'VE BEEN PRETTY BUSY...
AND I REALIZED SOME-THING TOO.
I LIKE WATCHING YOU PLAY...
...MORE THAN I LIKE PLAYING MYSELF.
...AIKA-NEE-CHAN, YOU'RE NOT PARTICULARLY GOOD AT THE PIANO OR ANYTHING...
...BUT I THOUGHT YOU LIKED PLAYING.
GIVING UP ON IT, JUST LIKE THAT?
THIS THING I LOVED SO MUCH?
GU (CLENCH)

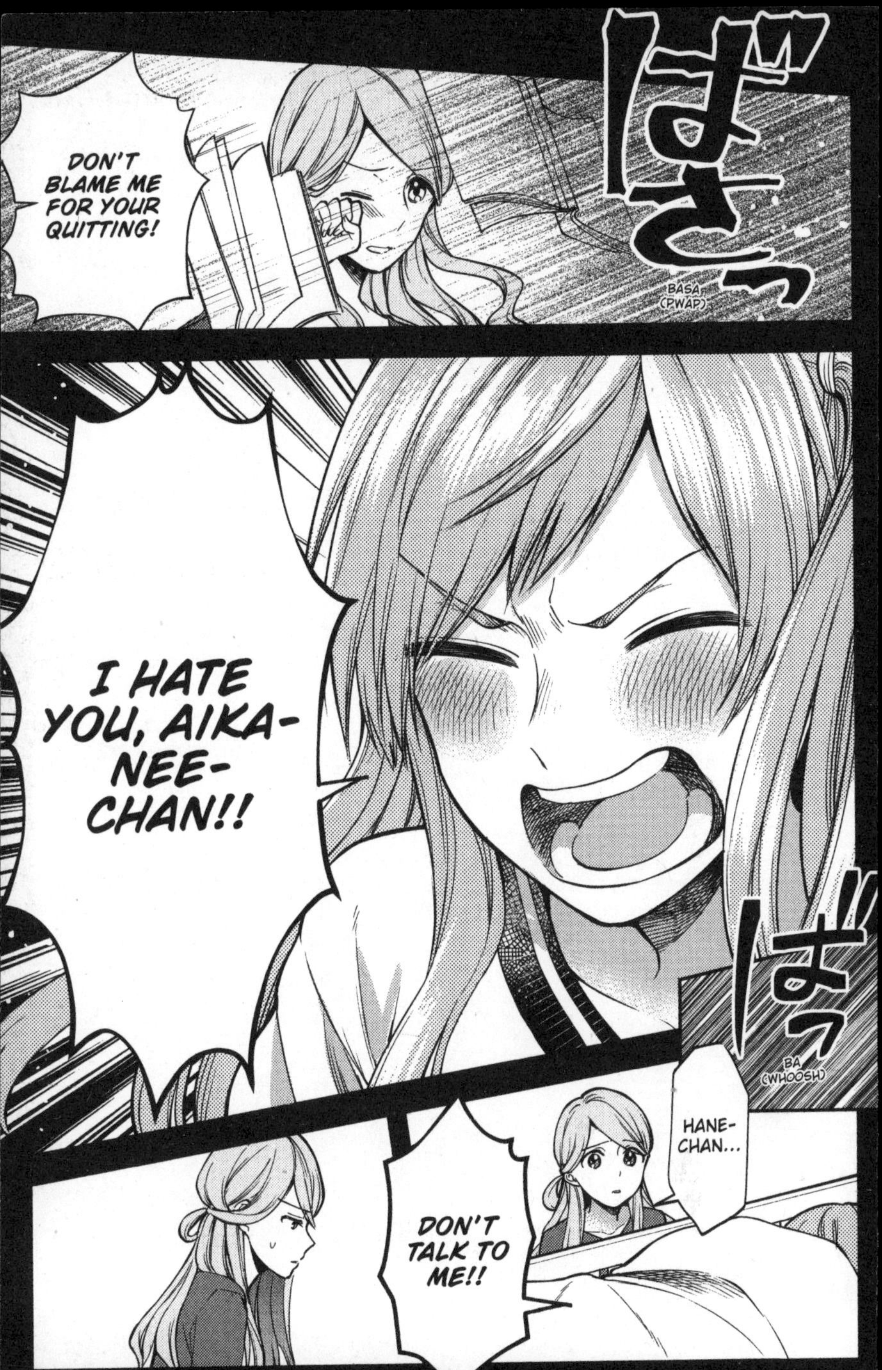
ばさっ
BASA (PWAP)
DON'T BLAME ME FOR YOUR QUITTING!
ばっ
BA (WHOOSH)
I HATE YOU, AIKA-NEE-CHAN!!
HANE-CHAN...
DON'T TALK TO ME!!

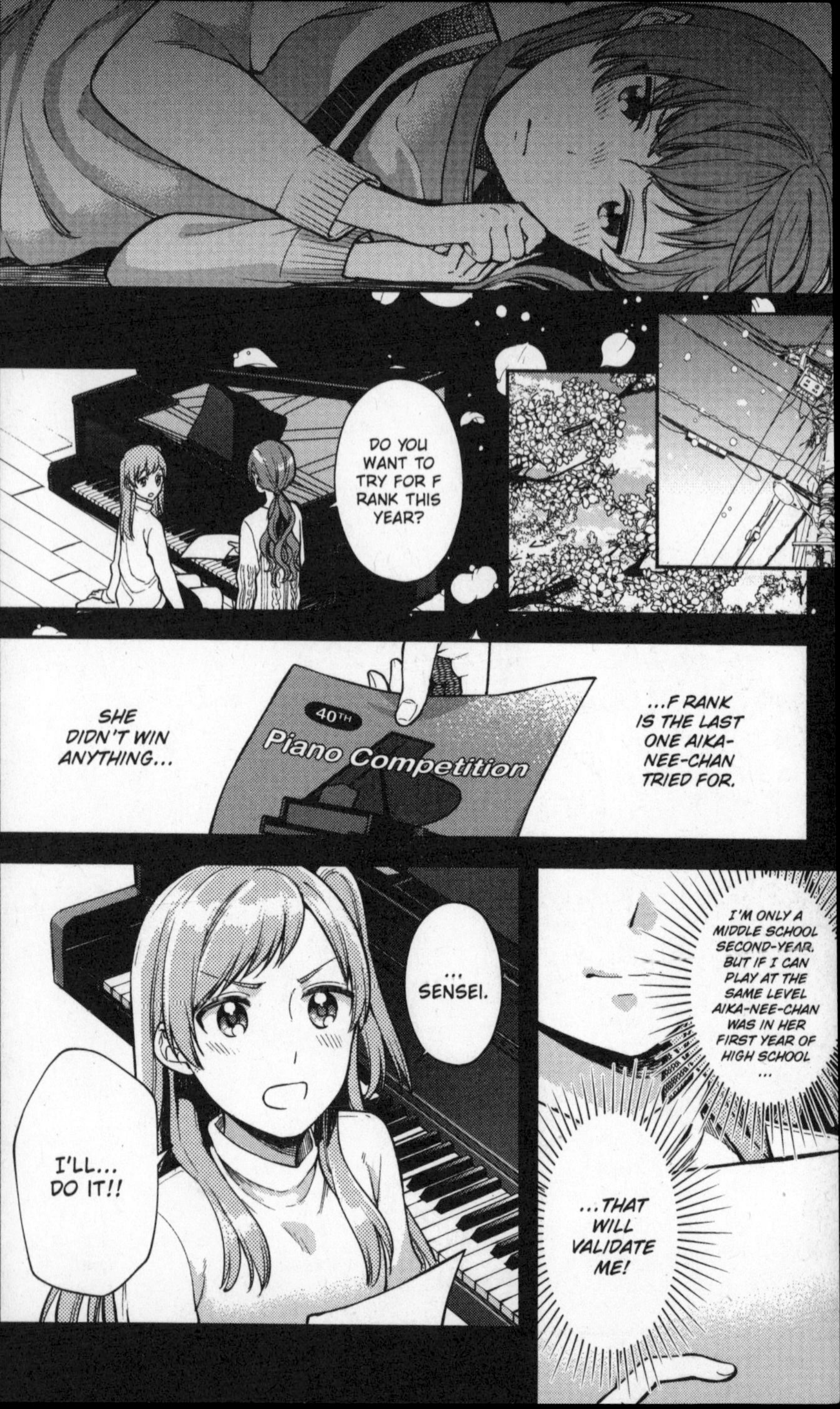
DO YOU WANT TO TRY FOR F RANK THIS YEAR?
...F RANK IS THE LAST ONE AIKA-NEE-CHAN TRIED FOR.
40TH
Piano Competition
SHE DIDN'T WIN ANYTHING...
I'M ONLY A MIDDLE SCHOOL SECOND-YEAR. BUT IF I CAN PLAY AT THE SAME LEVEL AIKA-NEE-CHAN WAS IN HER FIRST YEAR OF HIGH SCHOOL ...
...THAT WILL VALIDATE ME!
... SENSEI.
I'LL... DO IT!!

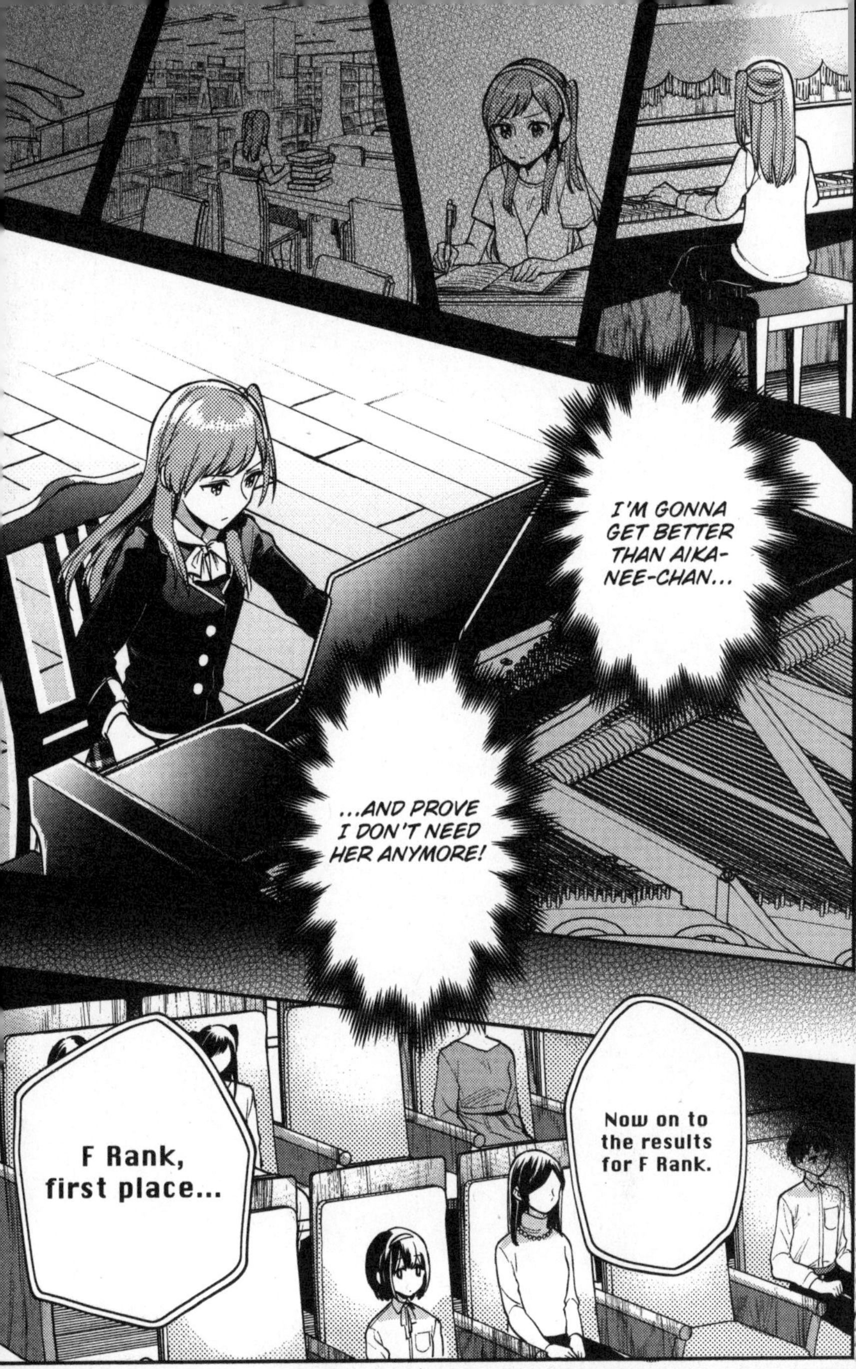
I'M GONNA GET BETTER THAN AIKA-NEE-CHAN...
...AND PROVE I DON'T NEED HER ANYMORE!
Now on to the results for F Rank.
F Rank, first place...

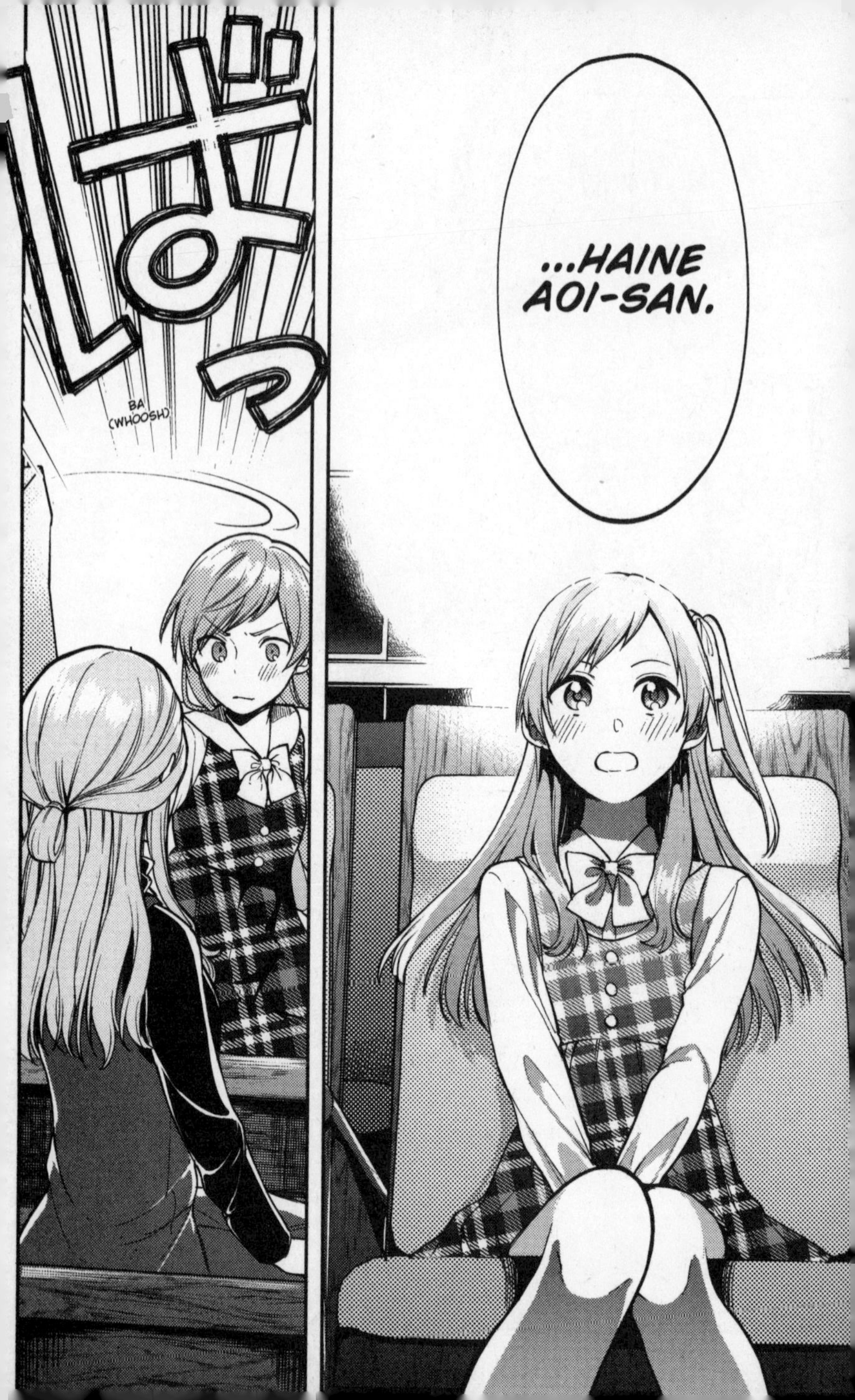
...HAINE AOI-SAN.
ばっ
BA (WHOOSH)

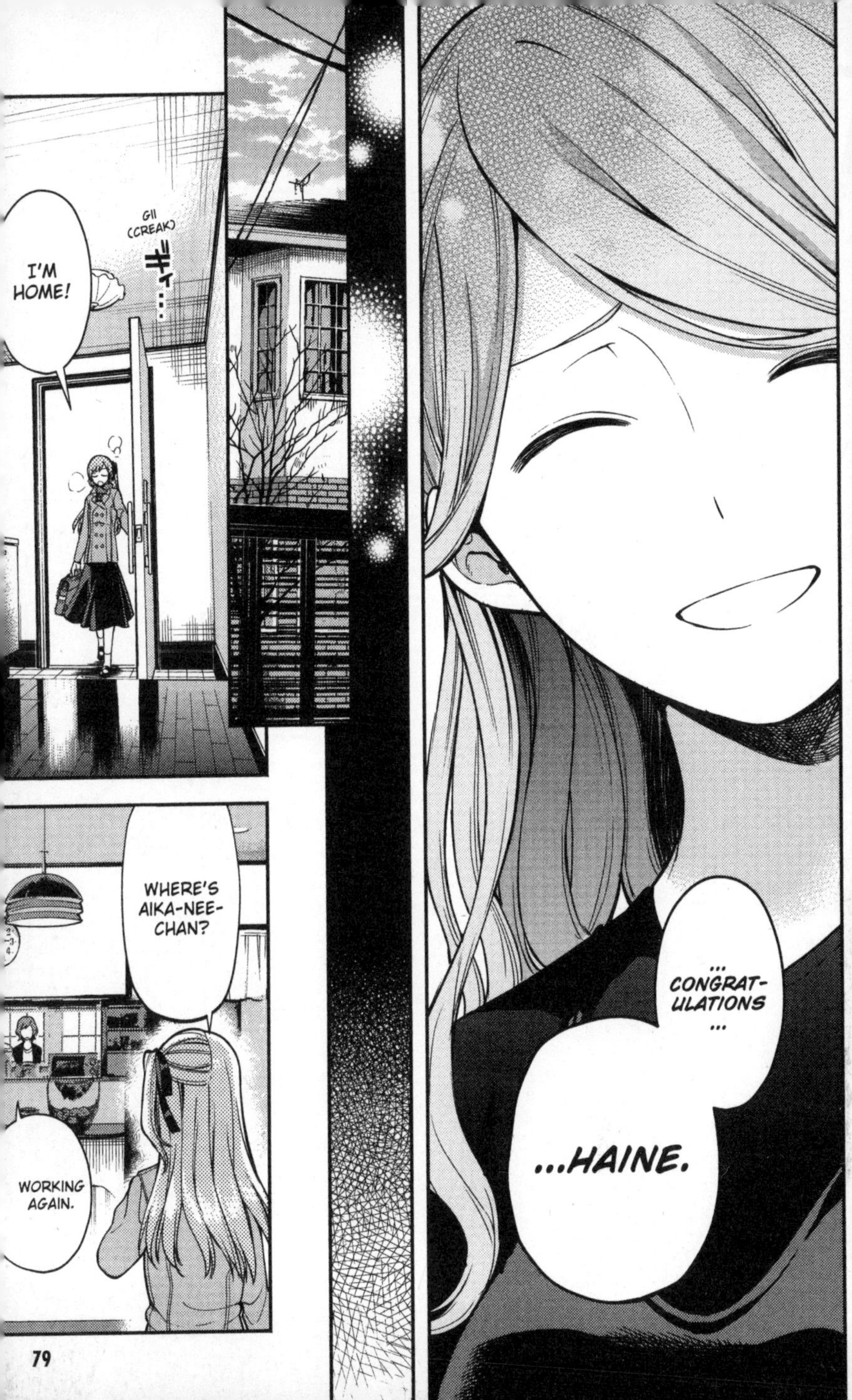
...CONGRATULATIONS...
...HAINE.
I'M HOME!
GII (CREAK)
ギィ...
WHERE'S AIKA-NEE-CHAN?
WORKING AGAIN.

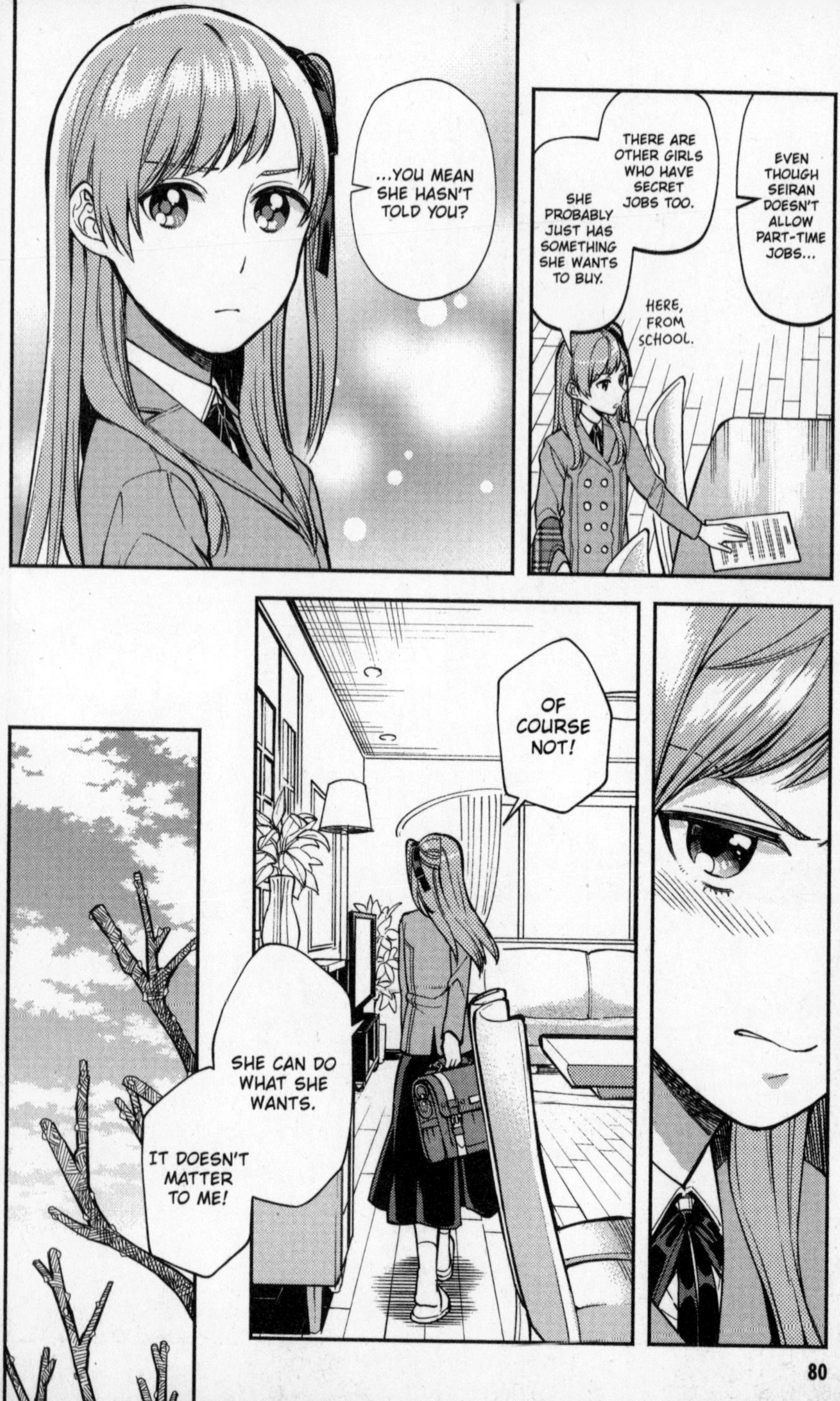
EVEN THOUGH SEIRAN DOESN'T ALLOW PART-TIME JOBS...
THERE ARE OTHER GIRLS WHO HAVE SECRET JOBS TOO.
SHE PROBABLY JUST HAS SOMETHING SHE WANTS TO BUY.
HERE, FROM SCHOOL.
...YOU MEAN SHE HASN'T TOLD YOU?
OF COURSE NOT!
SHE CAN DO WHAT SHE WANTS.
IT DOESN'T MATTER TO ME!

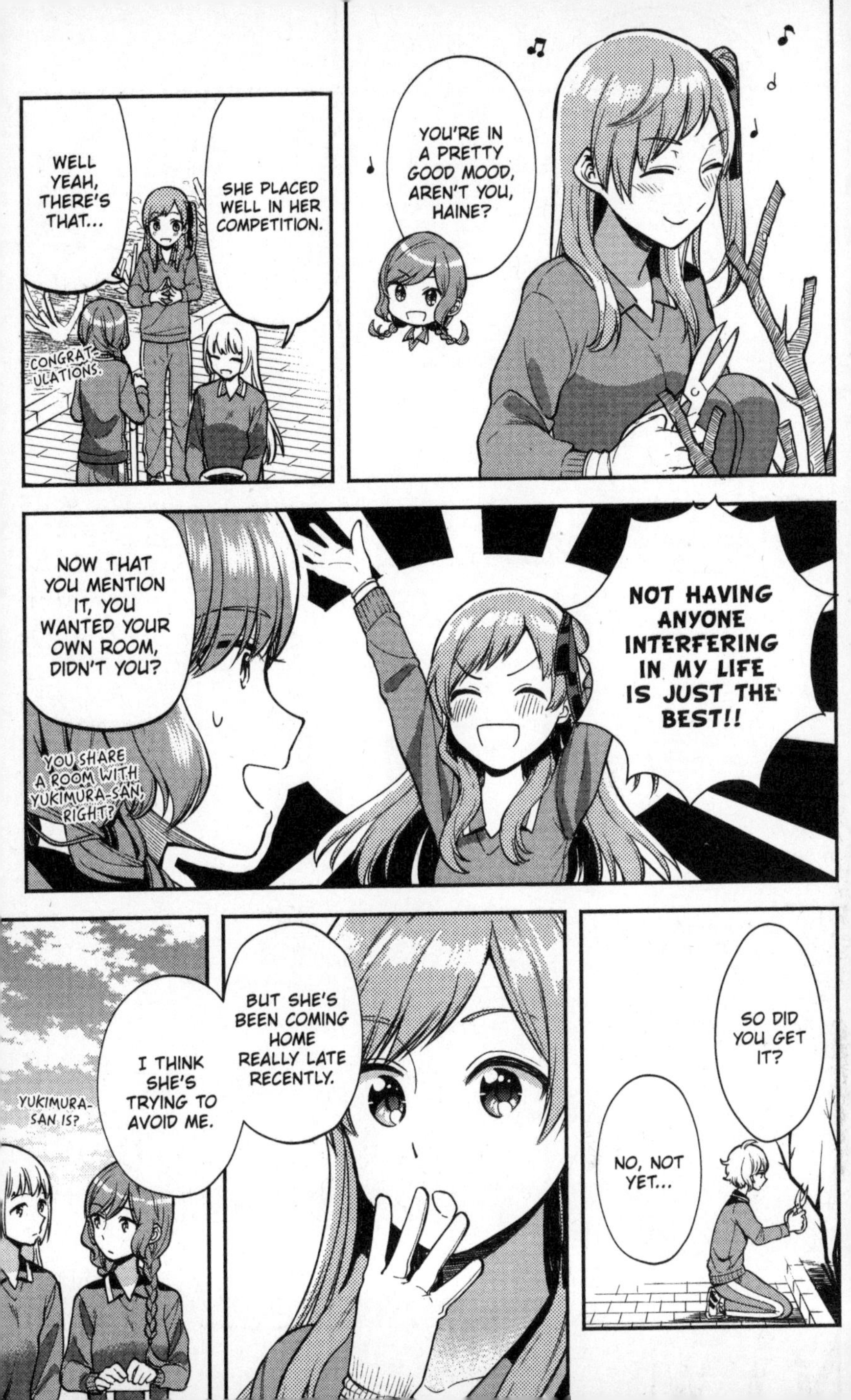
YOU'RE IN A PRETTY GOOD MOOD, AREN'T YOU, HAINE?
SHE PLACED WELL IN HER COMPETITION.
WELL YEAH, THERE'S THAT...
CONGRATULATIONS.
NOT HAVING ANYONE INTERFERING IN MY LIFE IS JUST THE BEST!!
NOW THAT YOU MENTION IT, YOU WANTED YOUR OWN ROOM, DIDN'T YOU?
YOU SHARE A ROOM WITH YUKIMURA-SAN, RIGHT?
SO DID YOU GET IT?
NO, NOT YET...
BUT SHE'S BEEN COMING HOME REALLY LATE RECENTLY.
I THINK SHE'S TRYING TO AVOID ME.
YUKIMURA-SAN IS?

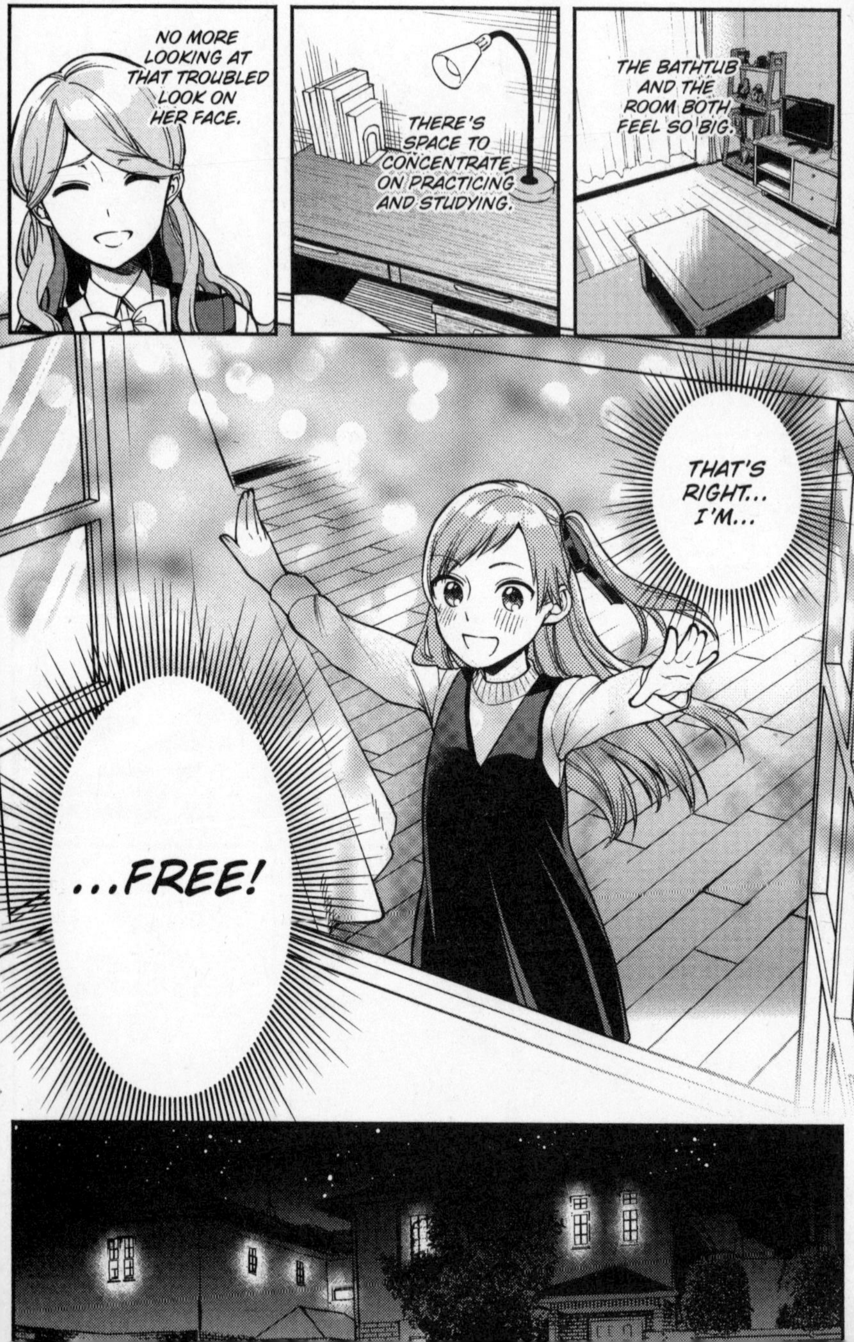
THE BATHTUB AND THE ROOM BOTH FEEL SO BIG.
THERE'S SPACE TO CONCENTRATE ON PRACTICING AND STUDYING.
NO MORE LOOKING AT THAT TROUBLED LOOK ON HER FACE.
THAT'S RIGHT... I'M...
...FREE!

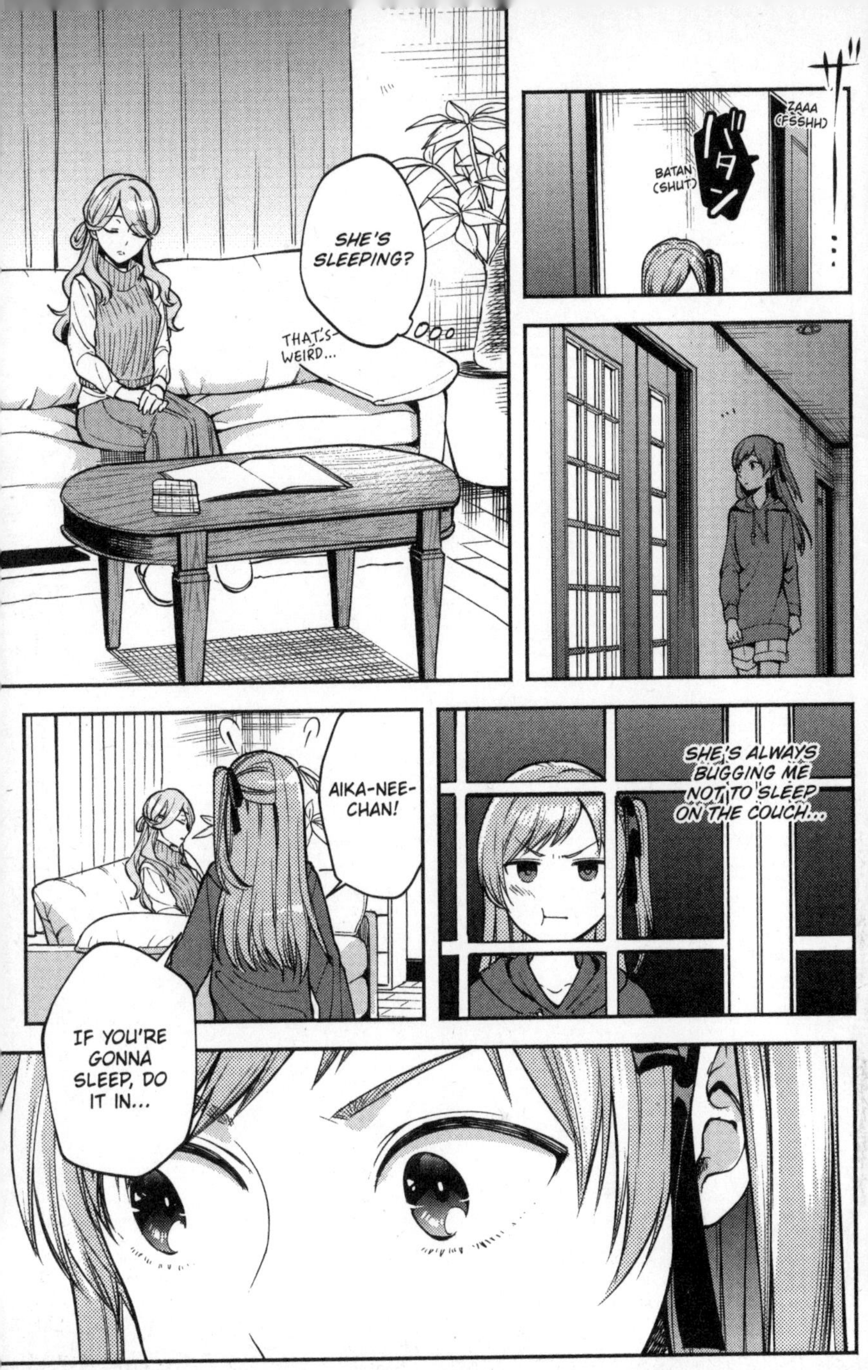

ZAAA (FSSHH)
BATAN (SHUT)
...
...
SHE'S SLEEPING?
THAT'S WEIRD...
SHE'S ALWAYS BUGGING ME NOT TO SLEEP ON THE COUCH...
AIKA-NEE-CHAN!
IF YOU'RE GONNA SLEEP, DO IT IN...

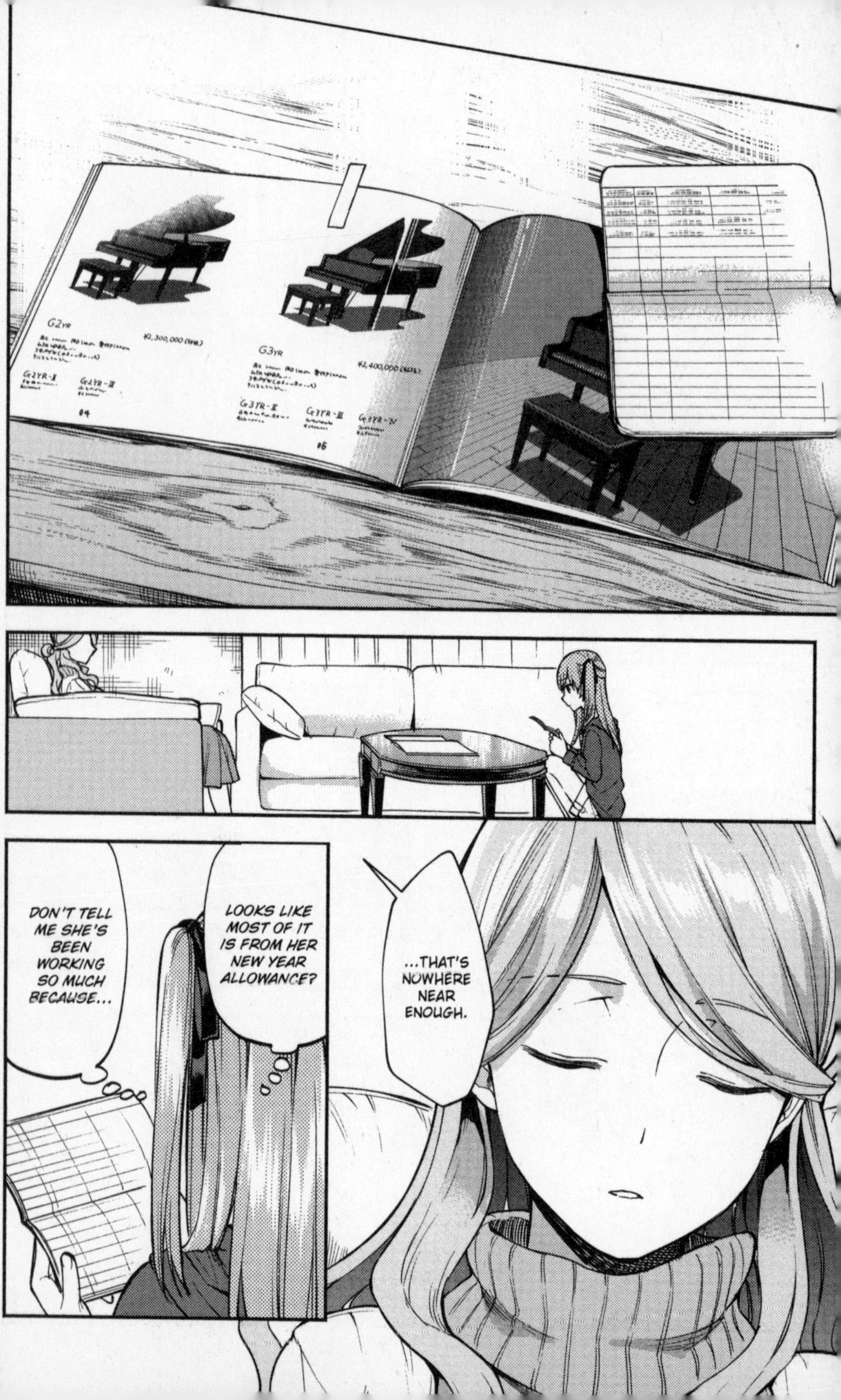
G2YR
G3YR
...THAT'S NOWHERE NEAR ENOUGH.
LOOKS LIKE MOST OF IT IS FROM HER NEW YEAR ALLOWANCE?
DON'T TELL ME SHE'S BEEN WORKING SO MUCH BECAUSE...

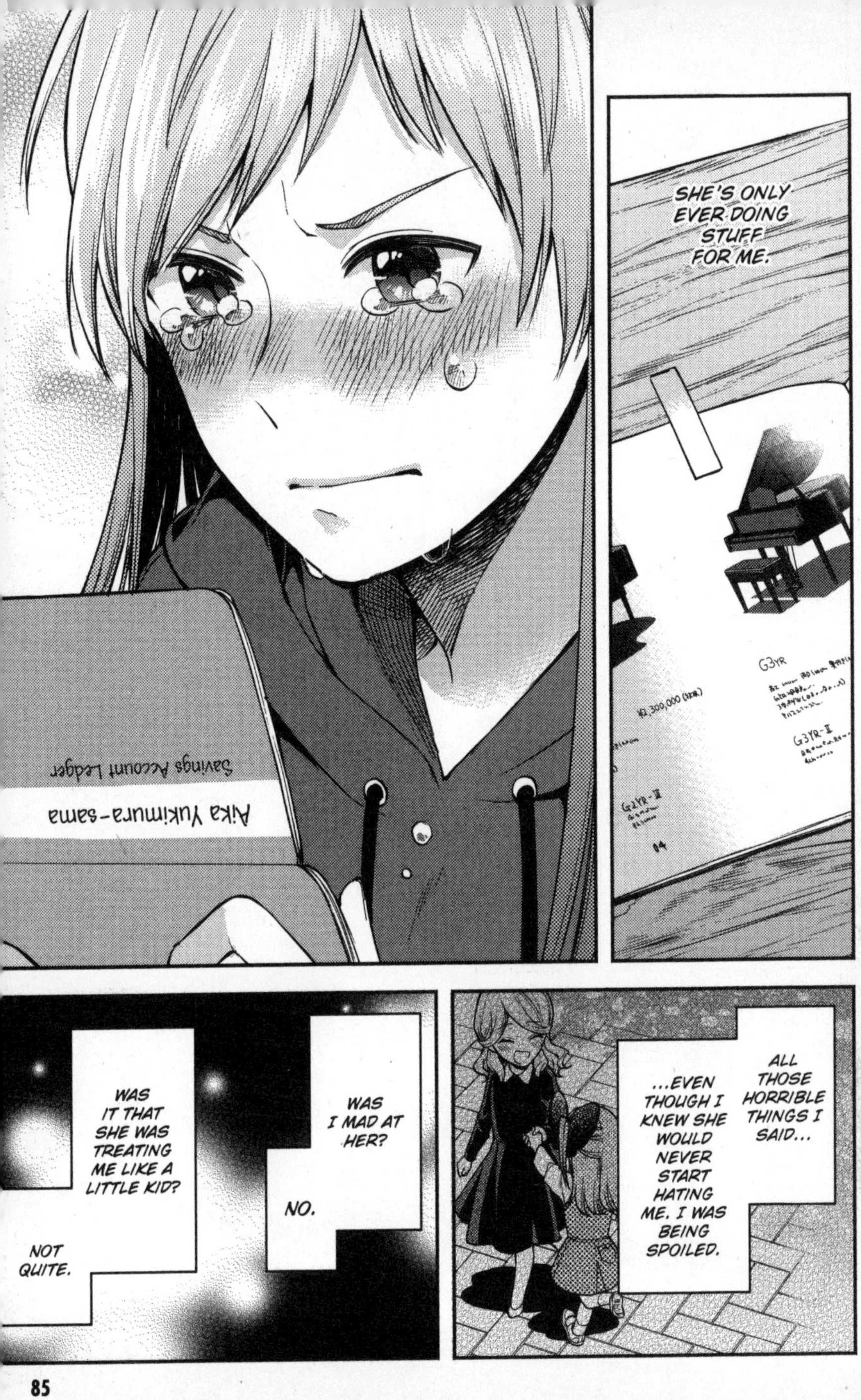
SHE'S ONLY EVER DOING STUFF FOR ME.
Savings Account Ledger
Aika Yukimura-sama
ALL THOSE HORRIBLE THINGS I SAID...
...EVEN THOUGH I KNEW SHE WOULD NEVER START HATING ME. I WAS BEING SPOILED.
WAS I MAD AT HER?
NO.
WAS IT THAT SHE WAS TREATING ME LIKE A LITTLE KID?
NOT QUITE.

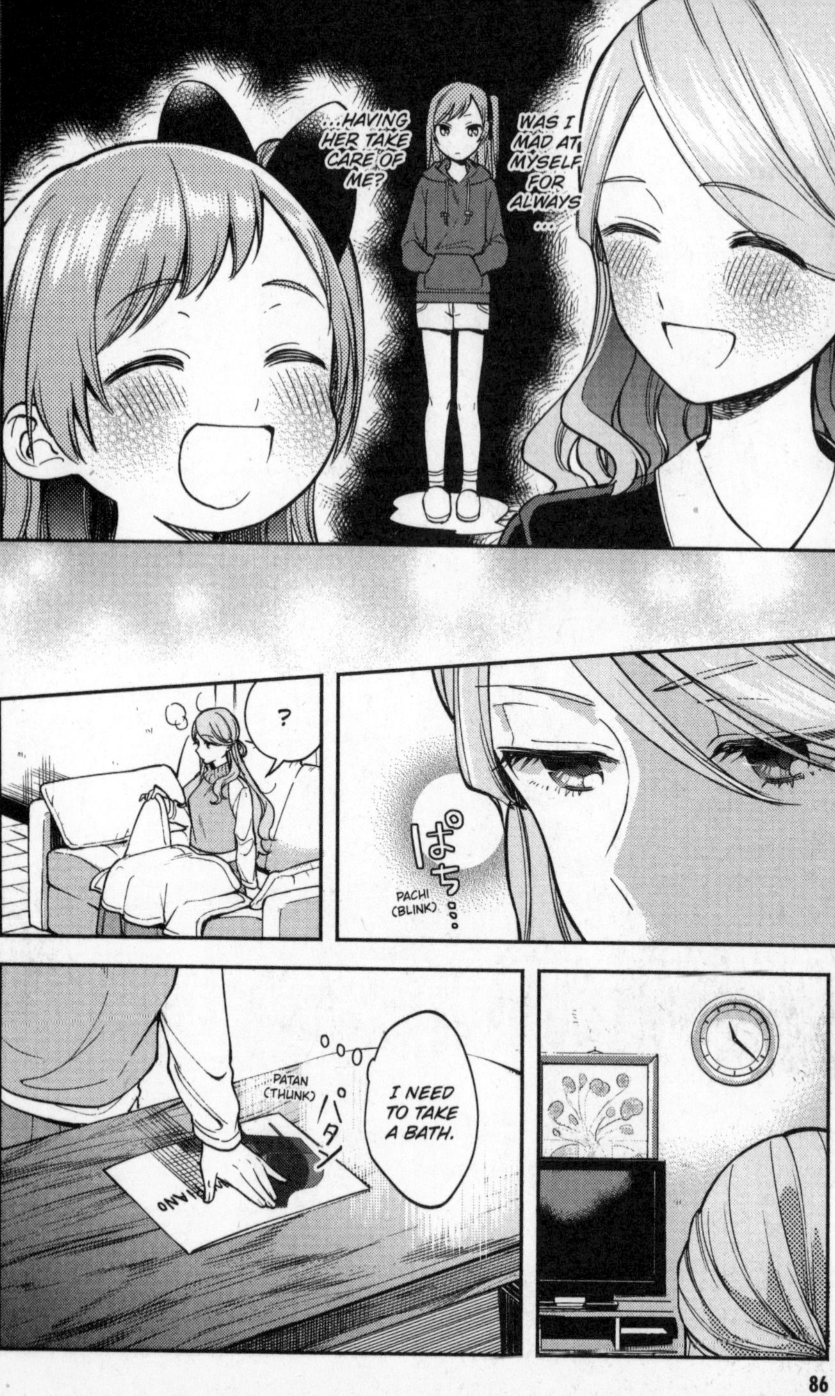
WAS I MAD AT MYSELF FOR ALWAYS ...
...HAVING HER TAKE CARE OF ME?
ぱち...
PACHI (BLINK)
?
I NEED TO TAKE A BATH.
パタン
PATAN (THUNK)

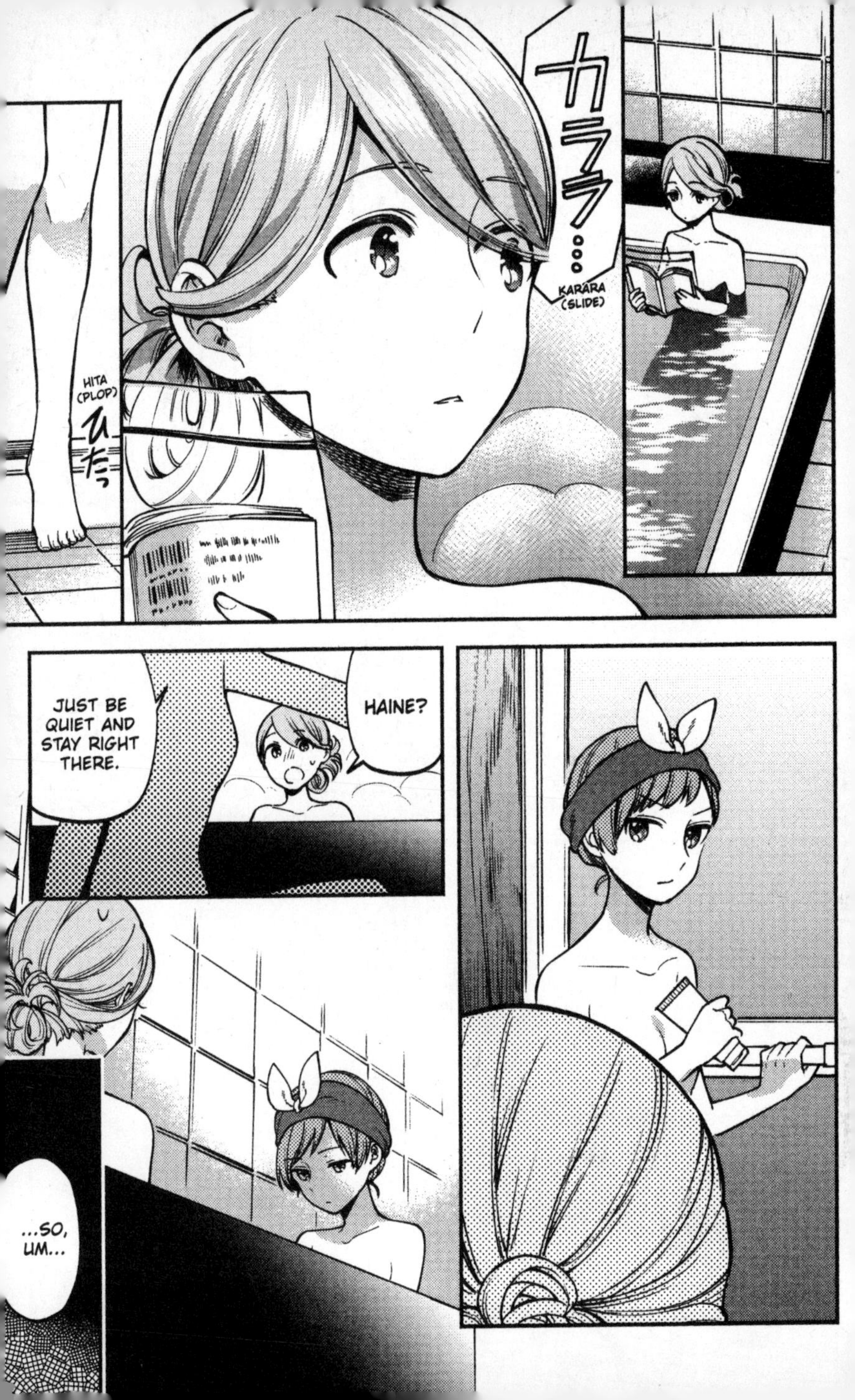
カララ…
KARARA (SLIDE)
HITA (PLOP)
ひたっ
HAINE?
JUST BE QUIET AND STAY RIGHT THERE.
...SO, UM...

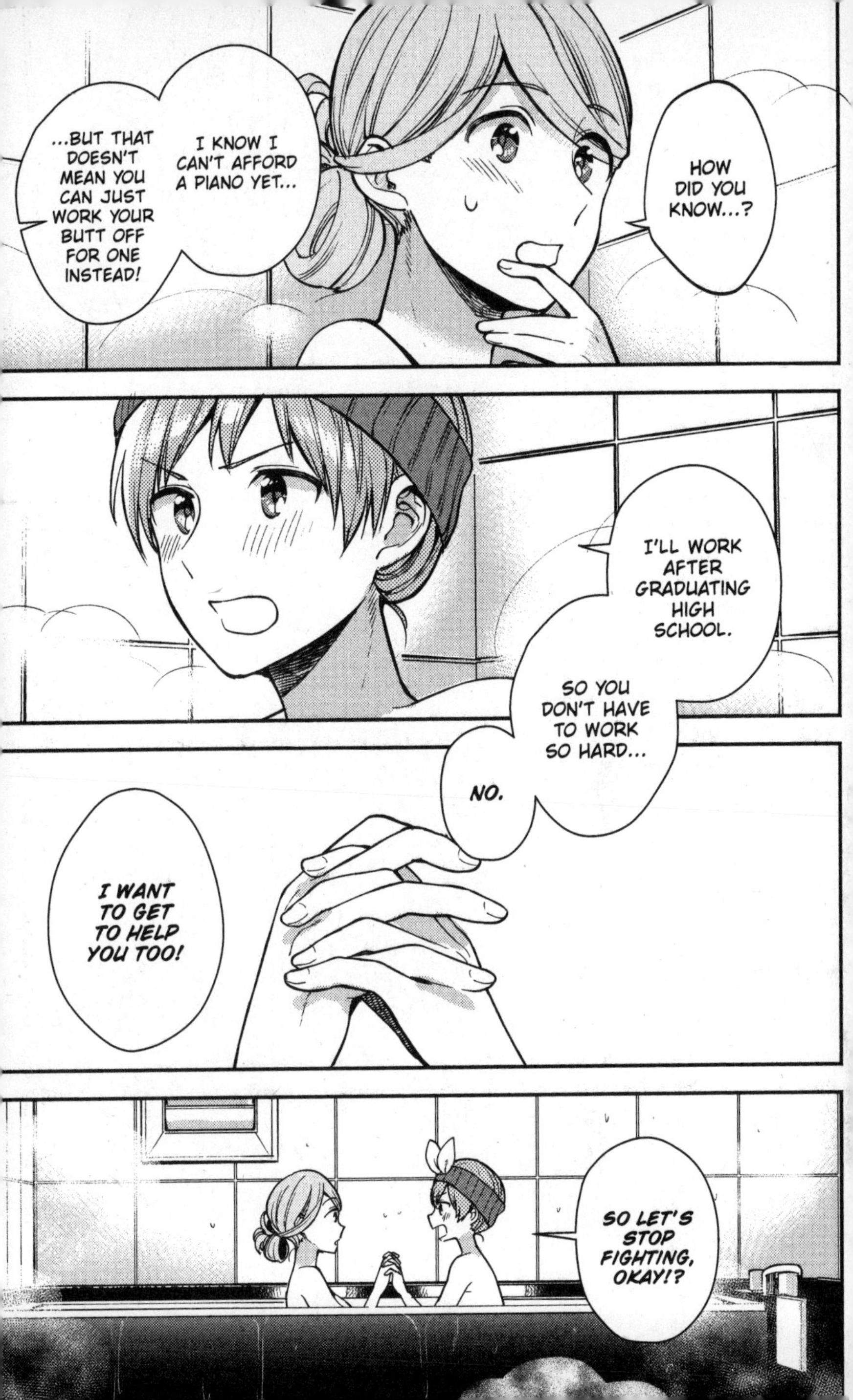
HOW DID YOU KNOW...?
I KNOW I CAN'T AFFORD A PIANO YET...
...BUT THAT DOESN'T MEAN YOU CAN JUST WORK YOUR BUTT OFF FOR ONE INSTEAD!
I'LL WORK AFTER GRADUATING HIGH SCHOOL.
SO YOU DON'T HAVE TO WORK SO HARD...
NO.
I WANT TO GET TO HELP YOU TOO!
SO LET'S STOP FIGHTING, OKAY!?

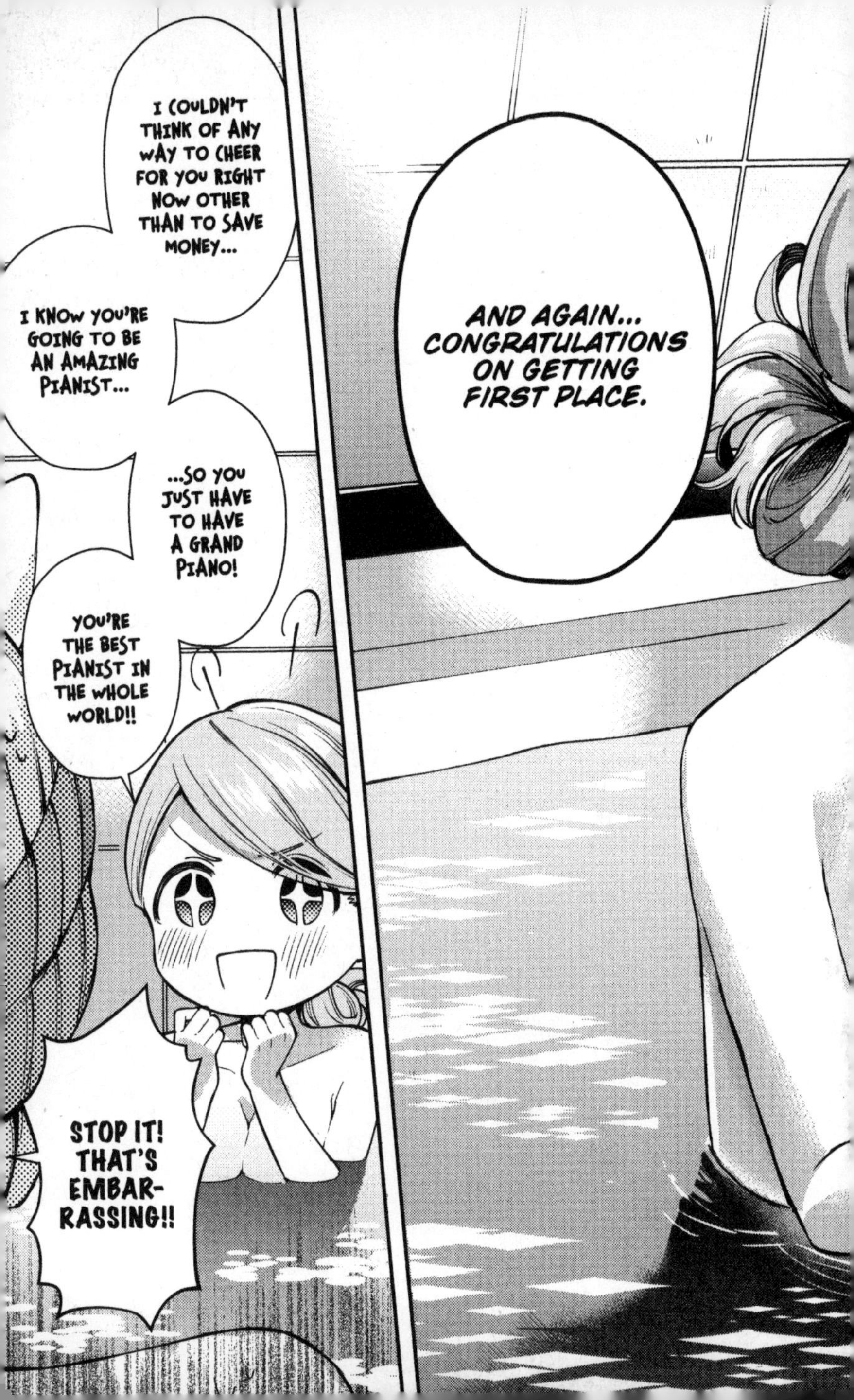
AND AGAIN... CONGRATULATIONS ON GETTING FIRST PLACE.
I COULDN'T THINK OF ANY WAY TO CHEER FOR YOU RIGHT NOW OTHER THAN TO SAVE MONEY...
I KNOW YOU'RE GOING TO BE AN AMAZING PIANIST...
...SO YOU JUST HAVE TO HAVE A GRAND PIANO!
YOU'RE THE BEST PIANIST IN THE WHOLE WORLD!!
STOP IT! THAT'S EMBAR-RASSING!!

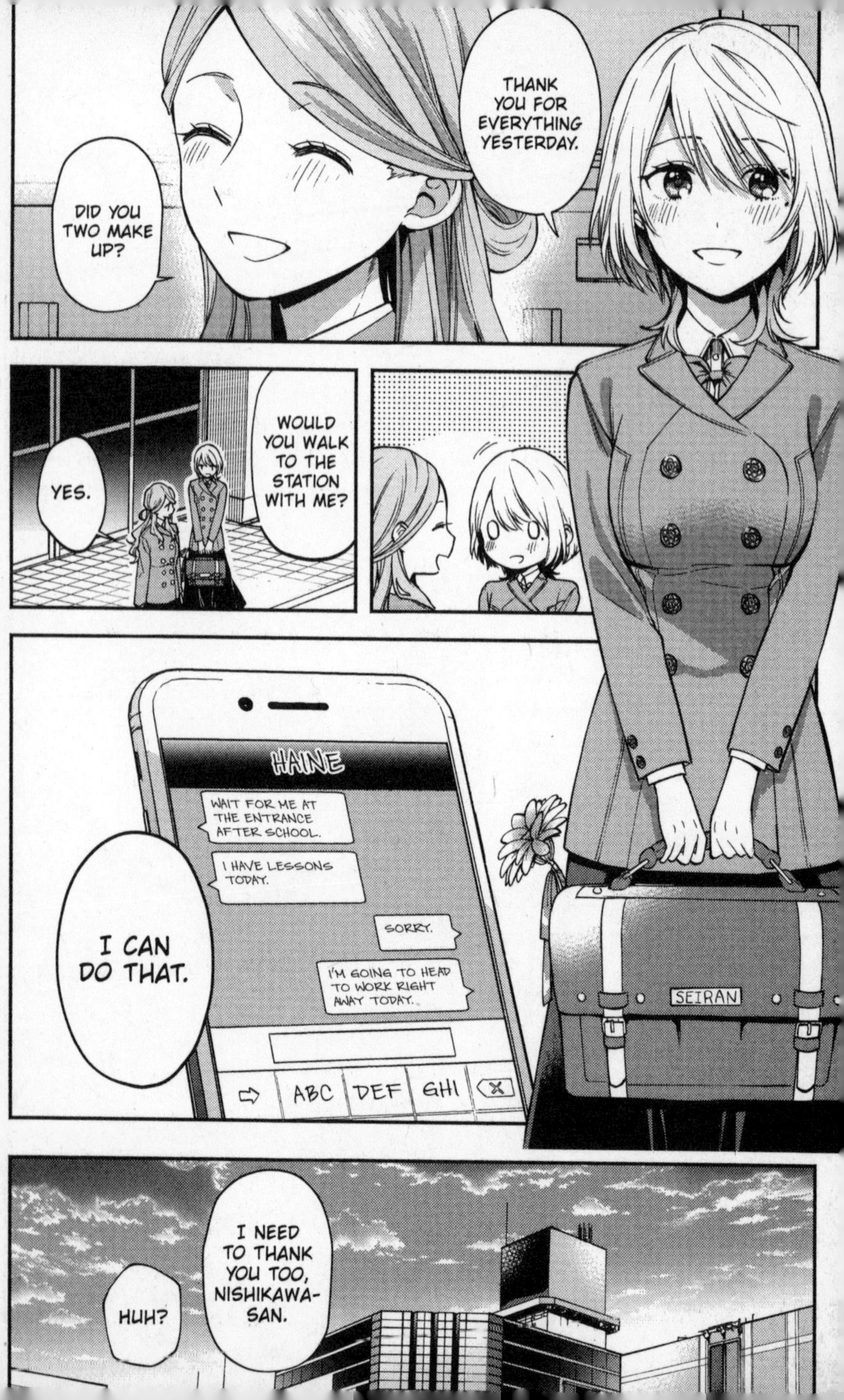
THANK YOU FOR EVERYTHING YESTERDAY.
DID YOU TWO MAKE UP?
WOULD YOU WALK TO THE STATION WITH ME?
YES.
HAINE
WAIT FOR ME AT THE ENTRANCE AFTER SCHOOL.
I HAVE LESSONS TODAY.
SORRY.
I'M GOING TO HEAD TO WORK RIGHT AWAY TODAY.
ABC DEF GHI
I CAN DO THAT.
SEIRAN
I NEED TO THANK YOU TOO, NISHIKAWA-SAN.
HUH?

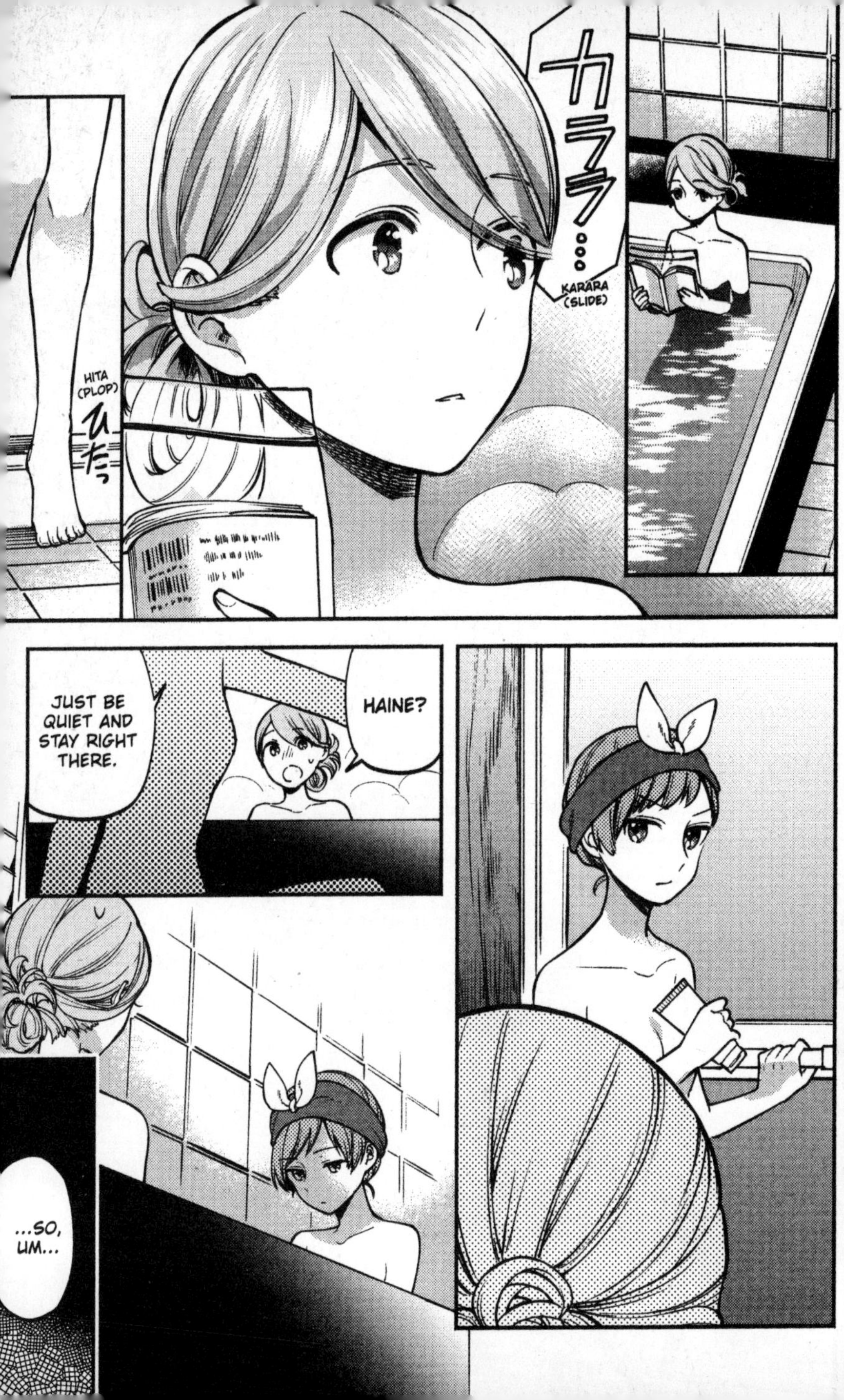
カララ…
KARARA (SLIDE)
ひたっ
HITA (PLOP)
HAINE?
JUST BE QUIET AND STAY RIGHT THERE.
...SO, UM...

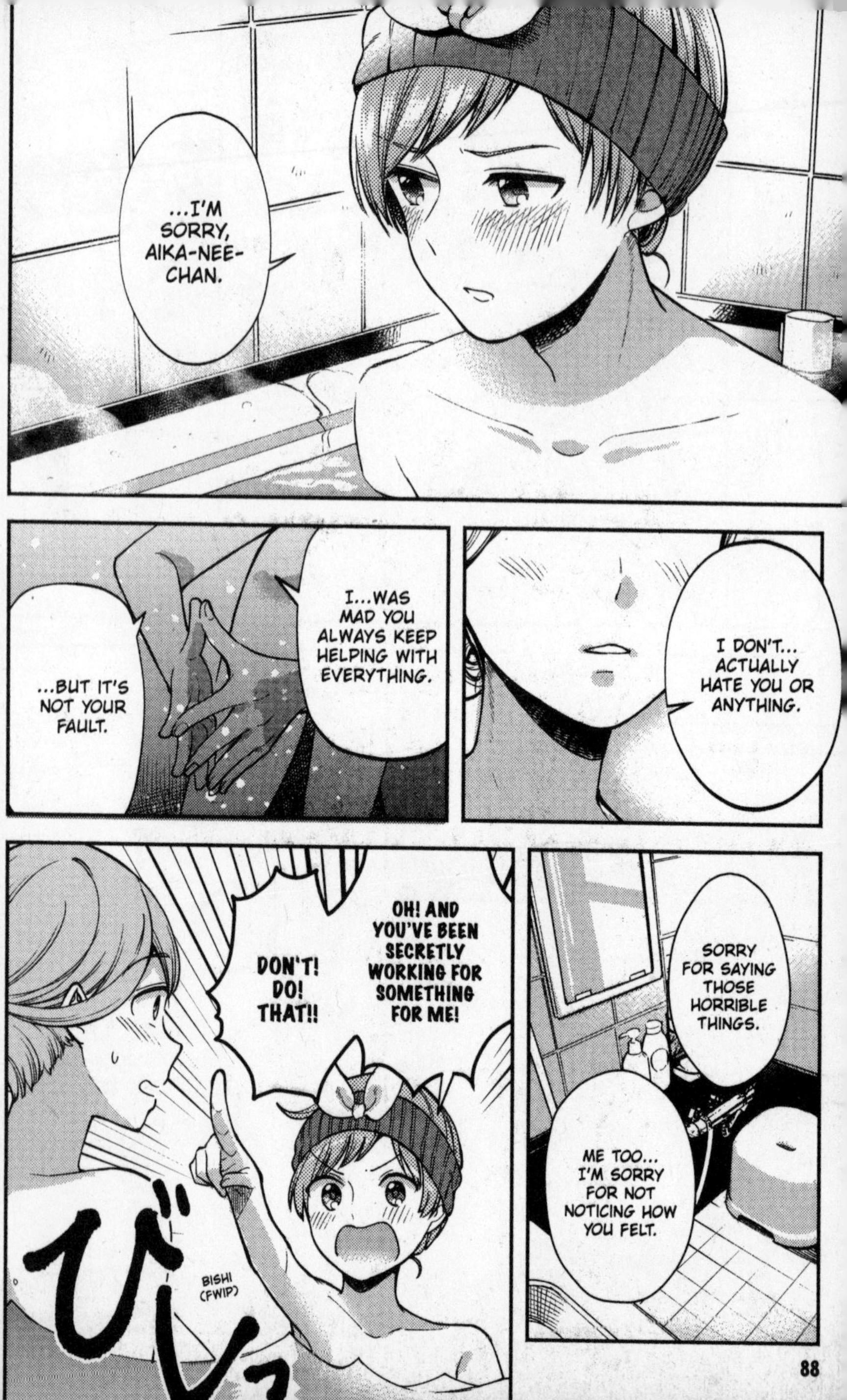
...I'M SORRY, AIKA-NEE-CHAN.
I DON'T... ACTUALLY HATE YOU OR ANYTHING.
I...WAS MAD YOU ALWAYS KEEP HELPING WITH EVERYTHING.
...BUT IT'S NOT YOUR FAULT.
SORRY FOR SAYING THOSE HORRIBLE THINGS.
ME TOO... I'M SORRY FOR NOT NOTICING HOW YOU FELT.
OH! AND YOU'VE BEEN SECRETLY WORKING FOR SOMETHING FOR ME!
DON'T! DO! THAT!!
BISHI (FWIP)

OKAY...
THANK YOU,
HANE-CHAN.

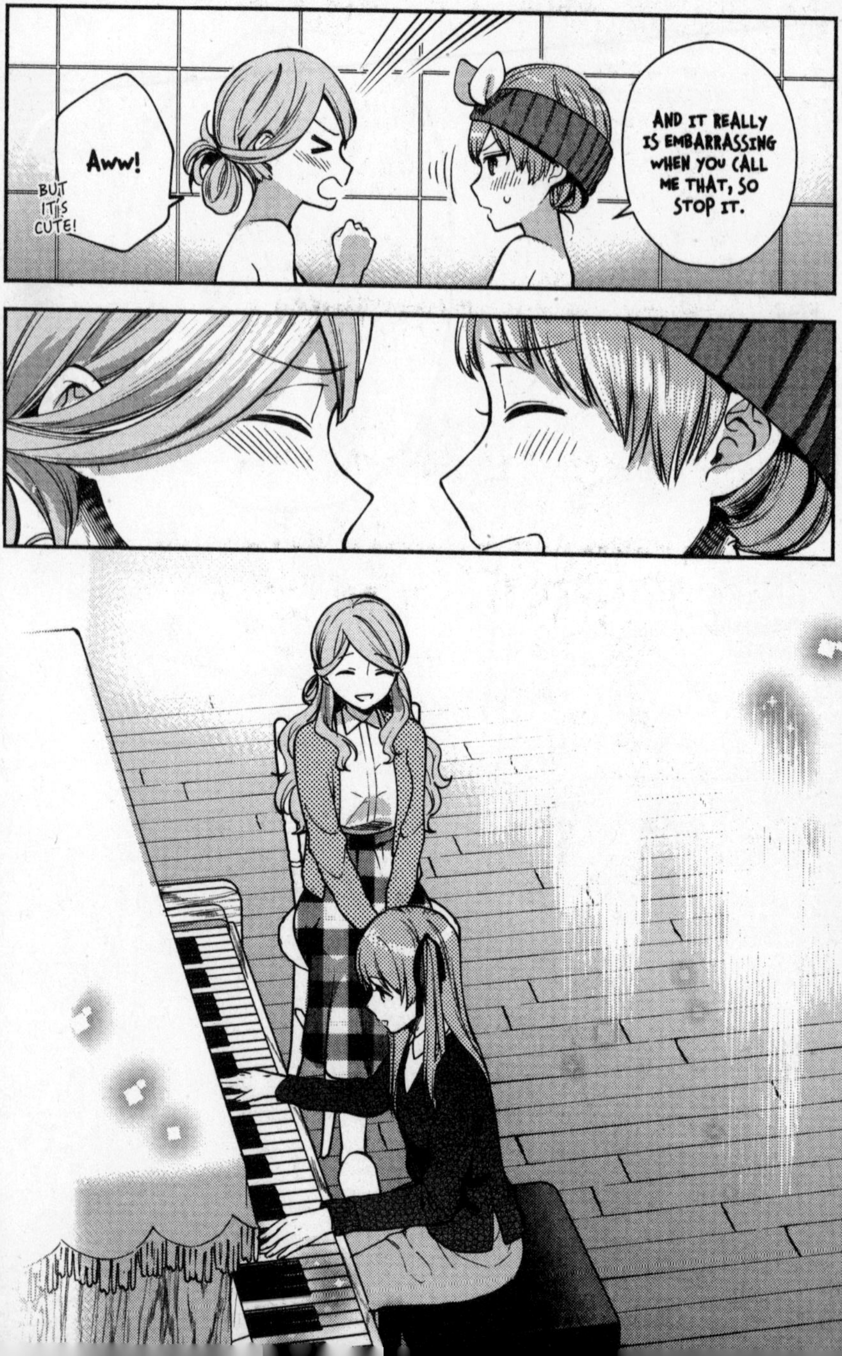

AND IT REALLY IS EMBARRASSING WHEN YOU CALL ME THAT, SO STOP IT.
Aww!
BUT IT'S CUTE!

KISS THEATER: WHAT'S BEHIND THE STORY!? ✶ PEOPLE OTHER THAN THE MAIN CHARACTERS HAVE STORIES TOO. HERE, WE PRESENT THE "LITTLE LOVE" STORIES HAPPENING BEHIND THE SCENES.

Everyone Is Different

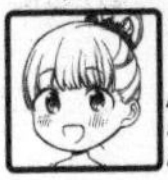

KAZUNA
HIGH SCHOOL SECOND-YEAR. LOVES THE PIANO.

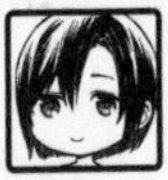

JUNKO
KAZUNA'S AUNT. SHE USED TO PLAY THE PIANO.

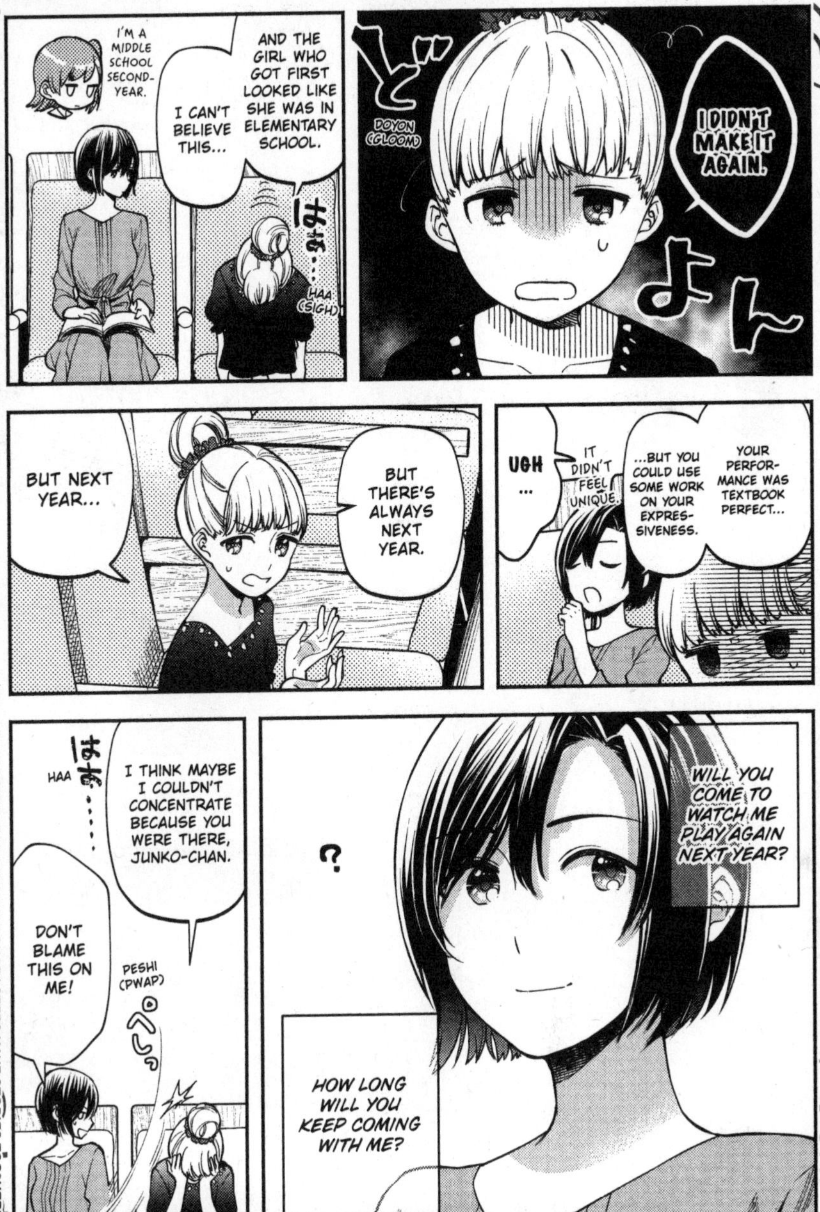
どよん
DOYON (GLOOM)
I DIDN'T MAKE IT AGAIN.
AND THE GIRL WHO GOT FIRST LOOKED LIKE SHE WAS IN ELEMENTARY SCHOOL.
I'M A MIDDLE SCHOOL SECOND-YEAR.
I CAN'T BELIEVE THIS...
はぁ…
HAA (SIGH)
YOUR PERFORMANCE WAS TEXTBOOK PERFECT...
...BUT YOU COULD USE SOME WORK ON YOUR EXPRESSIVENESS.
IT DIDN'T FEEL UNIQUE.
UGH...
BUT THERE'S ALWAYS NEXT YEAR.
BUT NEXT YEAR...
WILL YOU COME TO WATCH ME PLAY AGAIN NEXT YEAR?
?
HOW LONG WILL YOU KEEP COMING WITH ME?
はぁ……
HAA
I THINK MAYBE I COULDN'T CONCENTRATE BECAUSE YOU WERE THERE, JUNKO-CHAN.
DON'T BLAME THIS ON ME!
PESHI (PWAP)
ぺしっ

Aika Yukimura

Aika Yukimura

Third-year student in the Seiran Academy High School. She's Haine's mother's younger sister, which makes her Haine's aunt. She's fairly laid-back. She grew up with Haine and is like a sister to her. Taking care of Haine is one of her reasons for living. She has a part-time job at a donut shop.

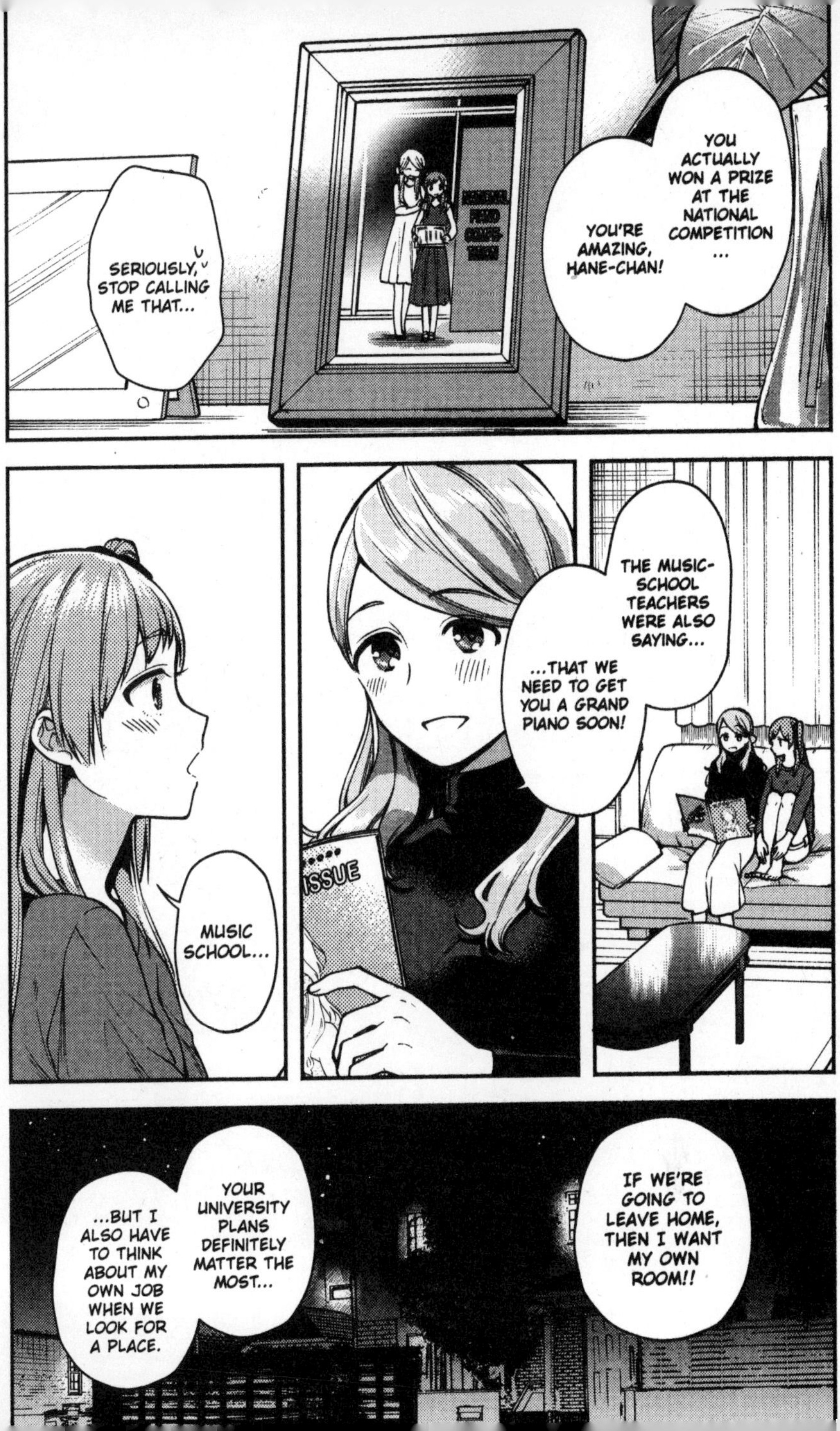

YOU ACTUALLY WON A PRIZE AT THE NATIONAL COMPETITION...
YOU'RE AMAZING, HANE-CHAN!
SERIOUSLY, STOP CALLING ME THAT...
THE MUSIC-SCHOOL TEACHERS WERE ALSO SAYING...
...THAT WE NEED TO GET YOU A GRAND PIANO SOON!
ISSUE
MUSIC SCHOOL...
IF WE'RE GOING TO LEAVE HOME, THEN I WANT MY OWN ROOM!!
YOUR UNIVERSITY PLANS DEFINITELY MATTER THE MOST...
...BUT I ALSO HAVE TO THINK ABOUT MY OWN JOB WHEN WE LOOK FOR A PLACE.

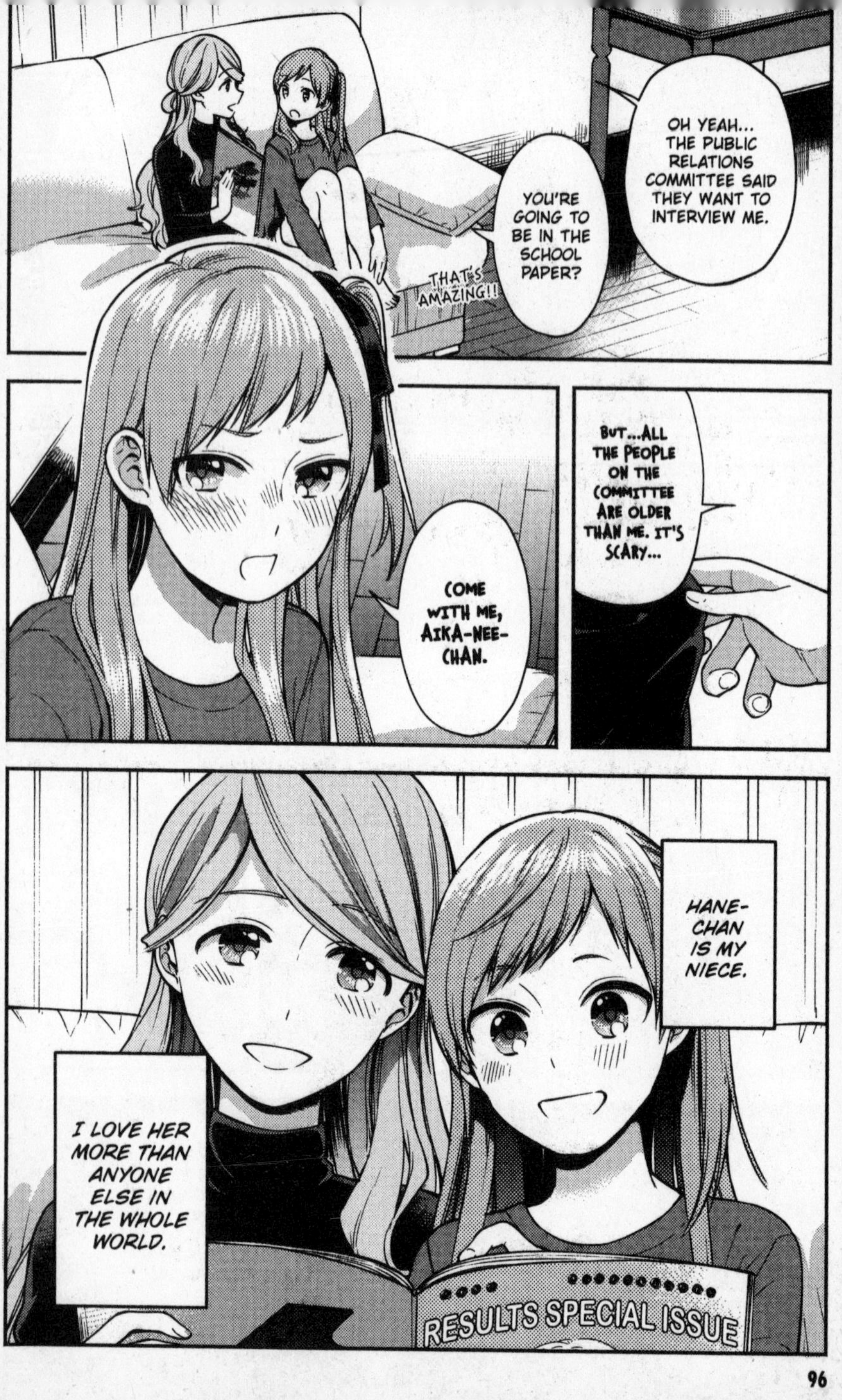
OH YEAH... THE PUBLIC RELATIONS COMMITTEE SAID THEY WANT TO INTERVIEW ME.
YOU'RE GOING TO BE IN THE SCHOOL PAPER?
THAT'S AMAZING!!
BUT...ALL THE PEOPLE ON THE COMMITTEE ARE OLDER THAN ME. IT'S SCARY...
COME WITH ME, AIKA-NEE-CHAN.
HANE-CHAN IS MY NIECE.
I LOVE HER MORE THAN ANYONE ELSE IN THE WHOLE WORLD.
RESULTS SPECIAL ISSUE

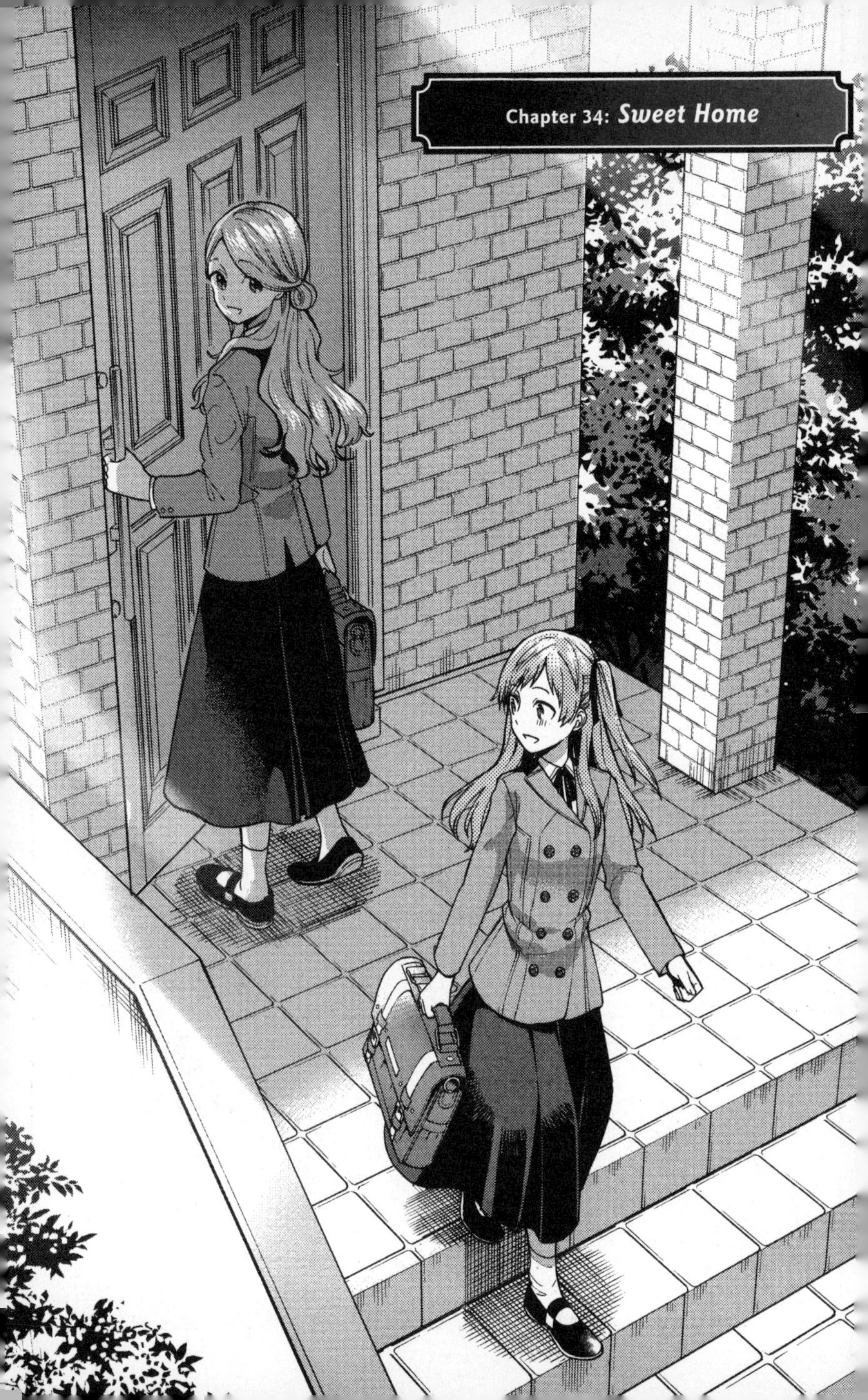
Chapter 34: Sweet Home

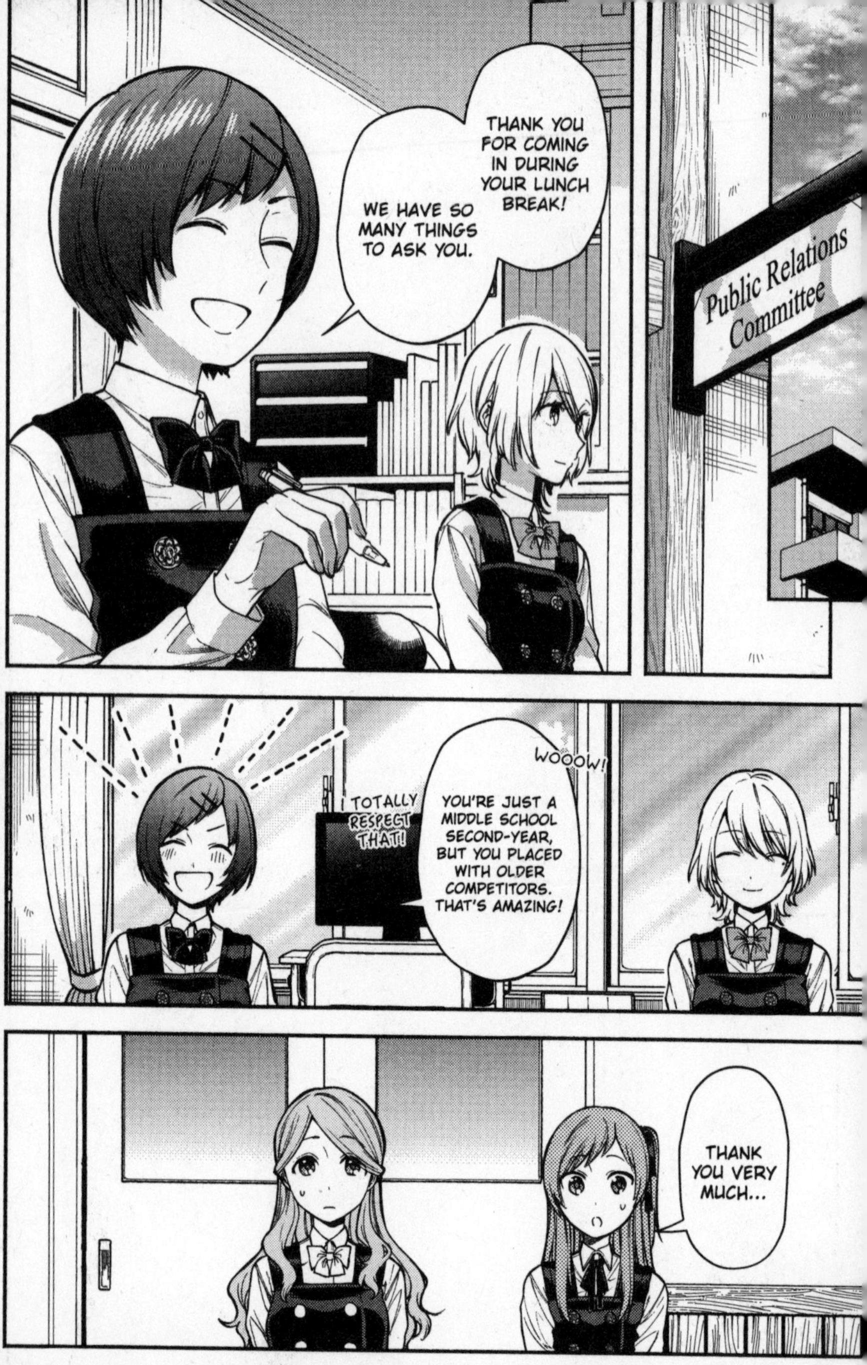
Public Relations Committee
THANK YOU FOR COMING IN DURING YOUR LUNCH BREAK!
WE HAVE SO MANY THINGS TO ASK YOU.
WOOOW!
YOU'RE JUST A MIDDLE SCHOOL SECOND-YEAR, BUT YOU PLACED WITH OLDER COMPETITORS. THAT'S AMAZING!
TOTALLY RESPECT THAT!
THANK YOU VERY MUCH...

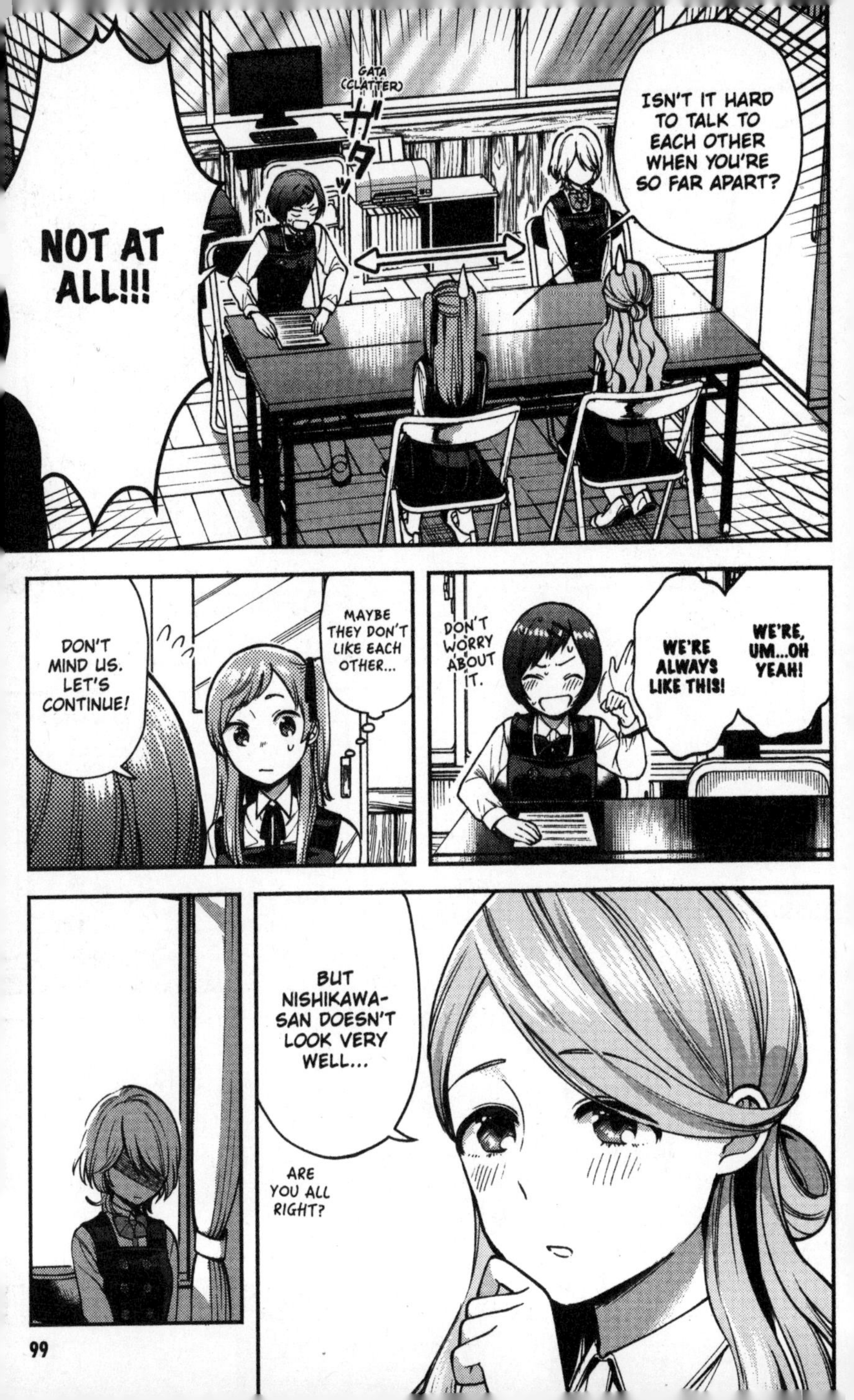

ISN'T IT HARD TO TALK TO EACH OTHER WHEN YOU'RE SO FAR APART?
GATA (CLATTER)
NOT AT ALL!!!
WE'RE, UM...OH YEAH!
WE'RE ALWAYS LIKE THIS!
DON'T WORRY ABOUT IT.
MAYBE THEY DON'T LIKE EACH OTHER...
DON'T MIND US. LET'S CONTINUE!
BUT NISHIKAWA-SAN DOESN'T LOOK VERY WELL...
ARE YOU ALL RIGHT?

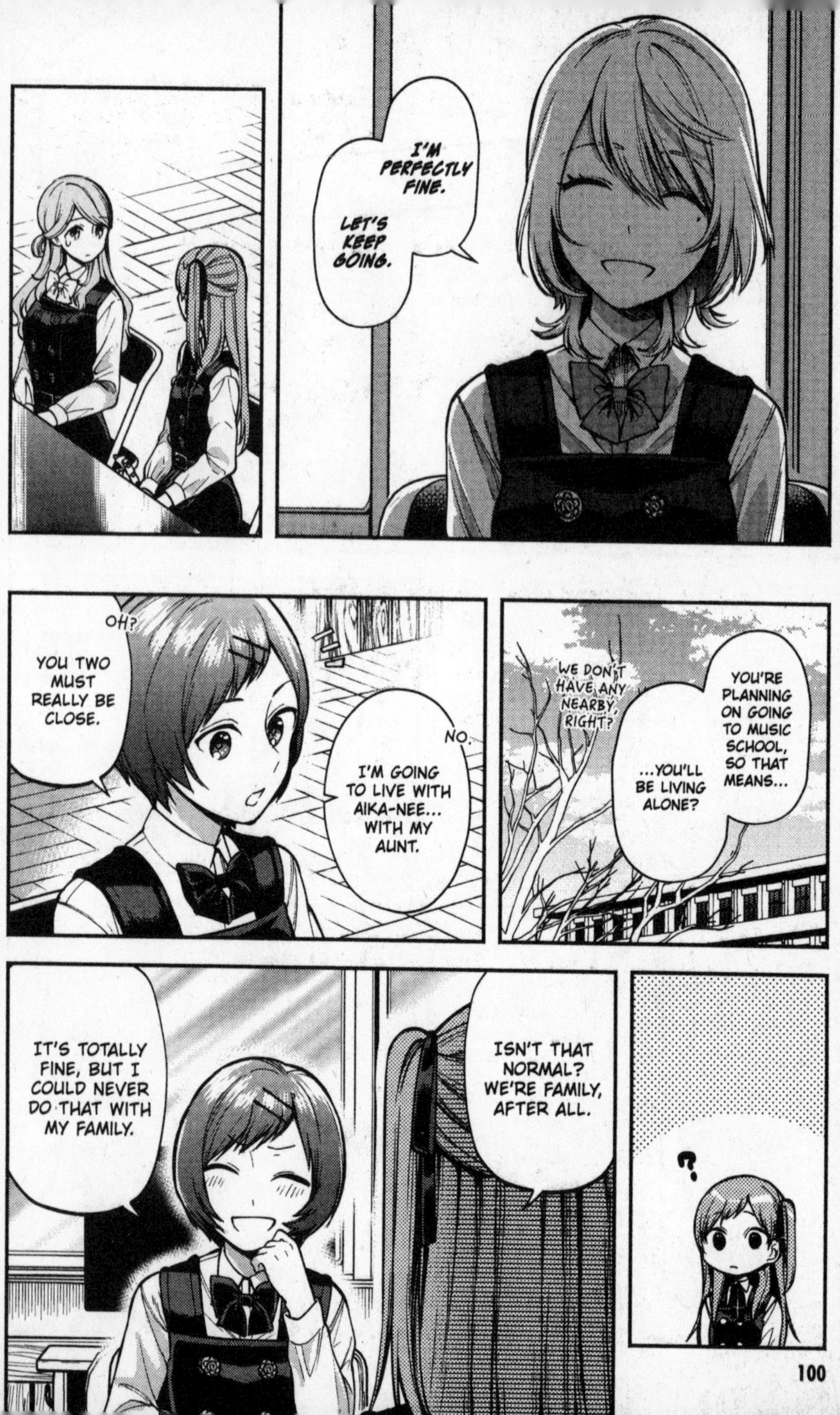
I'M PERFECTLY FINE.
LET'S KEEP GOING.
YOU'RE PLANNING ON GOING TO MUSIC SCHOOL, SO THAT MEANS...
...YOU'LL BE LIVING ALONE?
WE DON'T HAVE ANY NEARBY, RIGHT?
NO.
I'M GOING TO LIVE WITH AIKA-NEE... WITH MY AUNT.
OH?
YOU TWO MUST REALLY BE CLOSE.
?
ISN'T THAT NORMAL? WE'RE FAMILY, AFTER ALL.
IT'S TOTALLY FINE, BUT I COULD NEVER DO THAT WITH MY FAMILY.

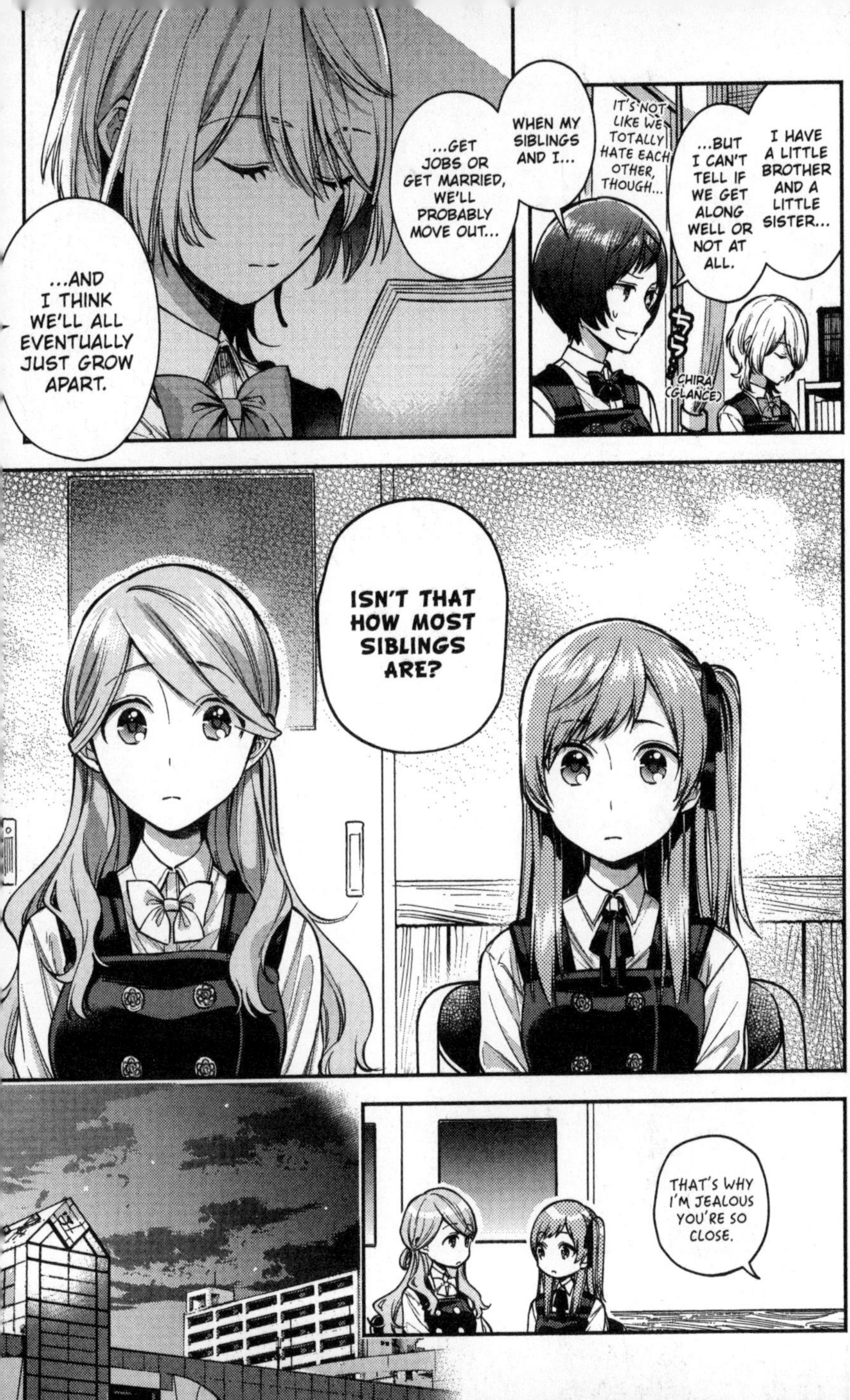
I HAVE A LITTLE BROTHER AND A LITTLE SISTER...
...BUT I CAN'T TELL IF WE GET ALONG WELL OR NOT AT ALL.
IT'S NOT LIKE WE TOTALLY HATE EACH OTHER, THOUGH...
CHIRA (GLANCE)
WHEN MY SIBLINGS AND I...
...GET JOBS OR GET MARRIED, WE'LL PROBABLY MOVE OUT...
...AND I THINK WE'LL ALL EVENTUALLY JUST GROW APART.
ISN'T THAT HOW MOST SIBLINGS ARE?
THAT'S WHY I'M JEALOUS YOU'RE SO CLOSE.

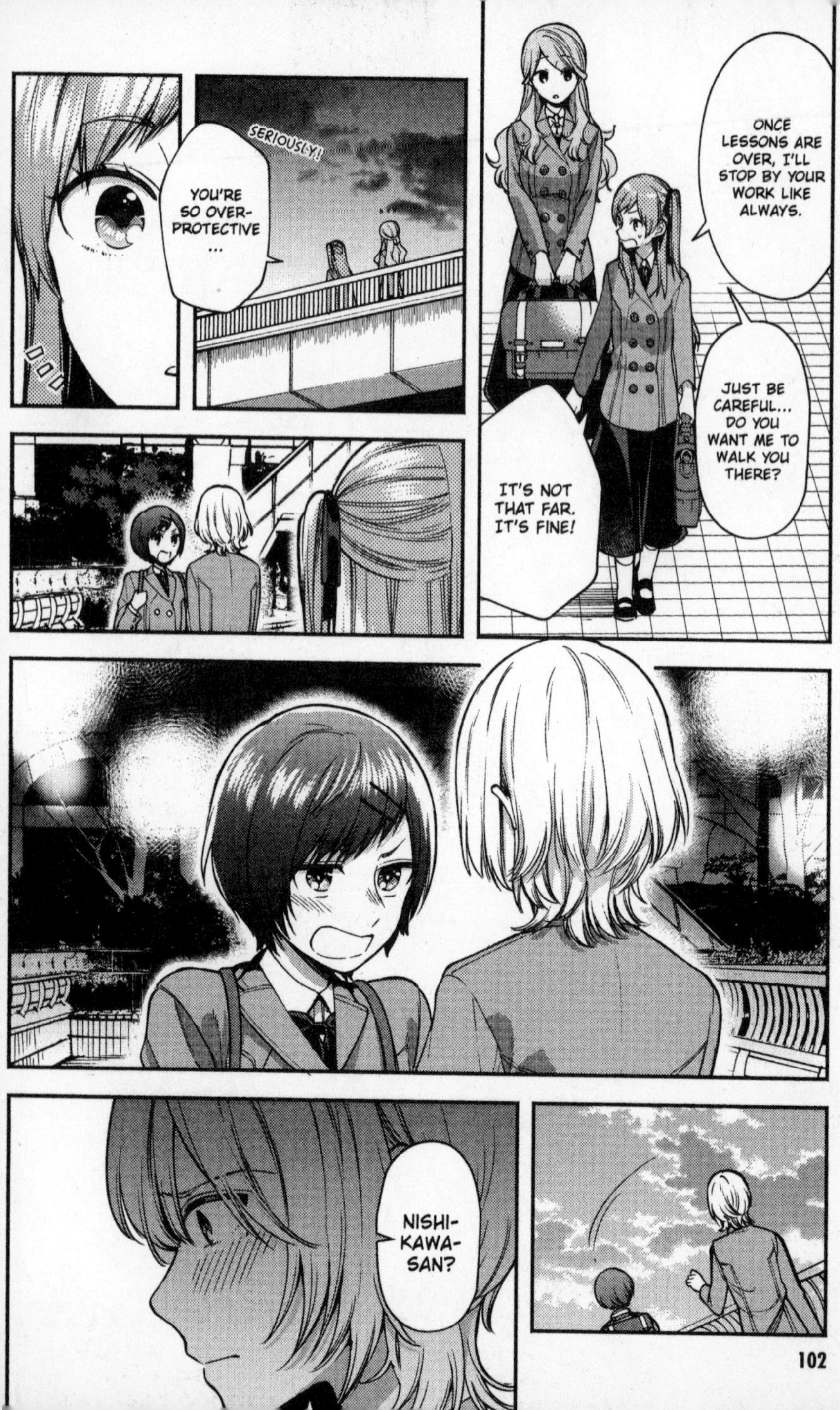
ONCE LESSONS ARE OVER, I'LL STOP BY YOUR WORK LIKE ALWAYS.
JUST BE CAREFUL... DO YOU WANT ME TO WALK YOU THERE?
IT'S NOT THAT FAR. IT'S FINE!
YOU'RE SO OVER-PROTECTIVE...
SERIOUSLY!
NISHI-KAWA-SAN?

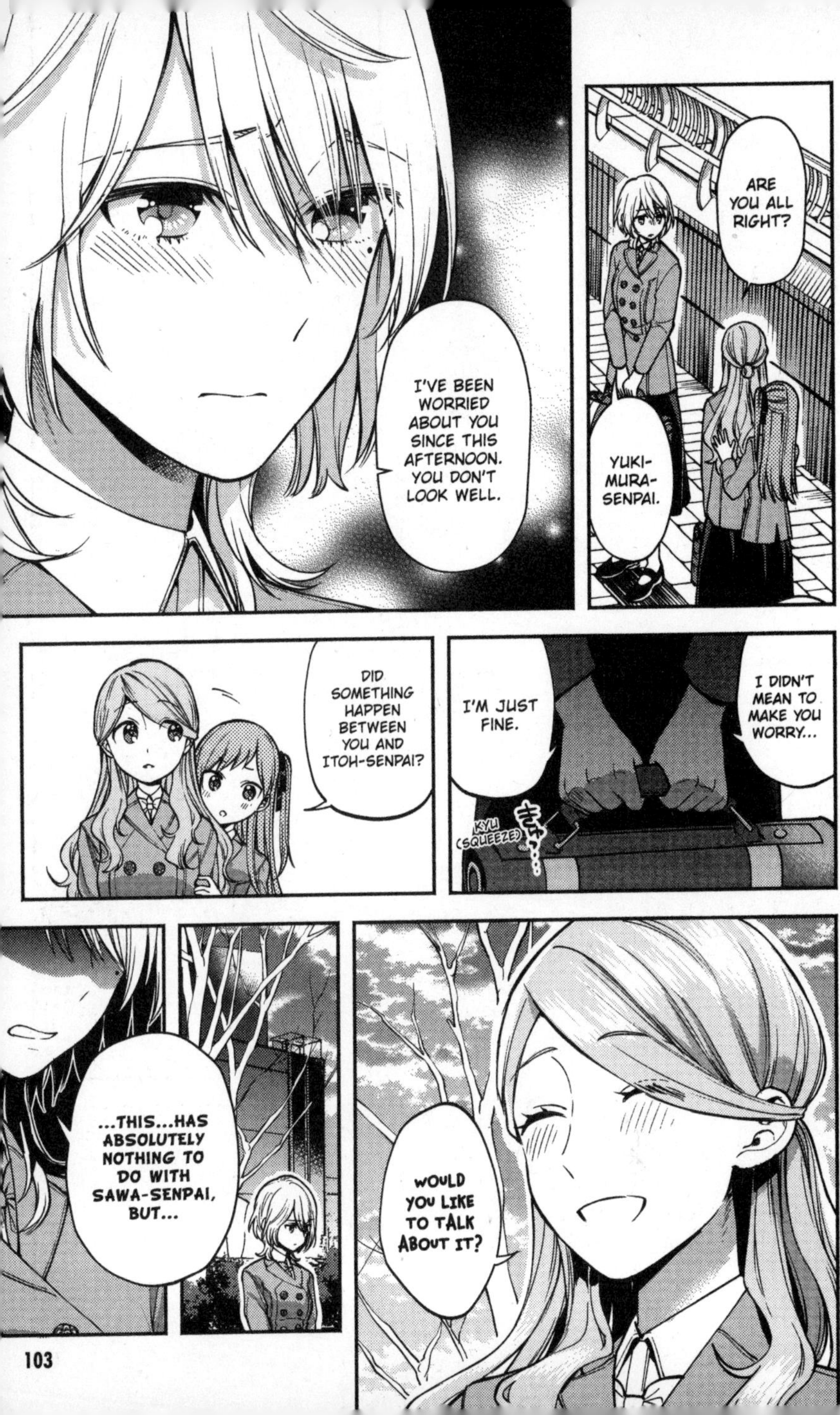
ARE YOU ALL RIGHT?
YUKI-MURA-SENPAI.
I'VE BEEN WORRIED ABOUT YOU SINCE THIS AFTERNOON. YOU DON'T LOOK WELL.
I DIDN'T MEAN TO MAKE YOU WORRY...
I'M JUST FINE.
KYU (SQUEEZE)
DID SOMETHING HAPPEN BETWEEN YOU AND ITOH-SENPAI?
WOULD YOU LIKE TO TALK ABOUT IT?
...THIS...HAS ABSOLUTELY NOTHING TO DO WITH SAWA-SENPAI, BUT...

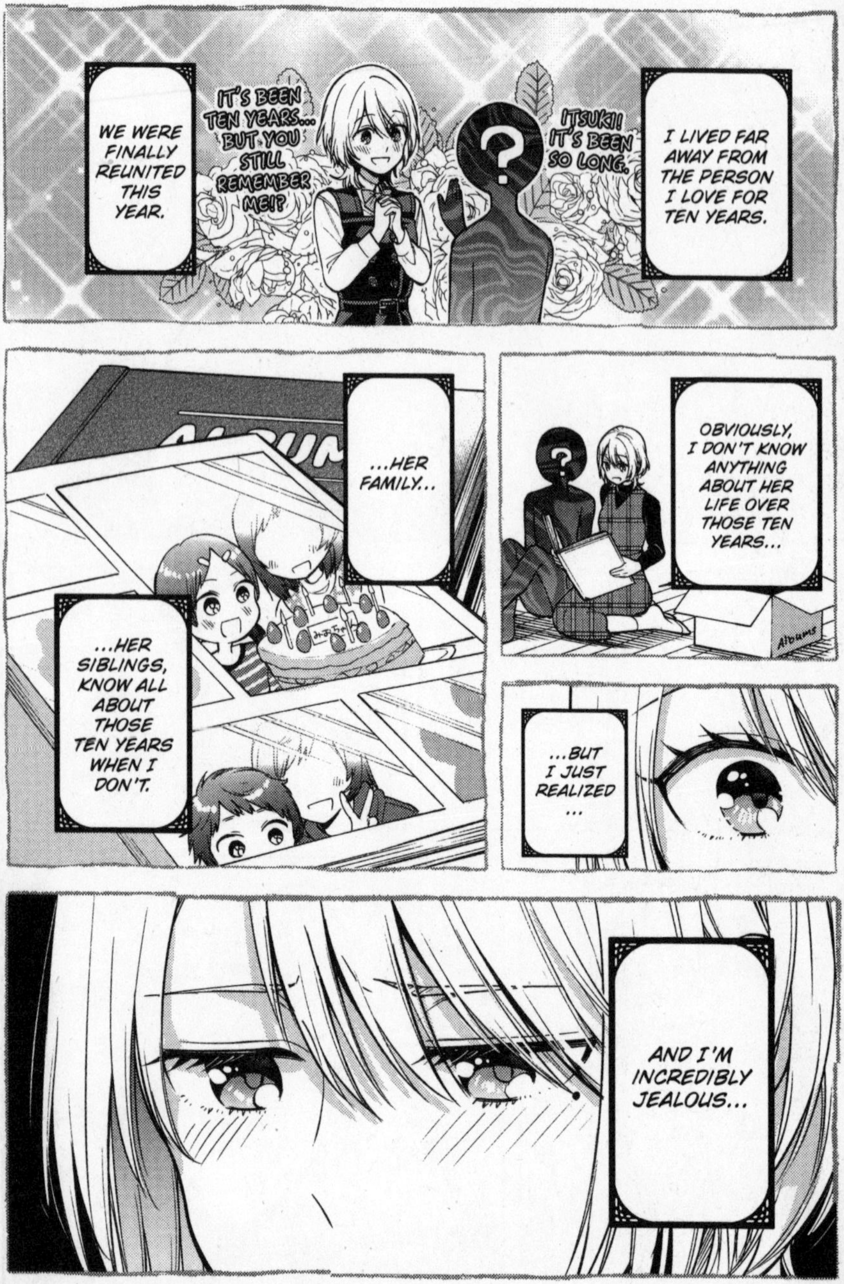
I LIVED FAR AWAY FROM THE PERSON I LOVE FOR TEN YEARS.
ITSUKI! IT'S BEEN SO LONG.
IT'S BEEN TEN YEARS... BUT YOU STILL REMEMBER ME!?
WE WERE FINALLY REUNITED THIS YEAR.
OBVIOUSLY, I DON'T KNOW ANYTHING ABOUT HER LIFE OVER THOSE TEN YEARS...
Albums
...BUT I JUST REALIZED...
...HER FAMILY...
...HER SIBLINGS, KNOW ALL ABOUT THOSE TEN YEARS WHEN I DON'T.
AND I'M INCREDIBLY JEALOUS...

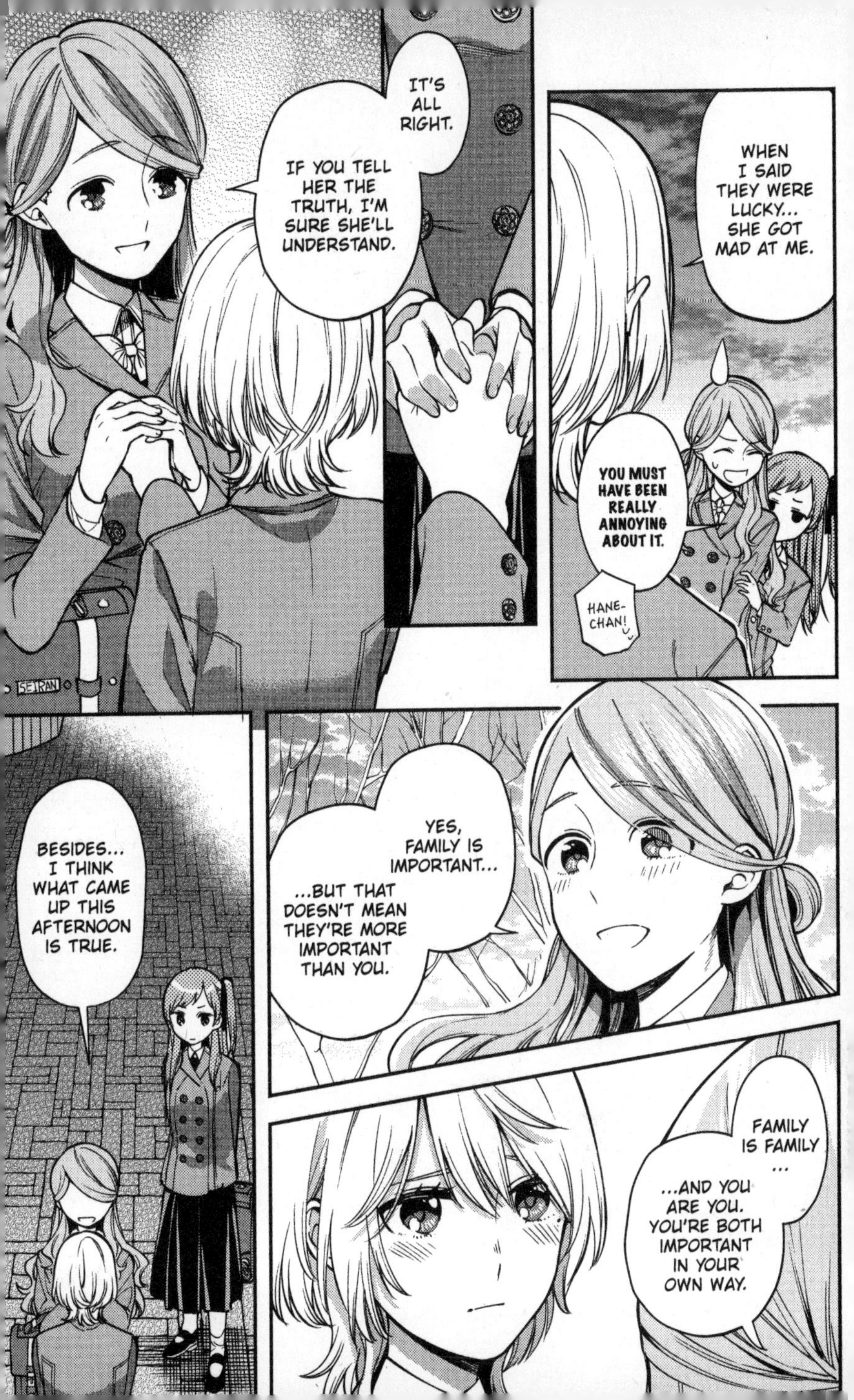
WHEN I SAID THEY WERE LUCKY... SHE GOT MAD AT ME.
YOU MUST HAVE BEEN REALLY ANNOYING ABOUT IT.
HANE-CHAN!
IT'S ALL RIGHT.
IF YOU TELL HER THE TRUTH, I'M SURE SHE'LL UNDERSTAND.
SEIRAN
YES, FAMILY IS IMPORTANT...
...BUT THAT DOESN'T MEAN THEY'RE MORE IMPORTANT THAN YOU.
FAMILY IS FAMILY...
...AND YOU ARE YOU. YOU'RE BOTH IMPORTANT IN YOUR OWN WAY.
BESIDES... I THINK WHAT CAME UP THIS AFTERNOON IS TRUE.

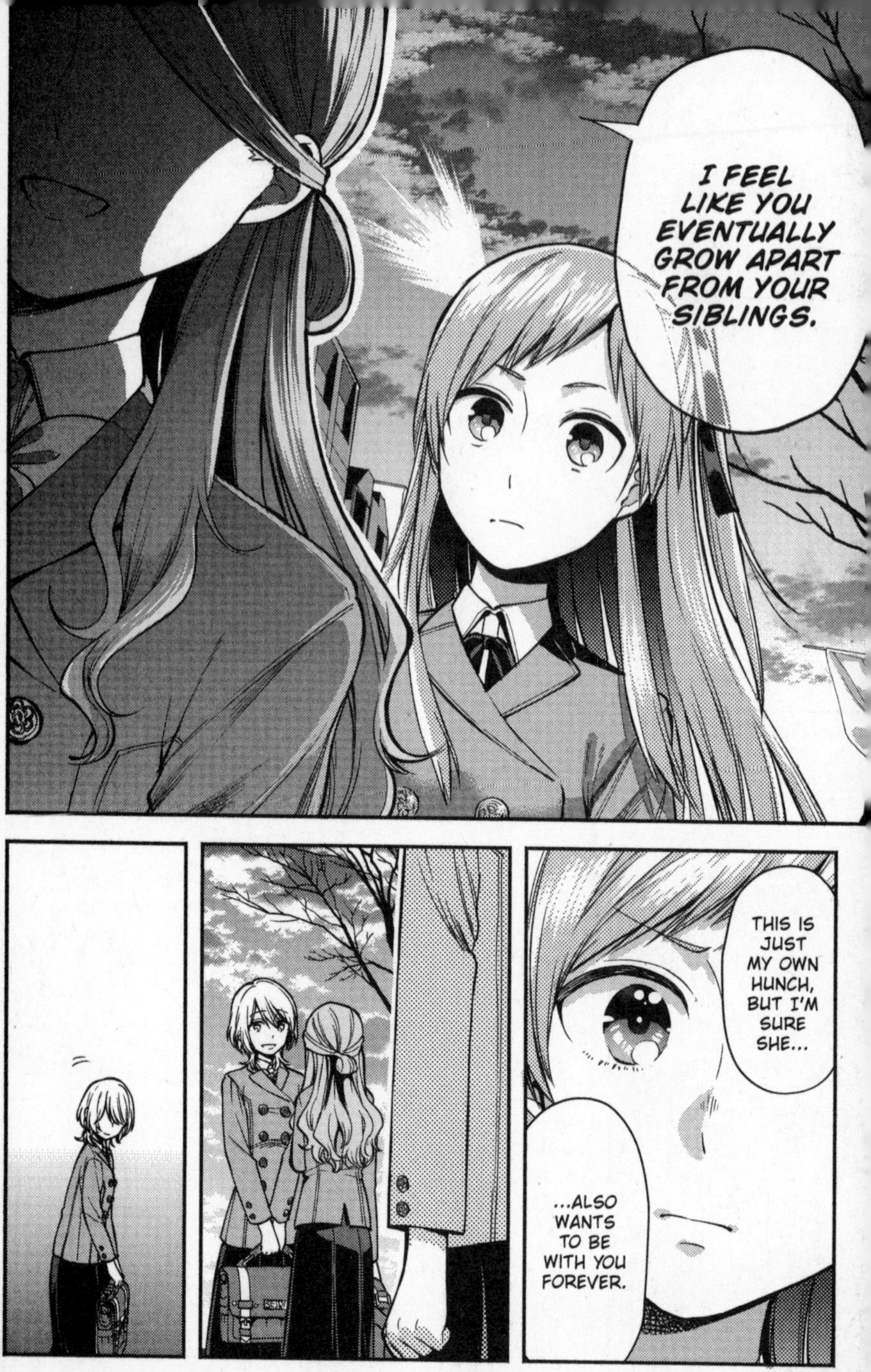
I FEEL LIKE YOU EVENTUALLY GROW APART FROM YOUR SIBLINGS.
THIS IS JUST MY OWN HUNCH, BUT I'M SURE SHE...
...ALSO WANTS TO BE WITH YOU FOREVER.

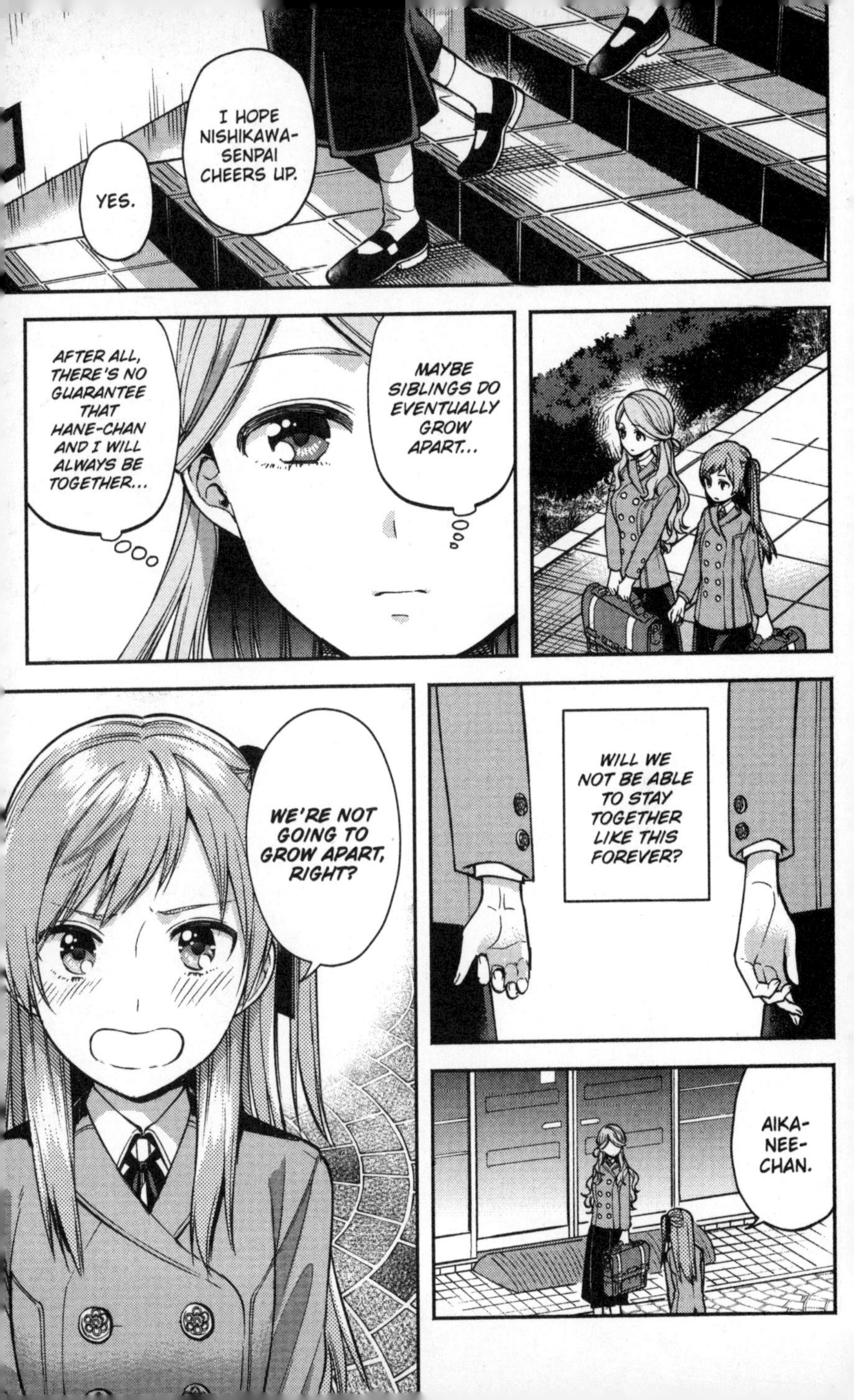
I HOPE NISHIKAWA-SENPAI CHEERS UP.
YES.
MAYBE SIBLINGS DO EVENTUALLY GROW APART...
AFTER ALL, THERE'S NO GUARANTEE THAT HANE-CHAN AND I WILL ALWAYS BE TOGETHER...
WILL WE NOT BE ABLE TO STAY TOGETHER LIKE THIS FOREVER?
AIKA-NEE-CHAN.
WE'RE NOT GOING TO GROW APART, RIGHT?

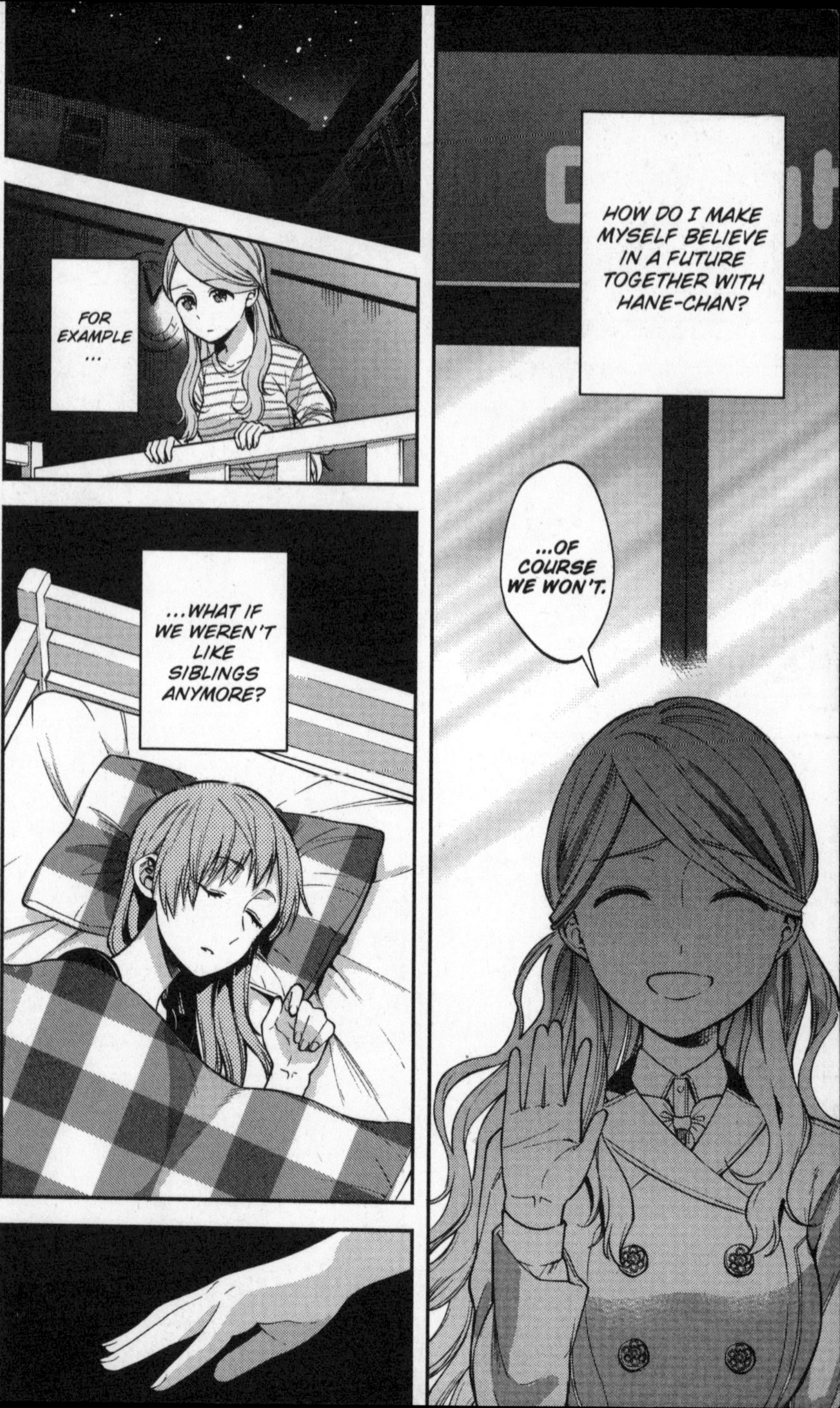
HOW DO I MAKE MYSELF BELIEVE IN A FUTURE TOGETHER WITH HANE-CHAN?
...OF COURSE WE WON'T.
FOR EXAMPLE ...
...WHAT IF WE WEREN'T LIKE SIBLINGS ANYMORE?

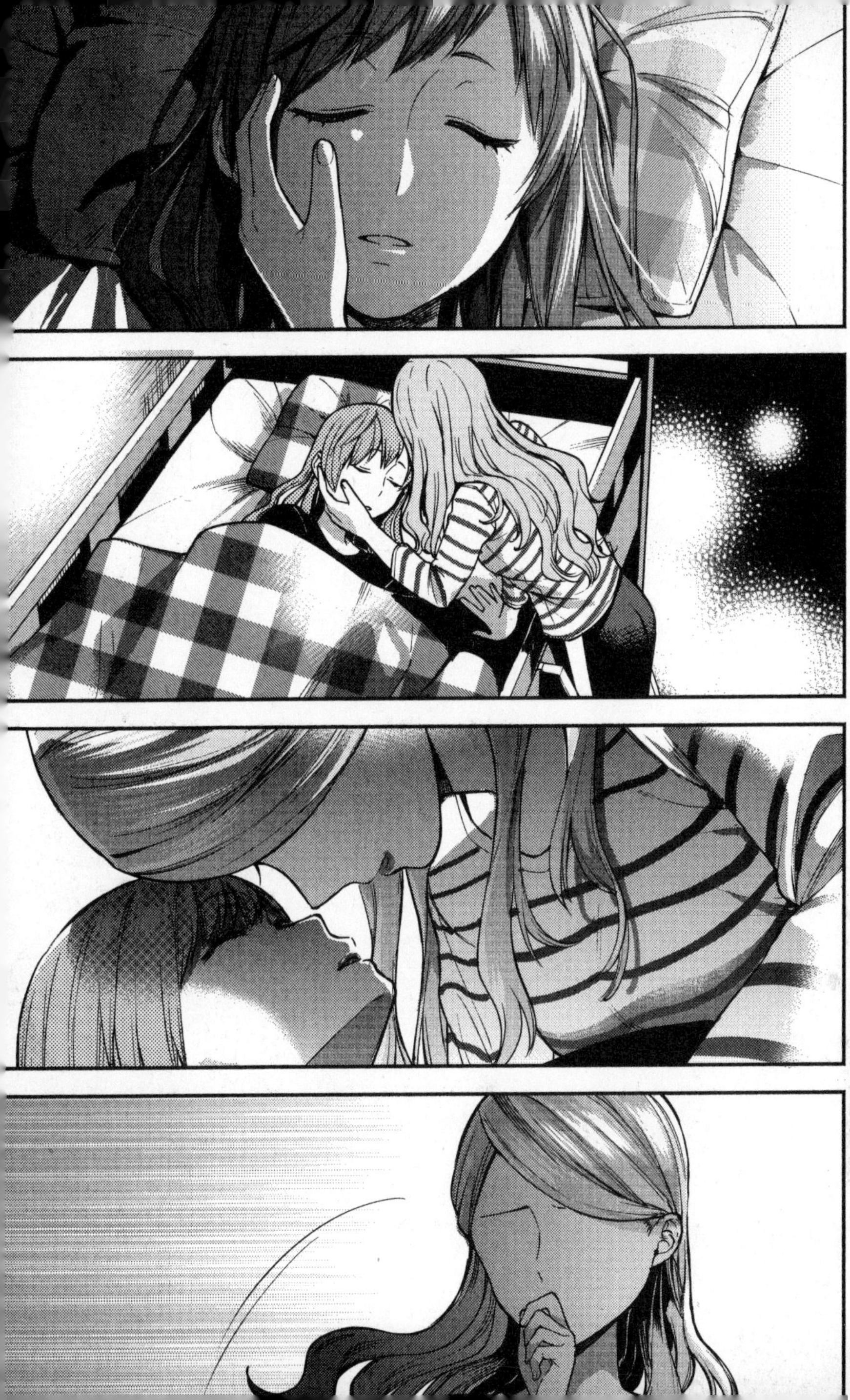

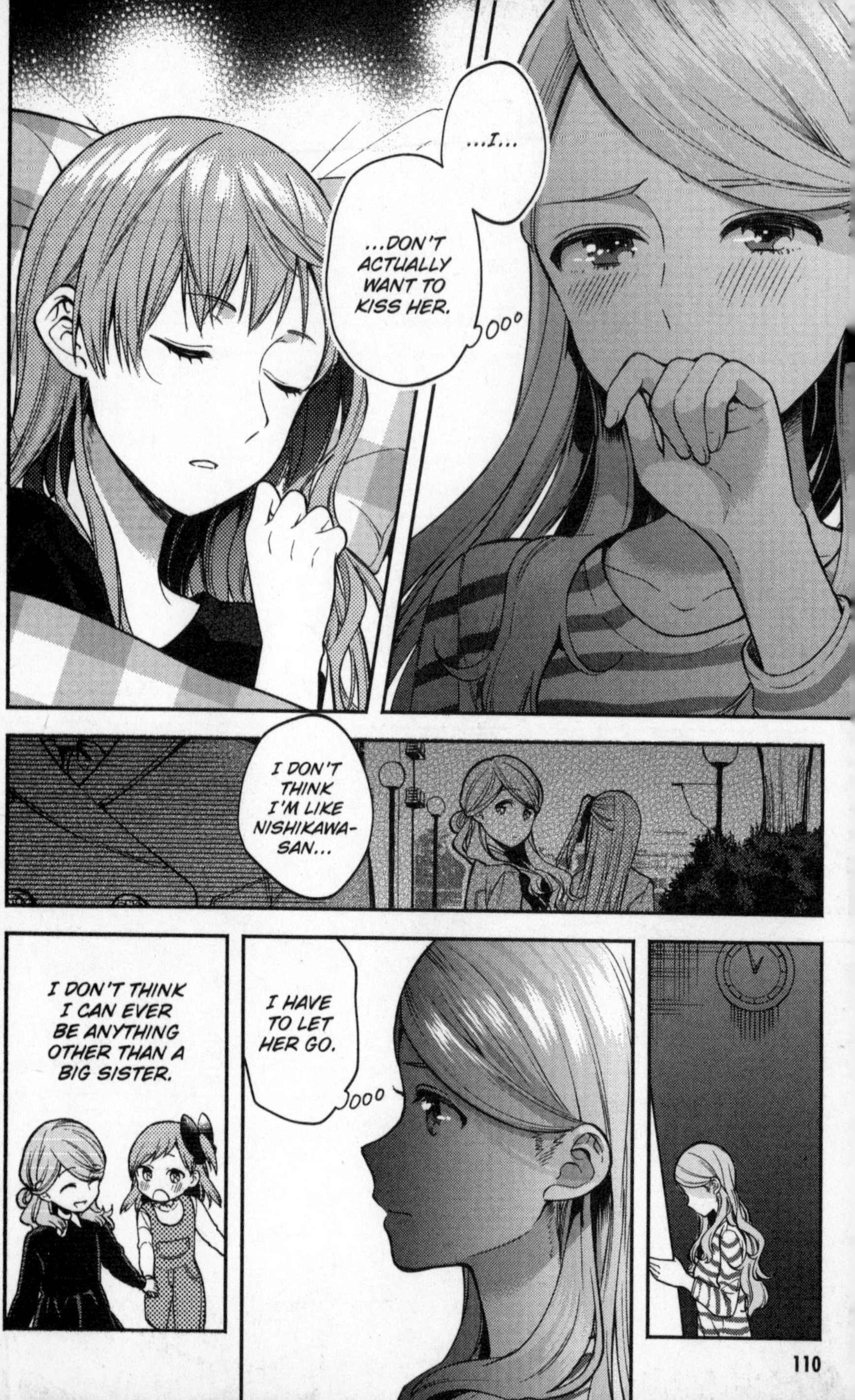
...I...
...DON'T ACTUALLY WANT TO KISS HER.
I DON'T THINK I'M LIKE NISHIKAWA-SAN...
I HAVE TO LET HER GO.
I DON'T THINK I CAN EVER BE ANYTHING OTHER THAN A BIG SISTER.

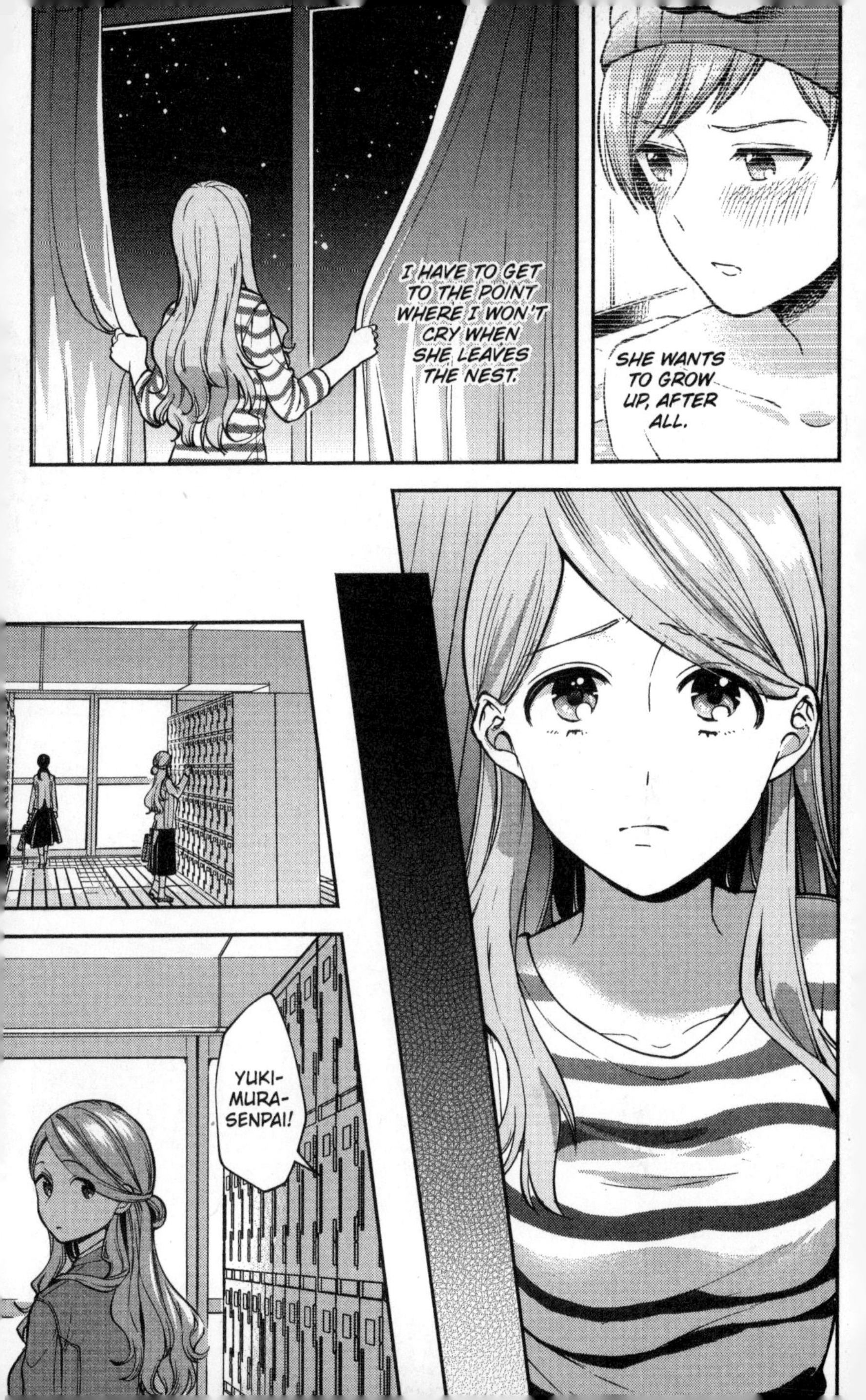
SHE WANTS TO GROW UP, AFTER ALL.
I HAVE TO GET TO THE POINT WHERE I WON'T CRY WHEN SHE LEAVES THE NEST.
YUKI-MURA-SENPAI!

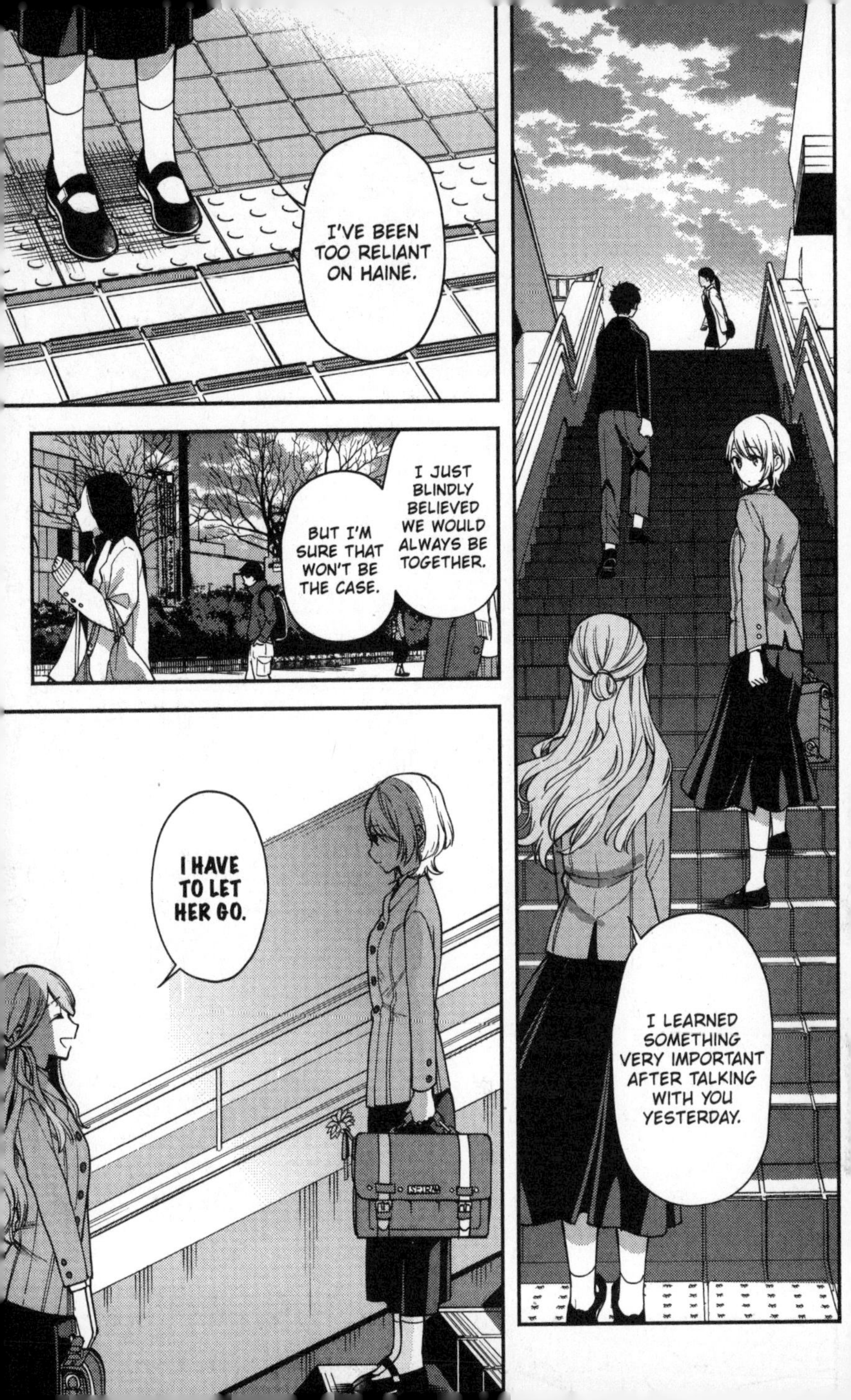
I LEARNED SOMETHING VERY IMPORTANT AFTER TALKING WITH YOU YESTERDAY.
I'VE BEEN TOO RELIANT ON HAINE.
I JUST BLINDLY BELIEVED WE WOULD ALWAYS BE TOGETHER.
BUT I'M SURE THAT WON'T BE THE CASE.
I HAVE TO LET HER GO.

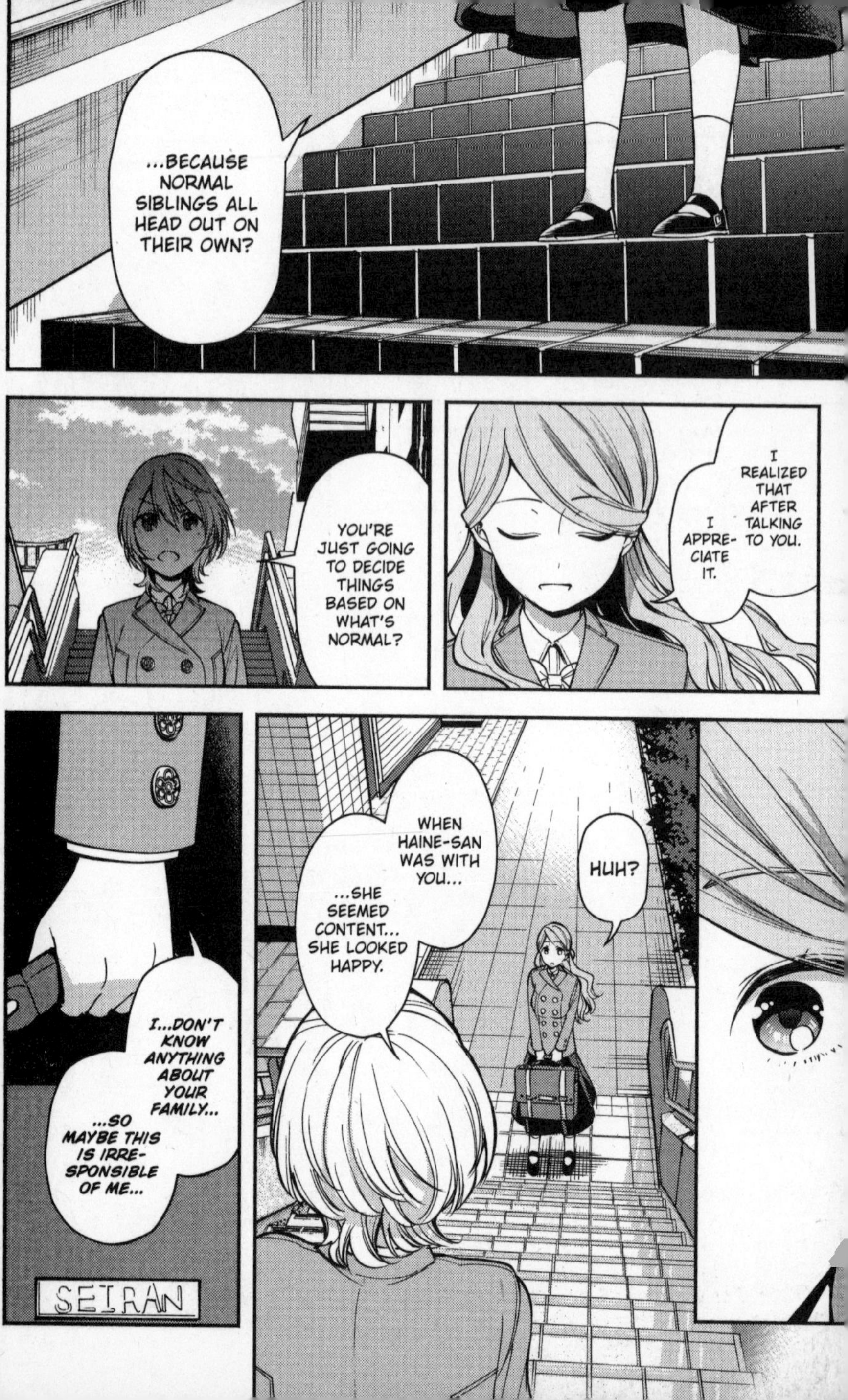
...BECAUSE NORMAL SIBLINGS ALL HEAD OUT ON THEIR OWN?
I REALIZED THAT AFTER TALKING TO YOU.
I APPRE-CIATE IT.
YOU'RE JUST GOING TO DECIDE THINGS BASED ON WHAT'S NORMAL?
HUH?
WHEN HAINE-SAN WAS WITH YOU...
...SHE SEEMED CONTENT... SHE LOOKED HAPPY.
I...DON'T KNOW ANYTHING ABOUT YOUR FAMILY...
...SO MAYBE THIS IS IRRE-SPONSIBLE OF ME...
SEIRAN

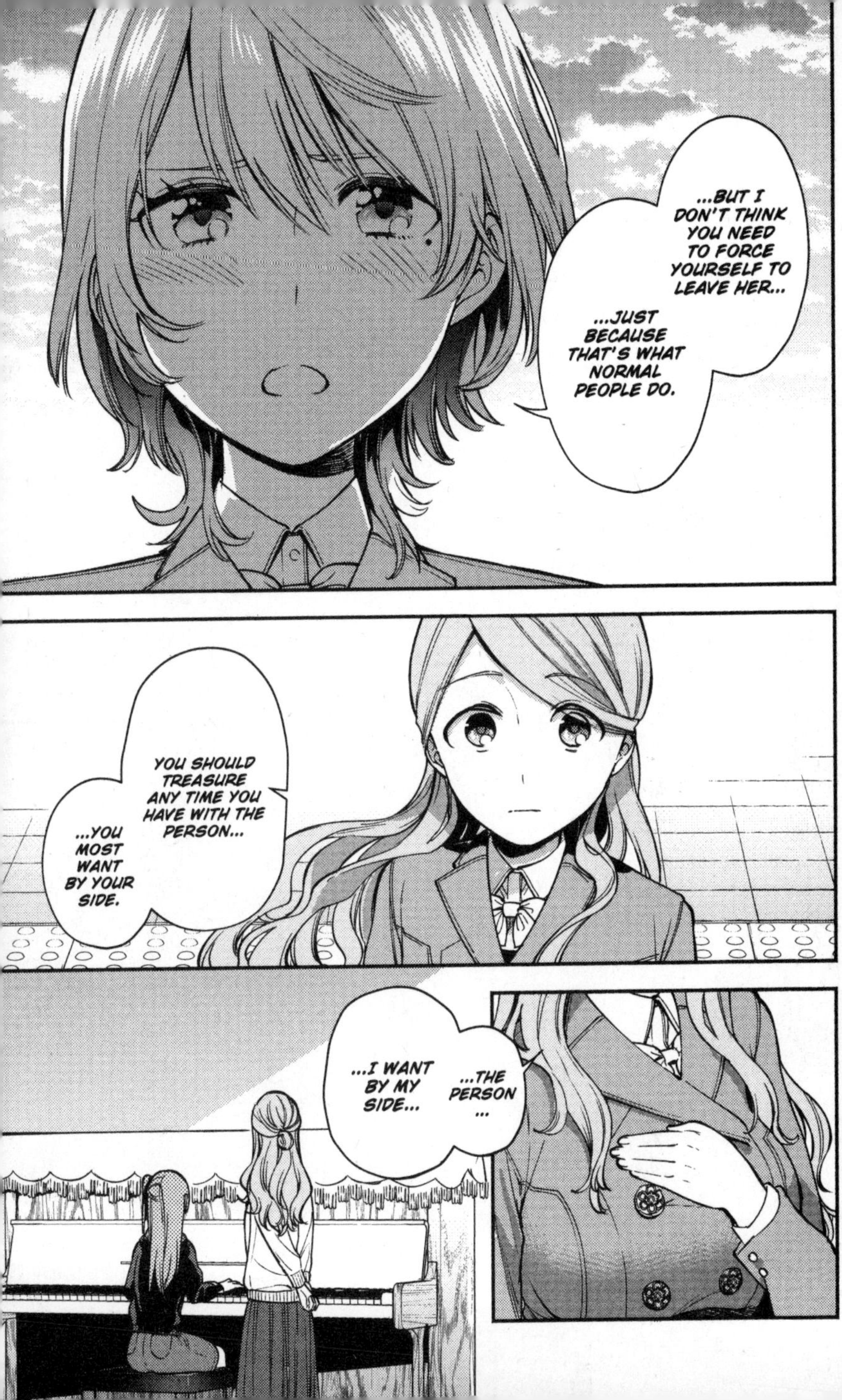
...BUT I DON'T THINK YOU NEED TO FORCE YOURSELF TO LEAVE HER...
...JUST BECAUSE THAT'S WHAT NORMAL PEOPLE DO.
YOU SHOULD TREASURE ANY TIME YOU HAVE WITH THE PERSON...
...YOU MOST WANT BY YOUR SIDE.
...THE PERSON ...
...I WANT BY MY SIDE...

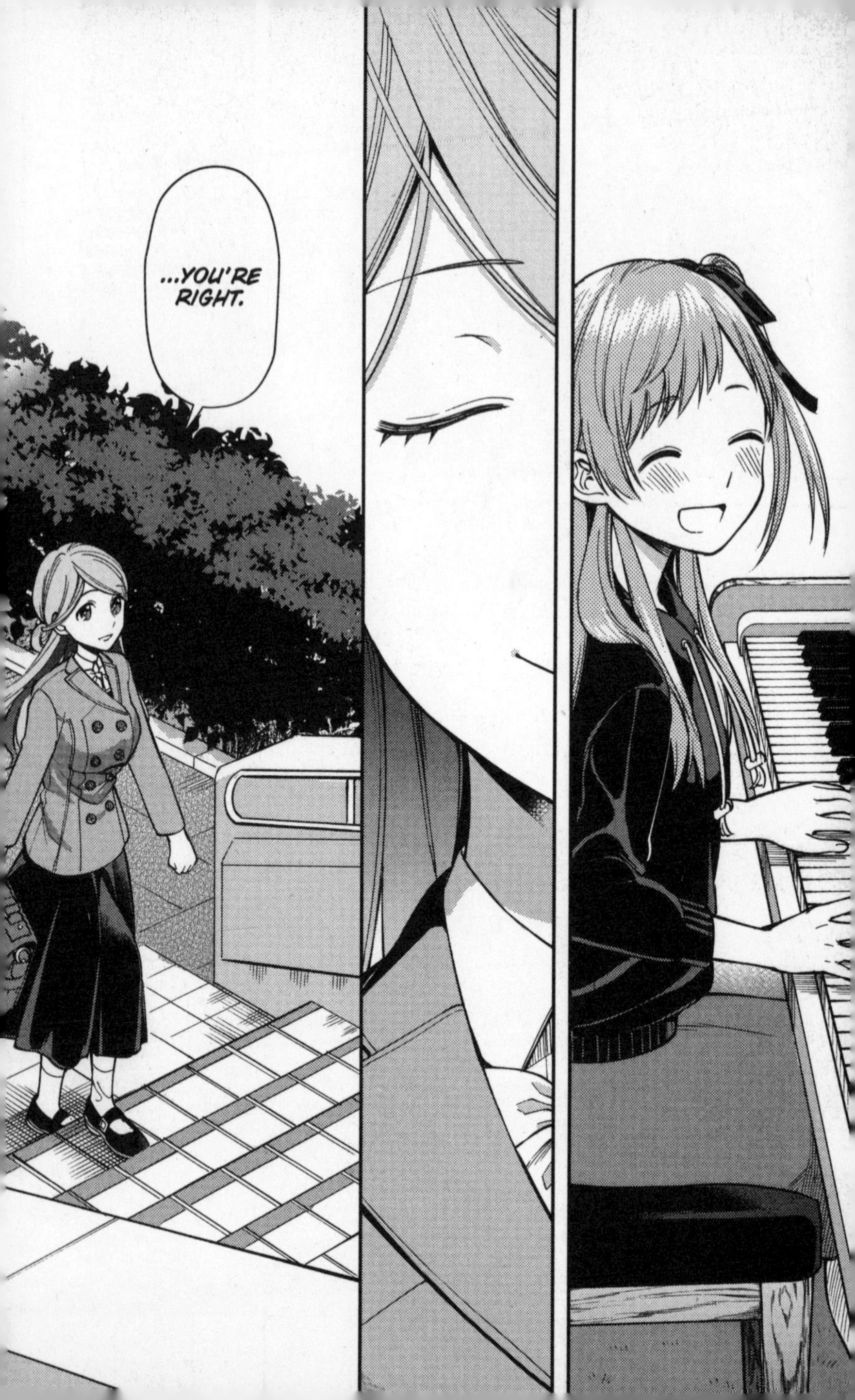
...YOU'RE RIGHT.

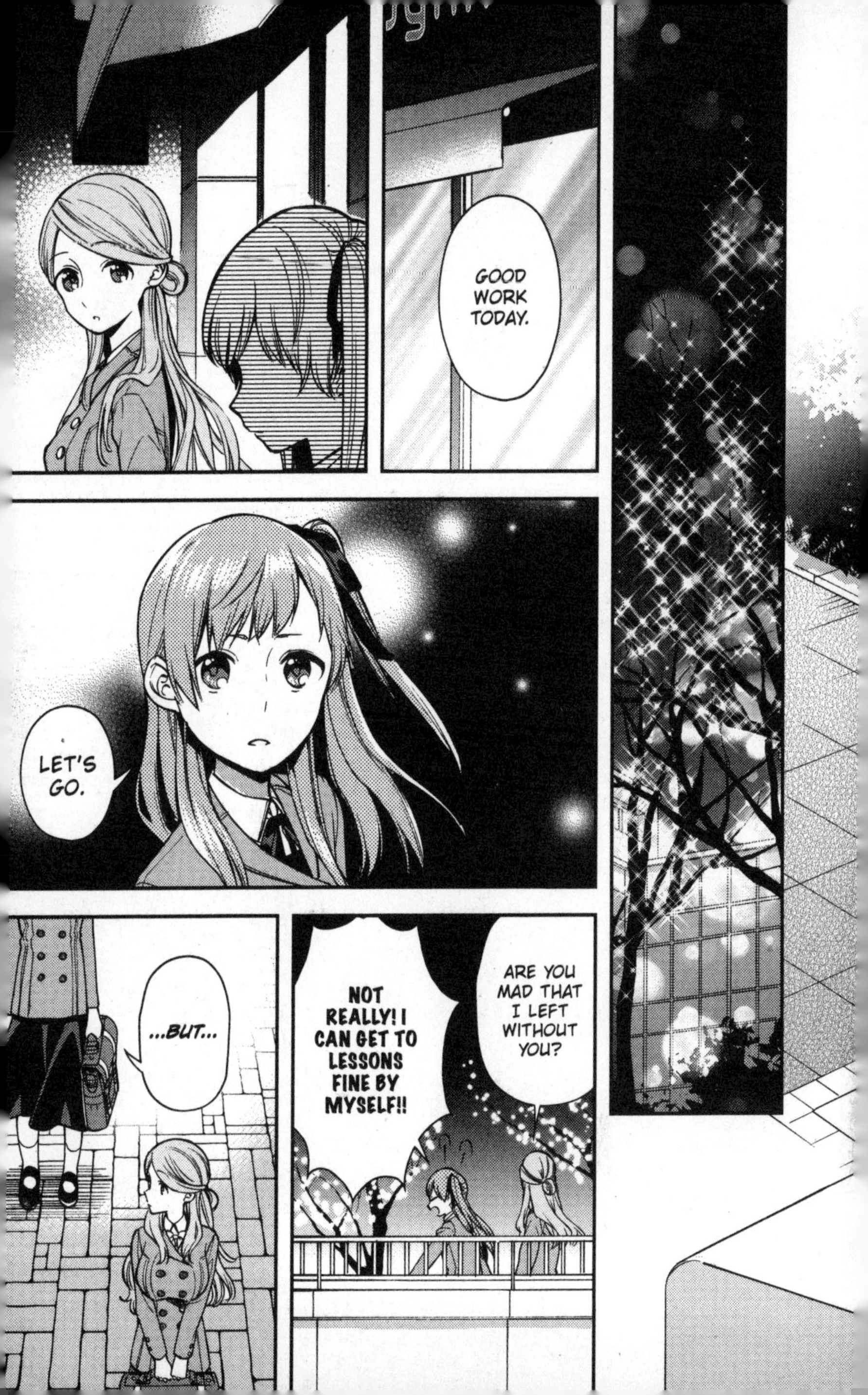
GOOD WORK TODAY.
LET'S GO.
ARE YOU MAD THAT I LEFT WITHOUT YOU?
NOT REALLY! I CAN GET TO LESSONS FINE BY MYSELF!!
...BUT...

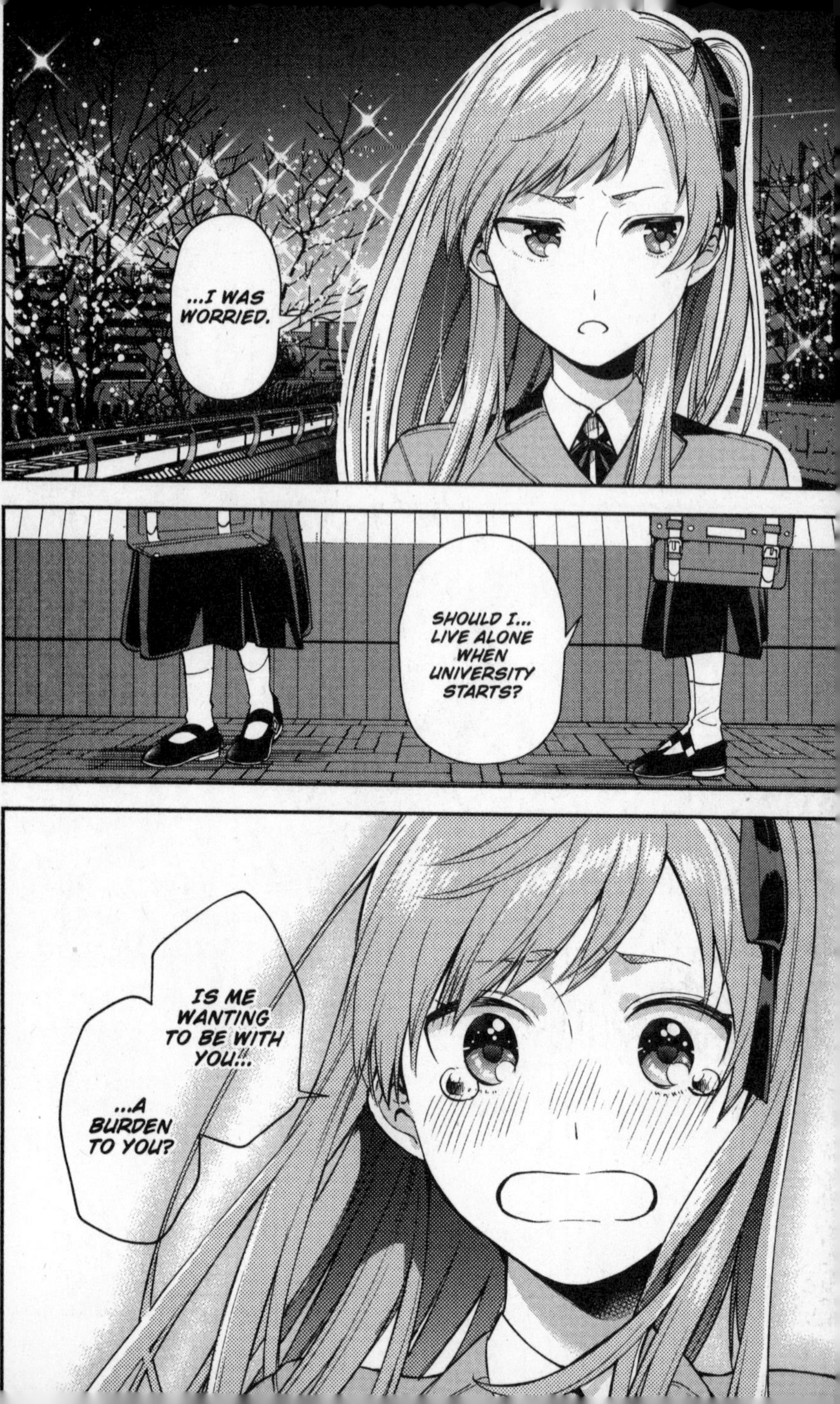
...I WAS WORRIED.
SHOULD I... LIVE ALONE WHEN UNIVERSITY STARTS?
IS ME WANTING TO BE WITH YOU!!...
...A BURDEN TO YOU?

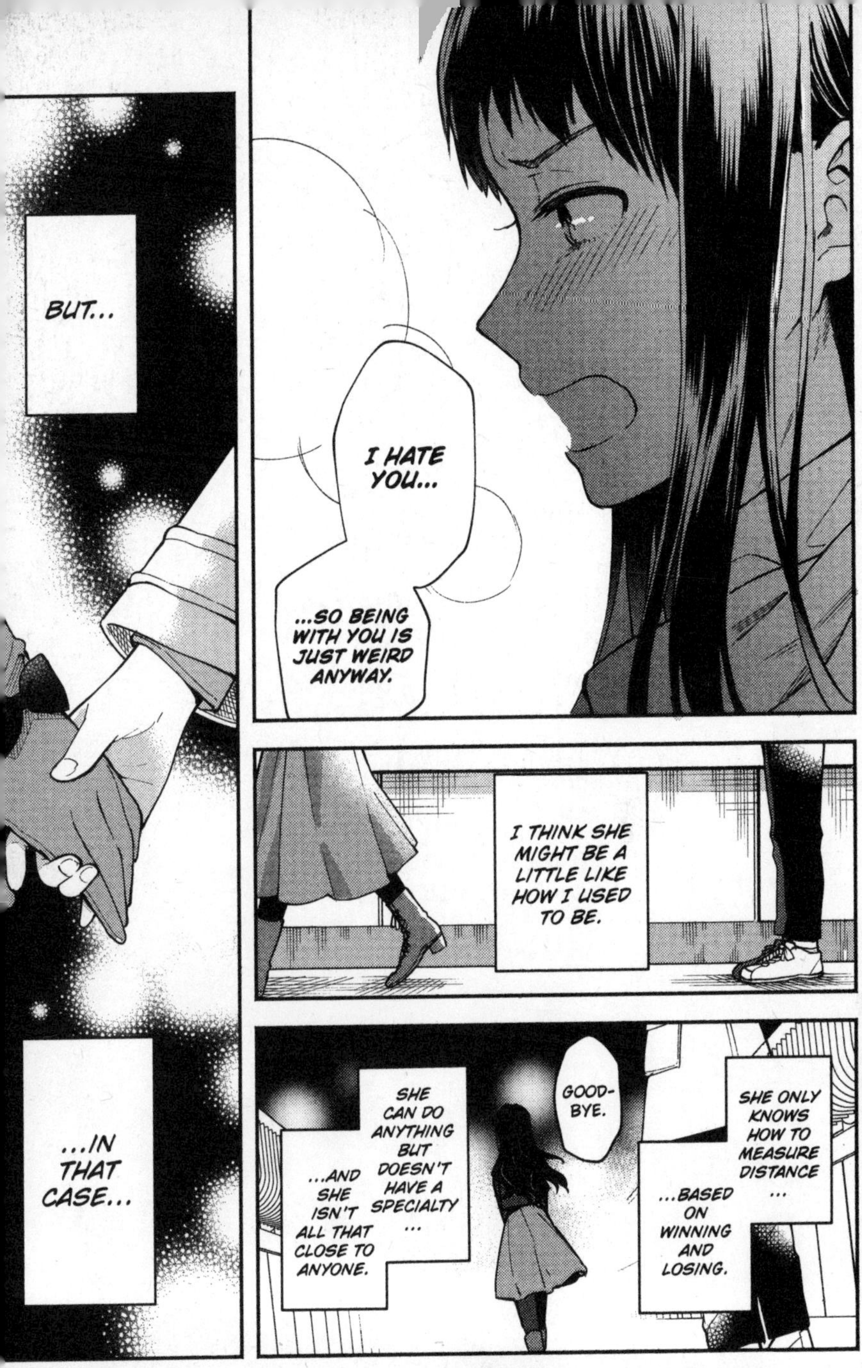

I HATE YOU...
...SO BEING WITH YOU IS JUST WEIRD ANYWAY.
I THINK SHE MIGHT BE A LITTLE LIKE HOW I USED TO BE.
SHE ONLY KNOWS HOW TO MEASURE DISTANCE...
...BASED ON WINNING AND LOSING.
GOOD-BYE.
SHE CAN DO ANYTHING BUT DOESN'T HAVE A SPECIALTY...
...AND SHE ISN'T ALL THAT CLOSE TO ANYONE.
BUT...
...IN THAT CASE...

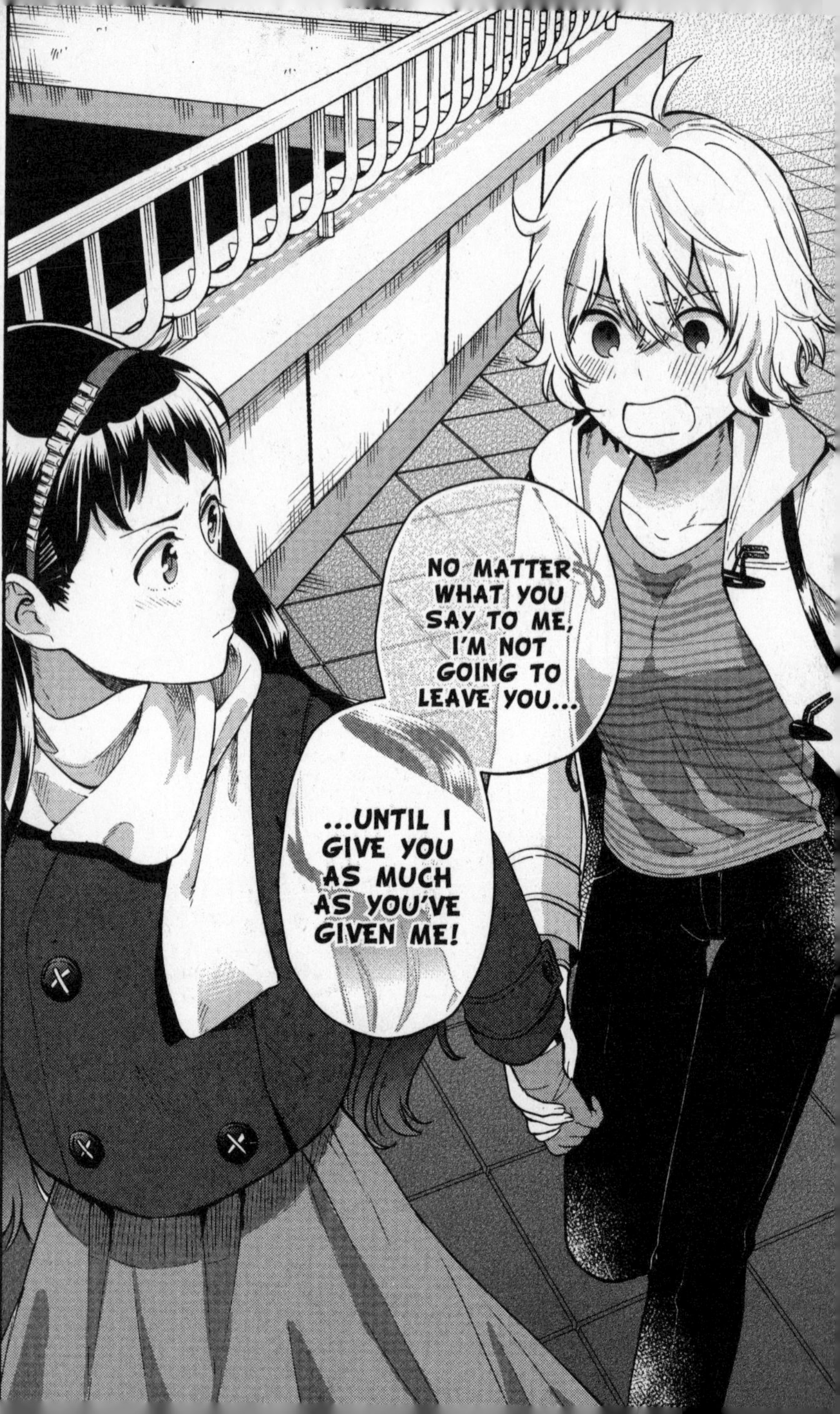
NO MATTER WHAT YOU SAY TO ME, I'M NOT GOING TO LEAVE YOU...
...UNTIL I GIVE YOU AS MUCH AS YOU'VE GIVEN ME!

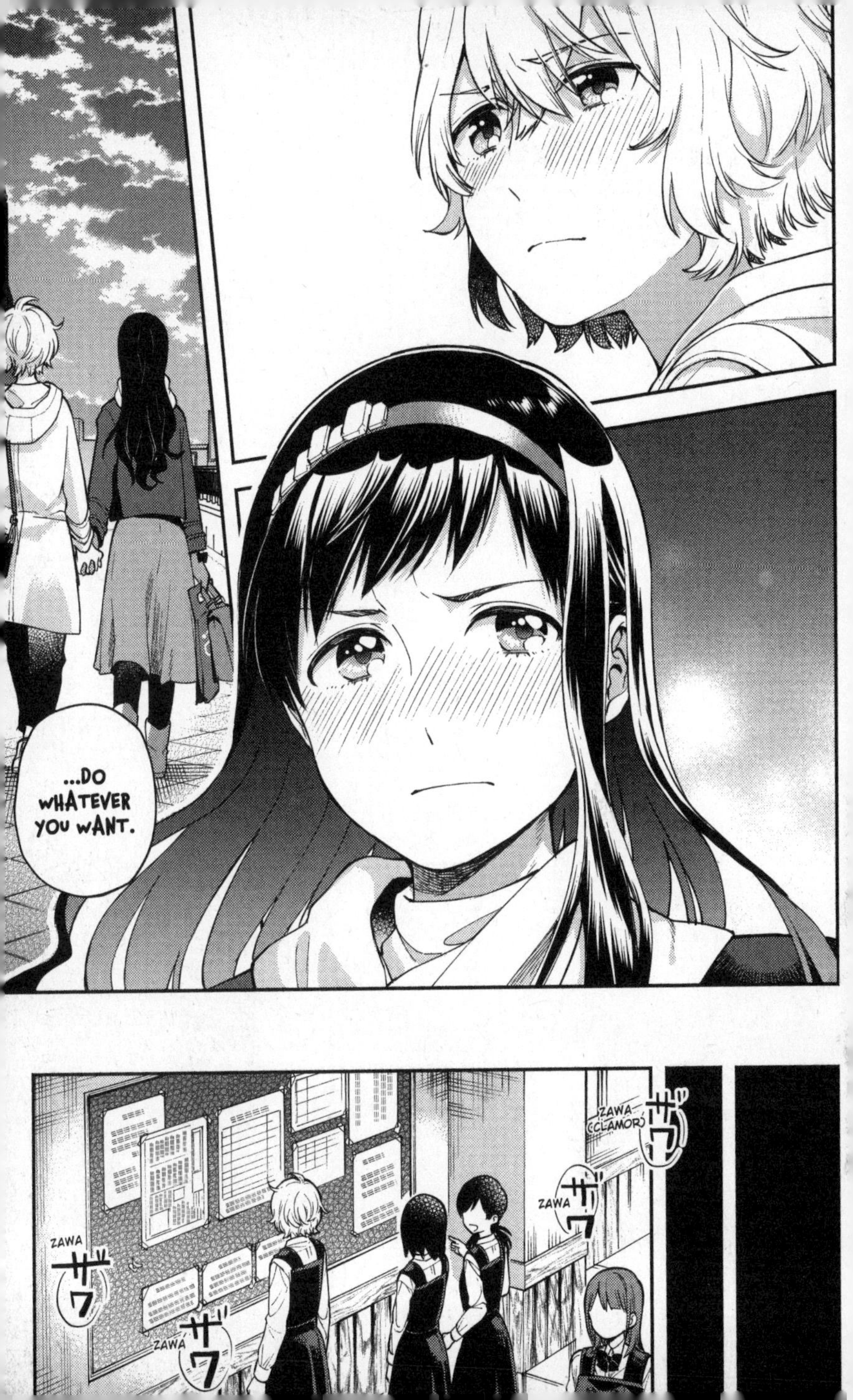
...DO WHATEVER YOU WANT.
ZAWA ザワ CLAMOR
ZAWA ザワ
ZAWA ザワ
ZAWA ザワ

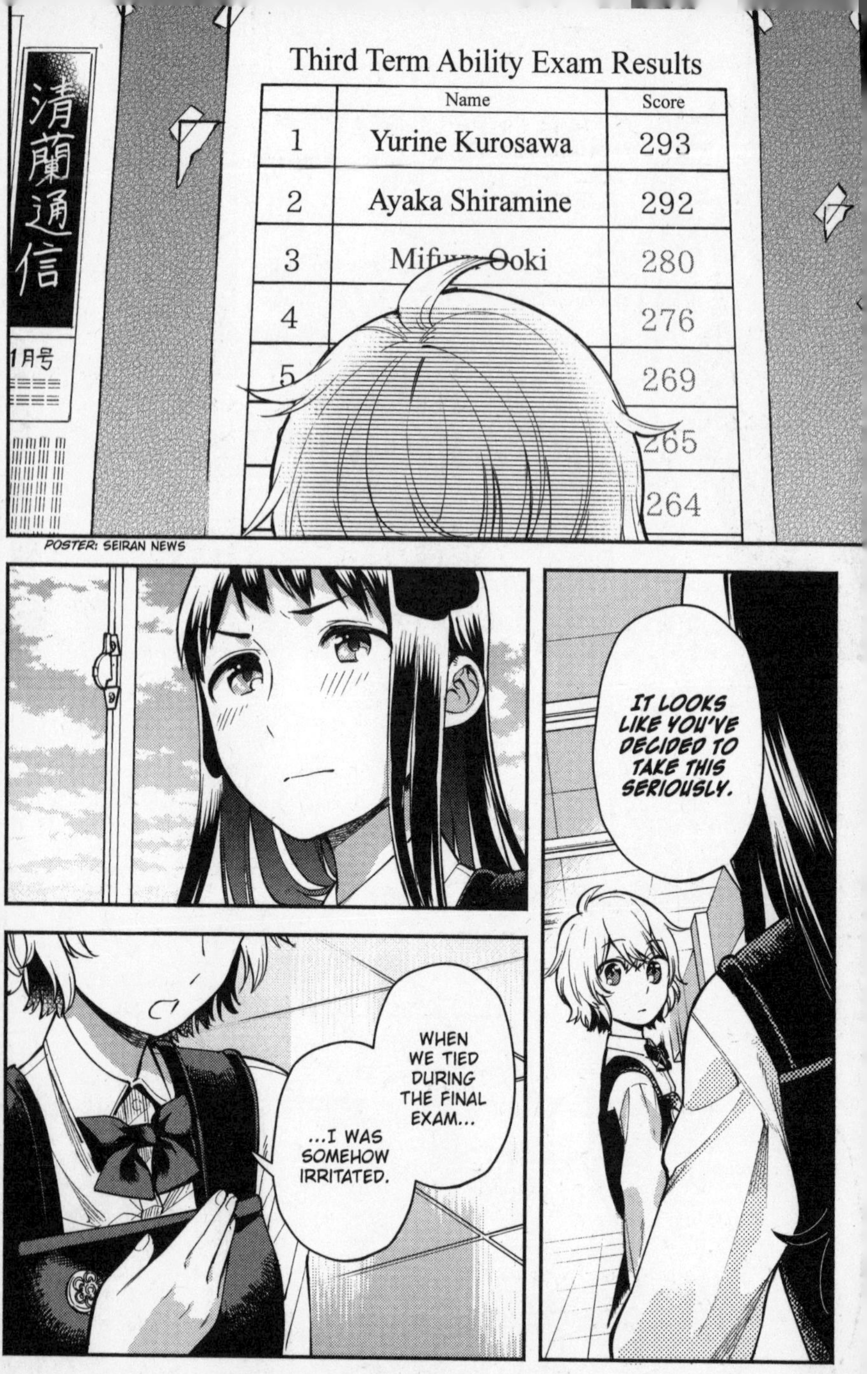
清蘭通信
1月号
Third Term Ability Exam Results
Name Score
1 Yurine Kurosawa 293
2 Ayaka Shiramine 292
3 Mifu Ooki 280
4 276
5 269
265
264
POSTER: SEIRAN NEWS
IT LOOKS LIKE YOU'VE DECIDED TO TAKE THIS SERIOUSLY.
WHEN WE TIED DURING THE FINAL EXAM...
...I WAS SOMEHOW IRRITATED.

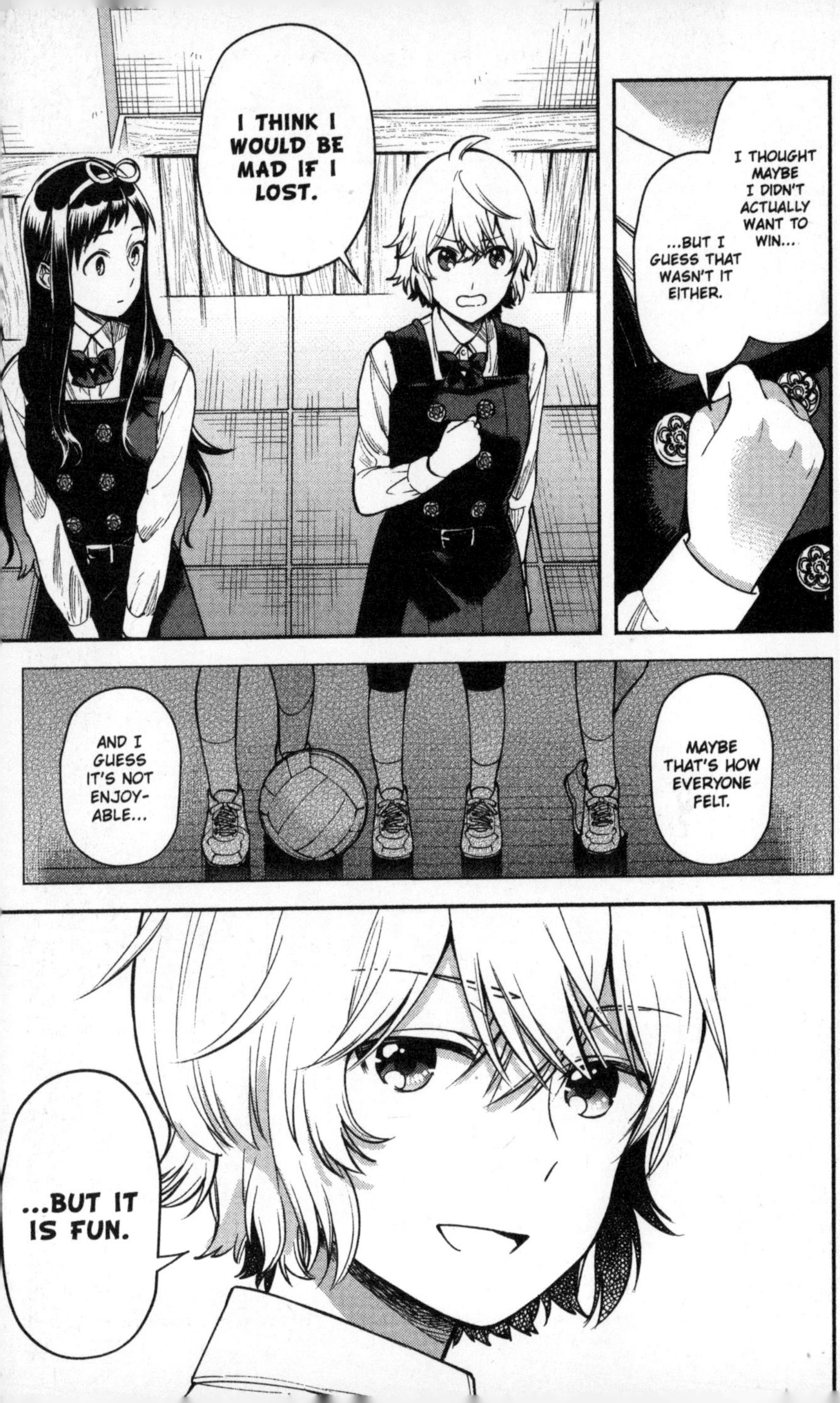
I THOUGHT MAYBE I DIDN'T ACTUALLY WANT TO WIN...
...BUT I GUESS THAT WASN'T IT EITHER.
I THINK I WOULD BE MAD IF I LOST.
MAYBE THAT'S HOW EVERYONE FELT.
AND I GUESS IT'S NOT ENJOY-ABLE...
...BUT IT IS FUN.

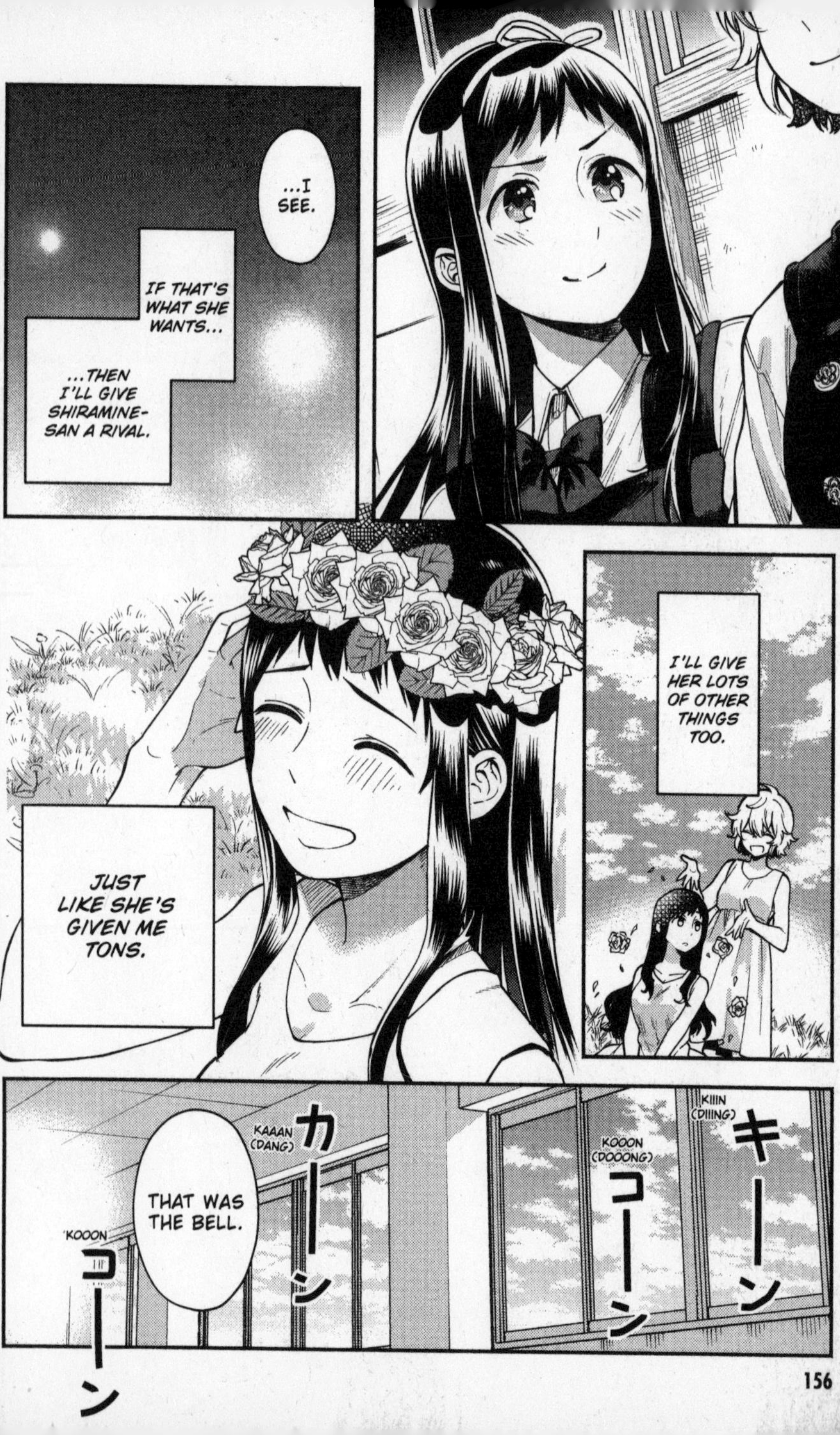
...I SEE.
IF THAT'S WHAT SHE WANTS...
...THEN I'LL GIVE SHIRAMINE-SAN A RIVAL.
I'LL GIVE HER LOTS OF OTHER THINGS TOO.
JUST LIKE SHE'S GIVEN ME TONS.
KIIN (DIIING)
キーン
KOOON (DOOONG)
コーン
THAT WAS THE BELL.
KAAAN (DANG)
カーン
KOOON
コーン

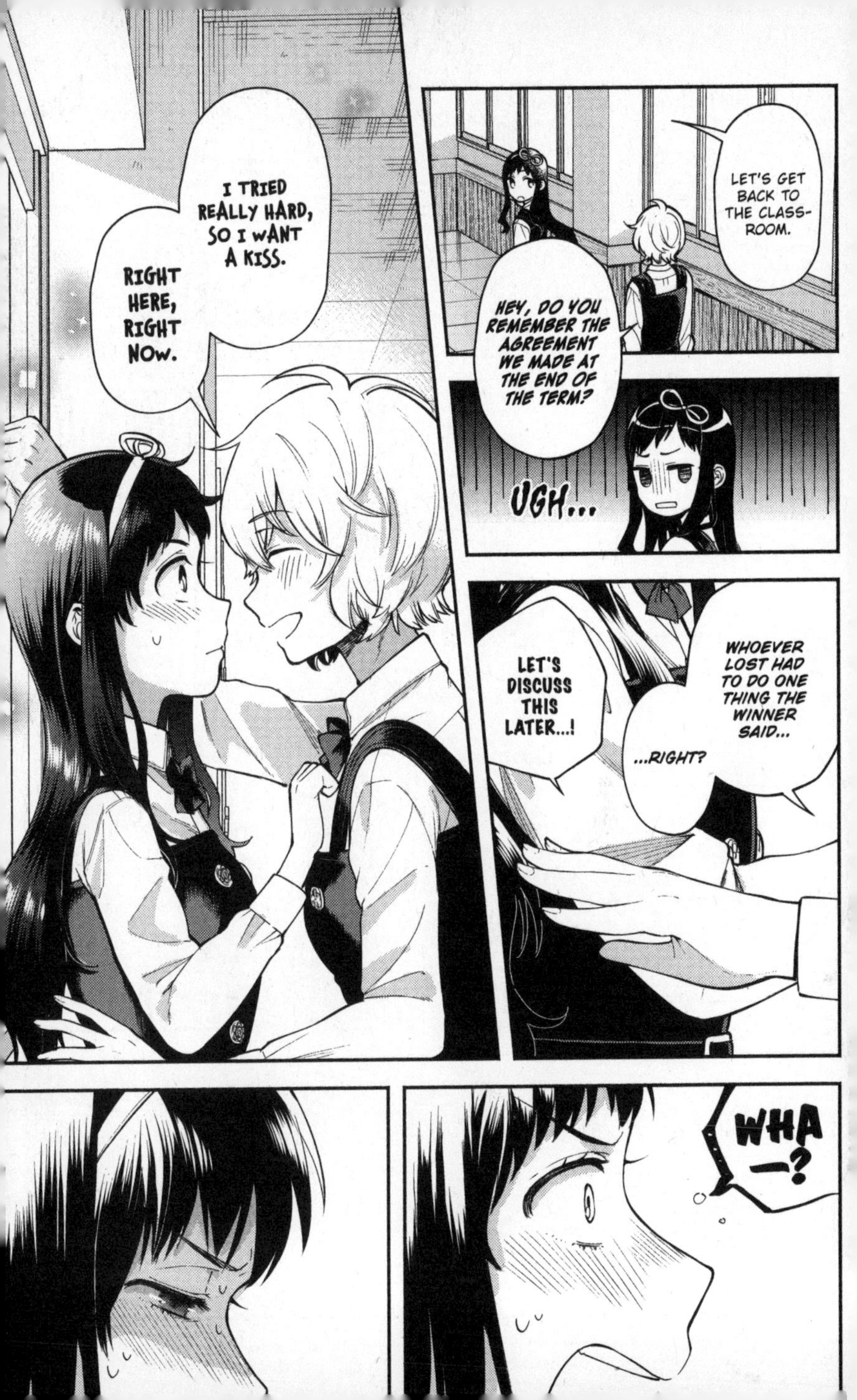
LET'S GET BACK TO THE CLASS-ROOM.
HEY, DO YOU REMEMBER THE AGREEMENT WE MADE AT THE END OF THE TERM?
UGH...
WHOEVER LOST HAD TO DO ONE THING THE WINNER SAID...
...RIGHT?
LET'S DISCUSS THIS LATER...!
I TRIED REALLY HARD, SO I WANT A KISS.
RIGHT HERE, RIGHT NOW.
WHA—?

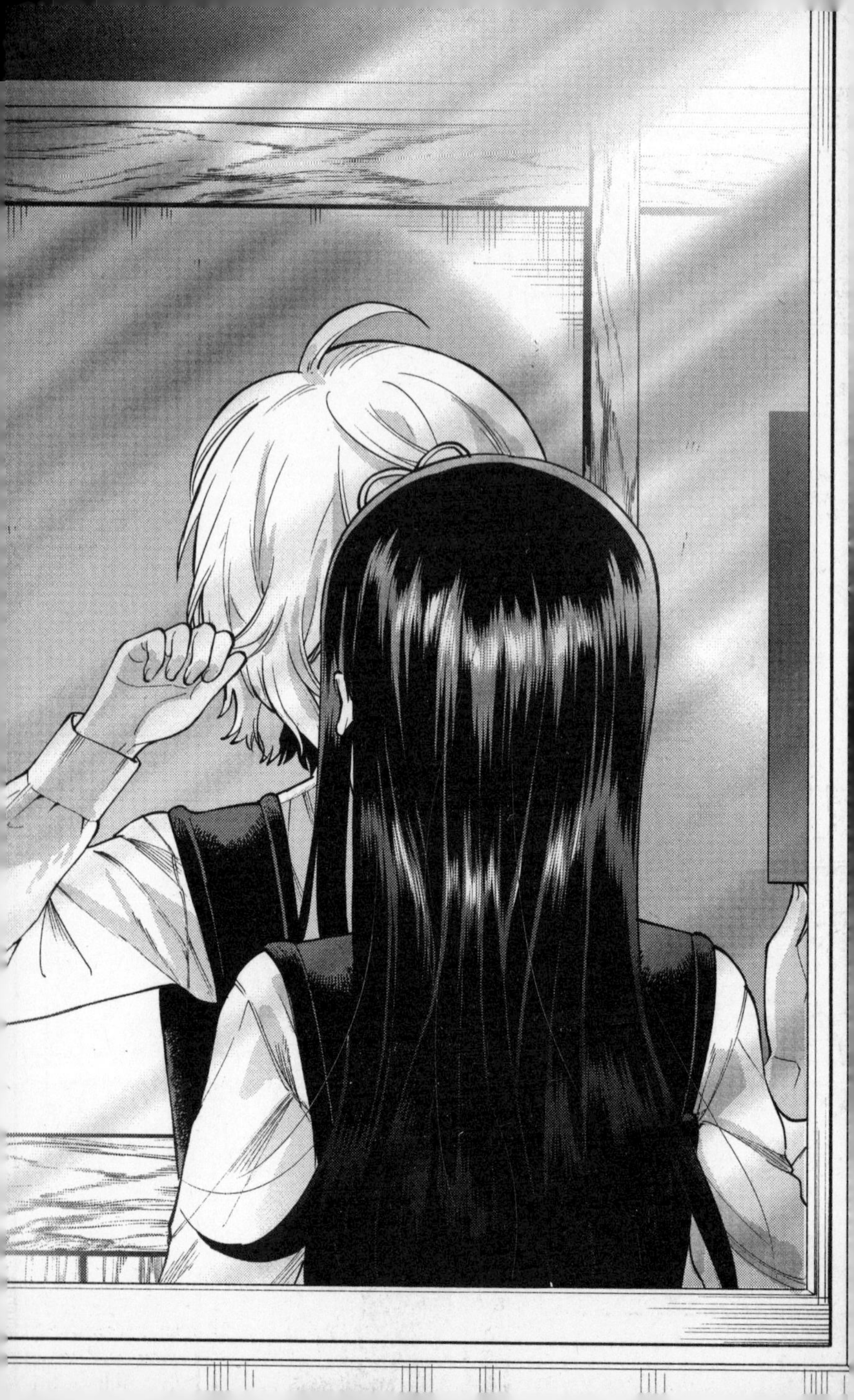

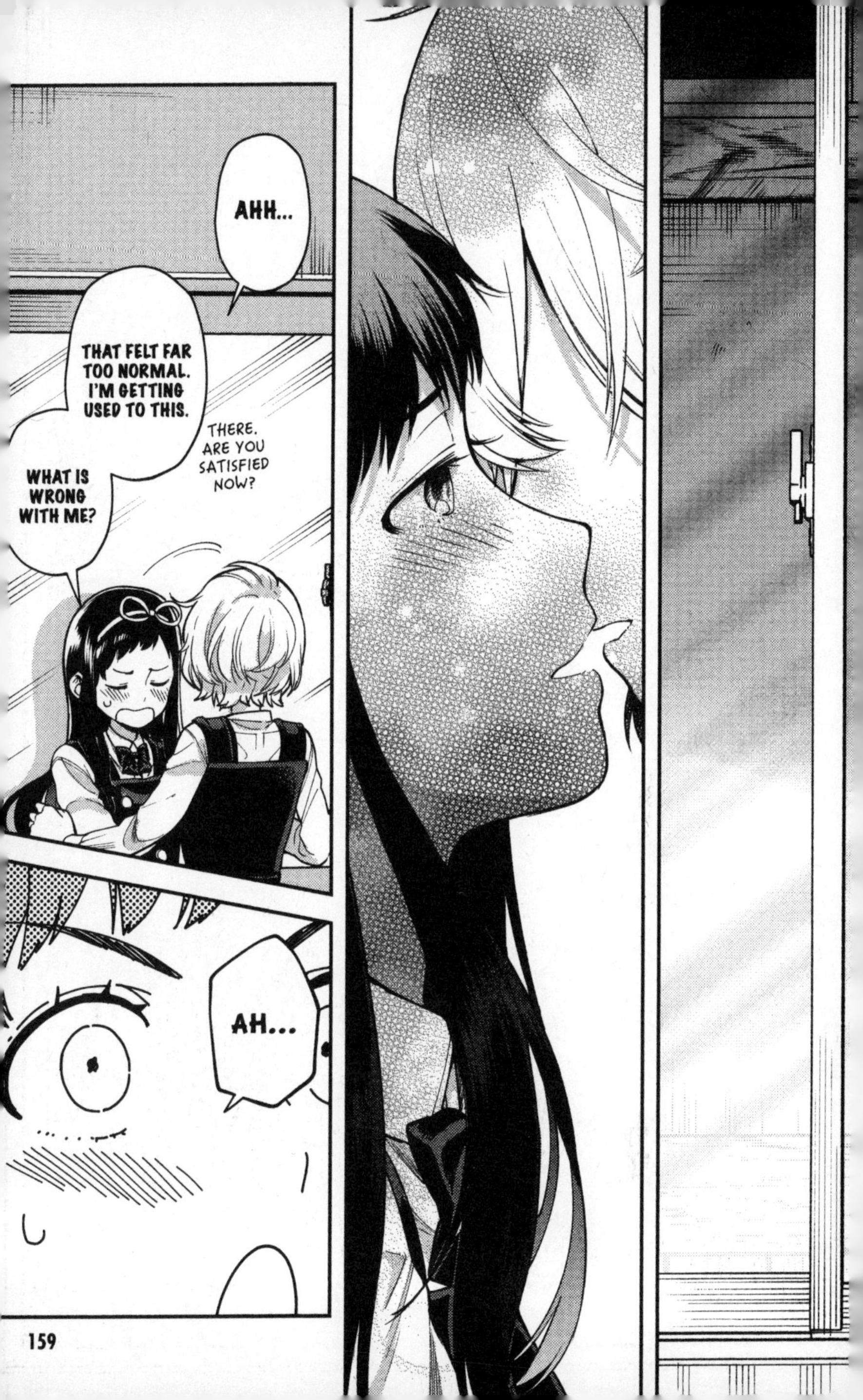
AHH...
THERE. ARE YOU SATISFIED NOW?
THAT FELT FAR TOO NORMAL. I'M GETTING USED TO THIS.
WHAT IS WRONG WITH ME?
AH...

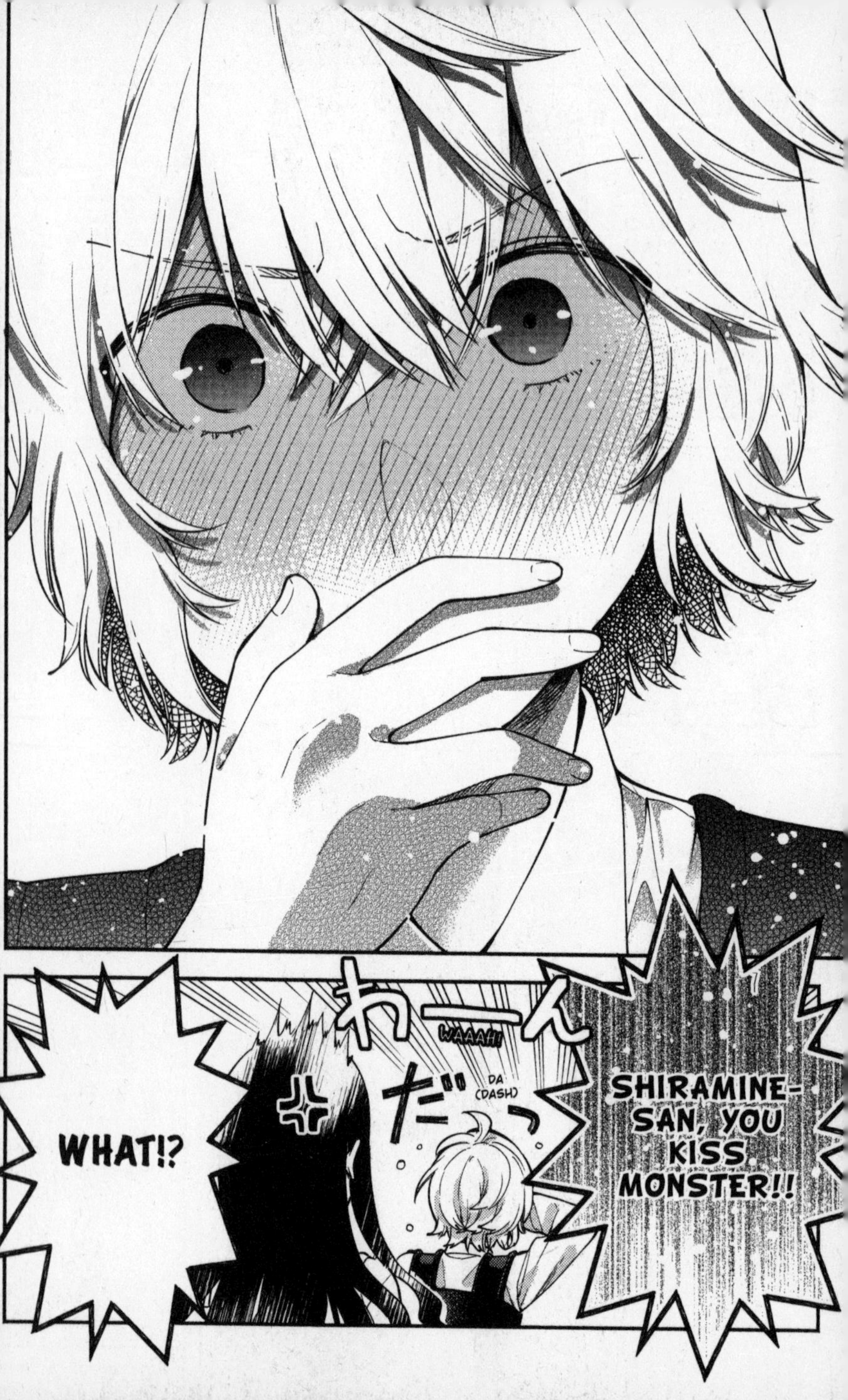
SHIRAMINE-SAN, YOU KISS MONSTER!!
わーん
WAAAH!!
だっ
DA (DASH)
WHAT!?

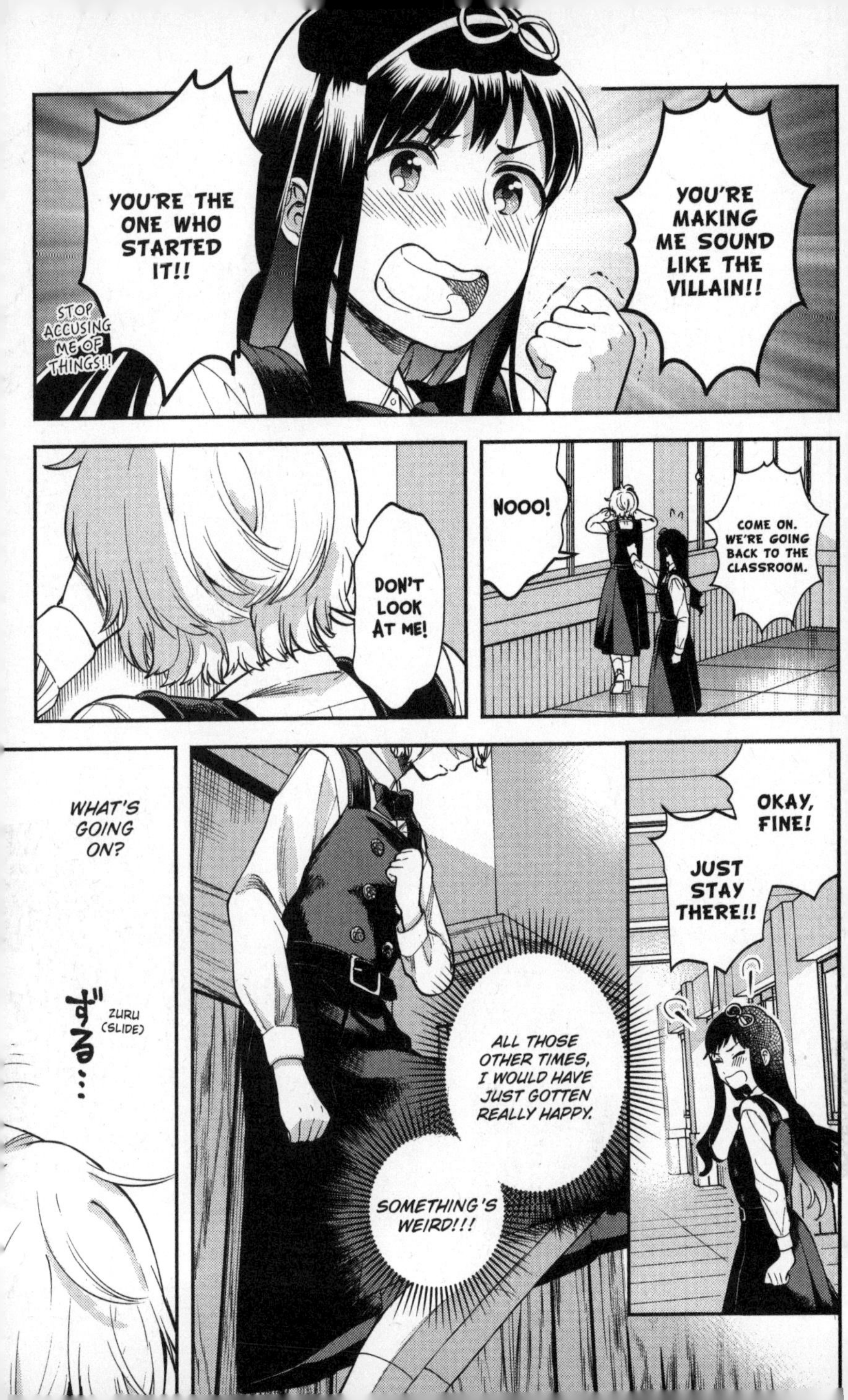
YOU'RE MAKING ME SOUND LIKE THE VILLAIN!!
YOU'RE THE ONE WHO STARTED IT!!
STOP ACCUSING ME OF THINGS!!
COME ON. WE'RE GOING BACK TO THE CLASSROOM.
NOOO!
DON'T LOOK AT ME!
OKAY, FINE!
JUST STAY THERE!!
ALL THOSE OTHER TIMES, I WOULD HAVE JUST GOTTEN REALLY HAPPY.
SOMETHING'S WEIRD!!!
WHAT'S GOING ON?
ずる…
ZURU (SLIDE)

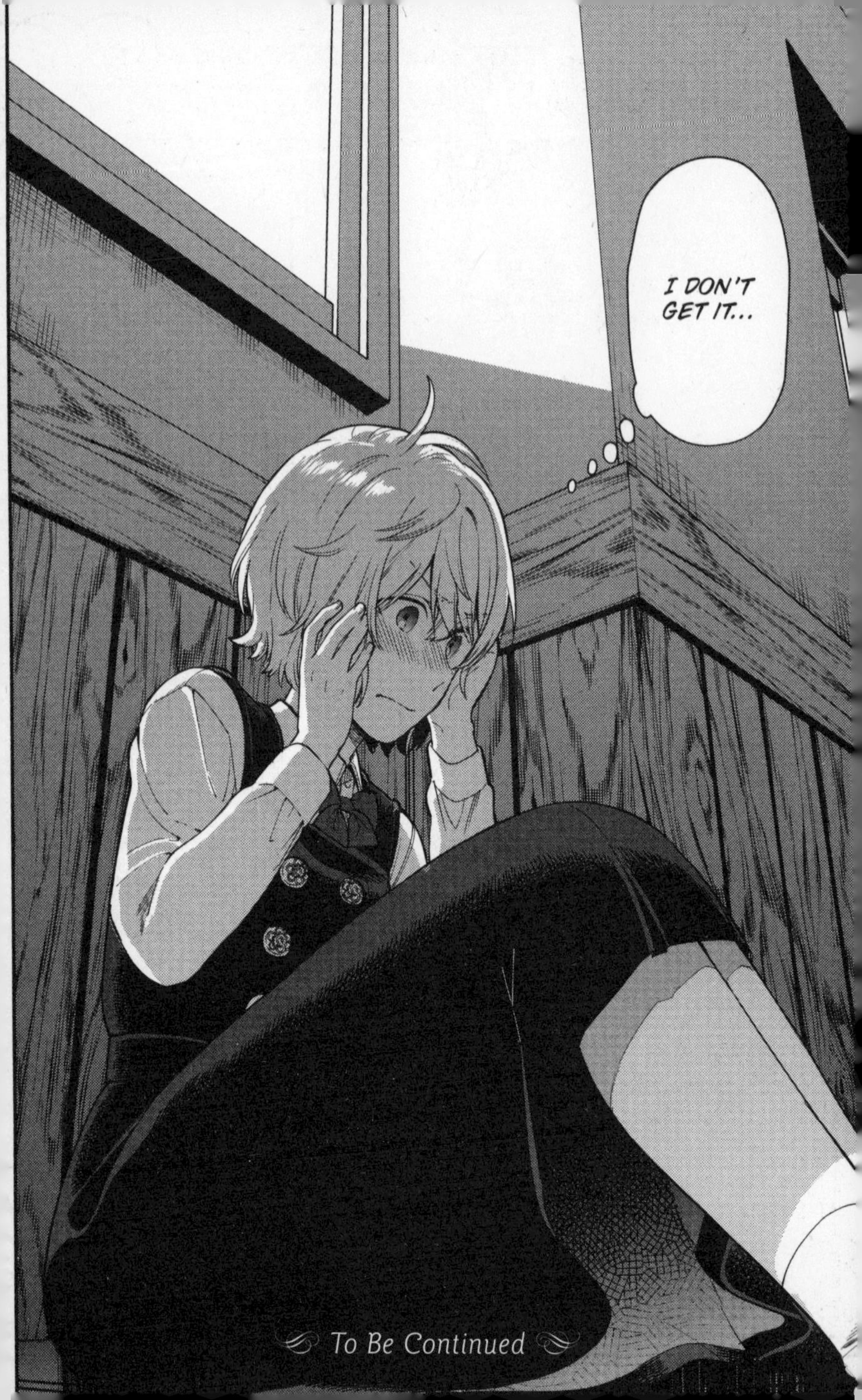
I DON'T GET IT...
To Be Continued

Christmas Eve

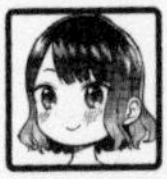

MIYUKI
TWENTY-FOUR YEARS OLD. SINGLE.

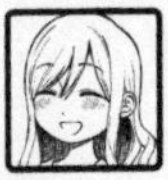

MIHO
TWENTY-FIVE YEARS OLD. SINGLE.

KISS THEATER: WHAT'S BEHIND THE STORY!? ✷ PEOPLE OTHER THAN THE MAIN CHARACTERS HAVE STORIES TOO. HERE, WE PRESENT THE "LITTLE LOVE" STORIES HAPPENING BEHIND THE SCENES.

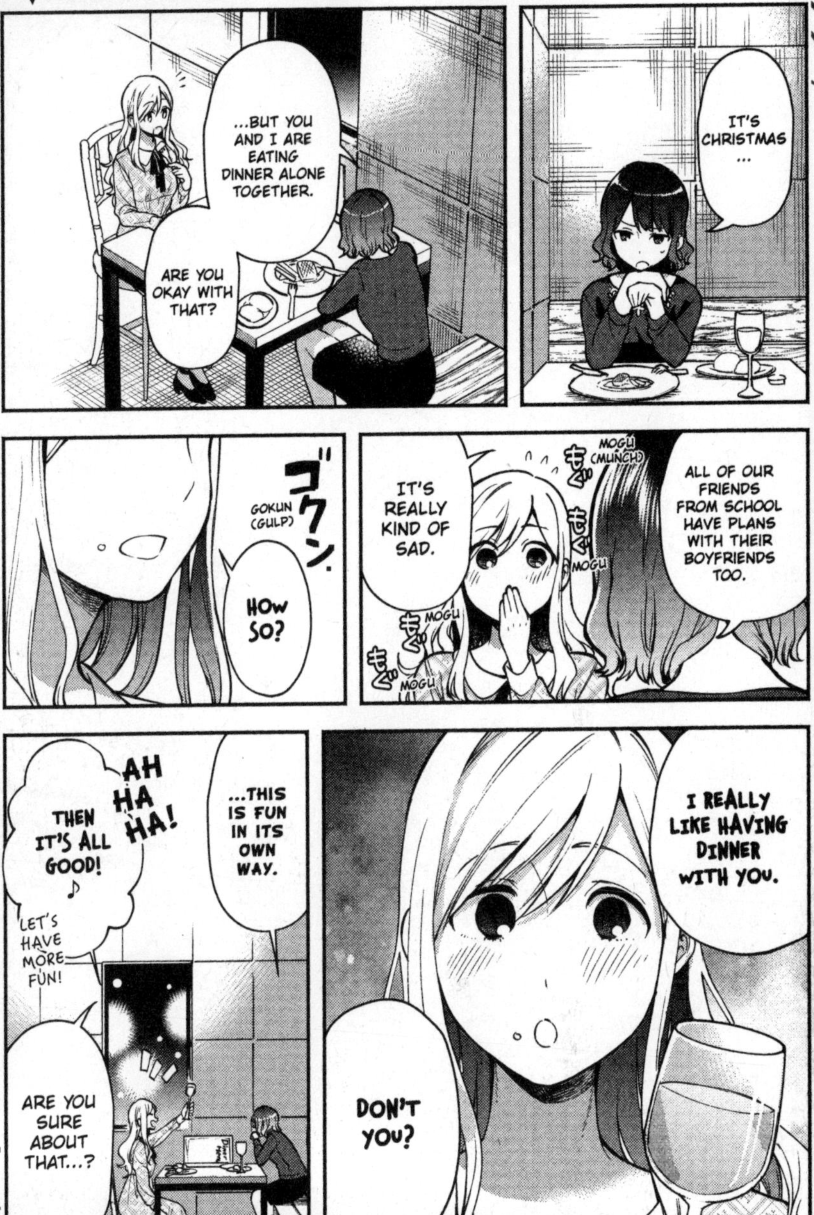
IT'S CHRISTMAS...
...BUT YOU AND I ARE EATING DINNER ALONE TOGETHER.
ARE YOU OKAY WITH THAT?
ALL OF OUR FRIENDS FROM SCHOOL HAVE PLANS WITH THEIR BOYFRIENDS TOO.
MOGU (MUNCH)
MOGU
IT'S REALLY KIND OF SAD.
MOGU
MOGU
GOKUN (GULP)
HOW SO?
I REALLY LIKE HAVING DINNER WITH YOU.
DON'T YOU?
...THIS IS FUN IN ITS OWN WAY.
THEN IT'S ALL GOOD! ♪
AH HA HA!
LET'S HAVE MORE FUN!
ARE YOU SURE ABOUT THAT...?

Kiss and White Lily for My Dearest Girl
Side Stories

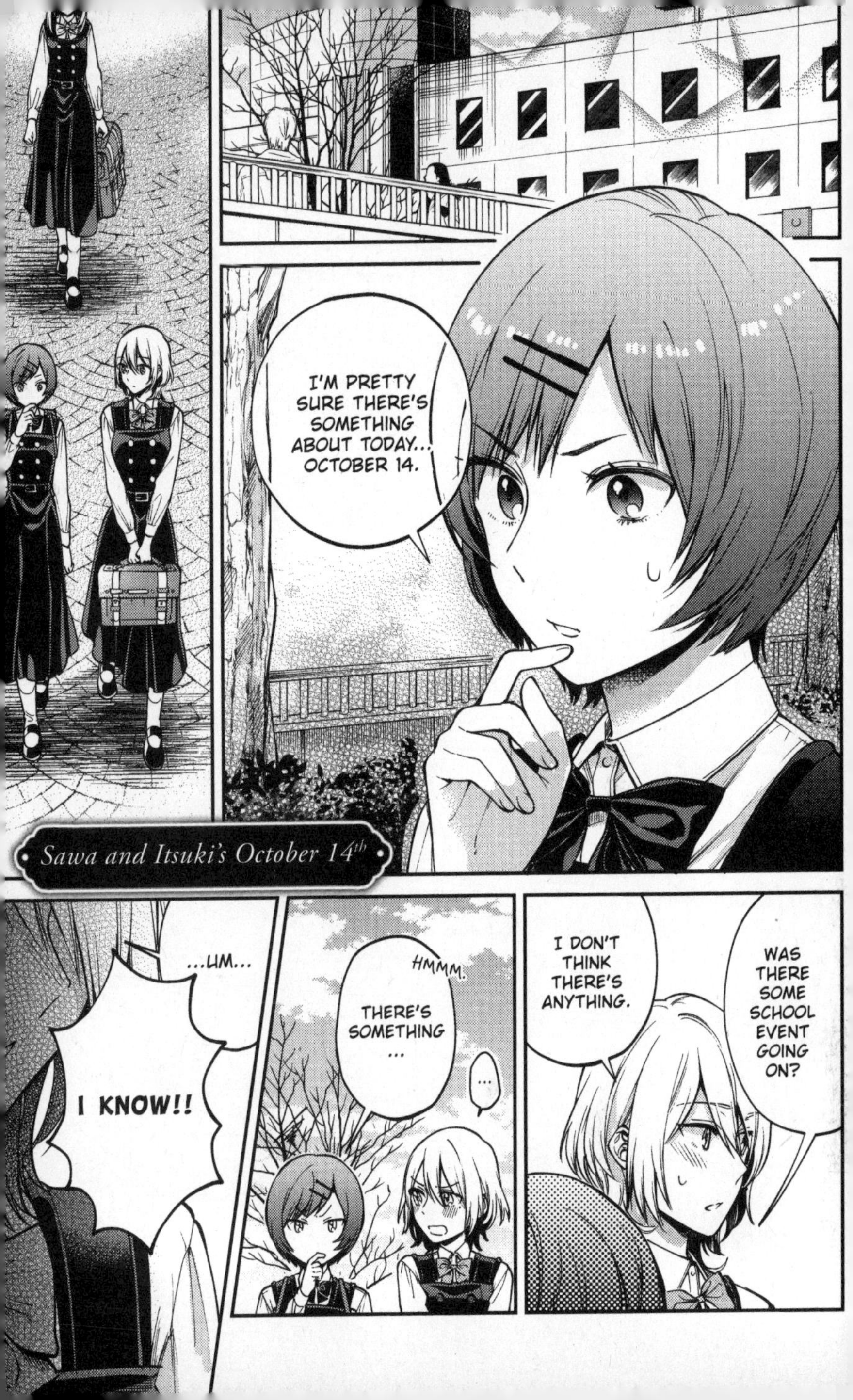
I'M PRETTY SURE THERE'S SOMETHING ABOUT TODAY... OCTOBER 14.
Sawa and Itsuki's October 14th
WAS THERE SOME SCHOOL EVENT GOING ON?
I DON'T THINK THERE'S ANYTHING.
HMMM.
THERE'S SOMETHING...
...
...UM...
I KNOW!!

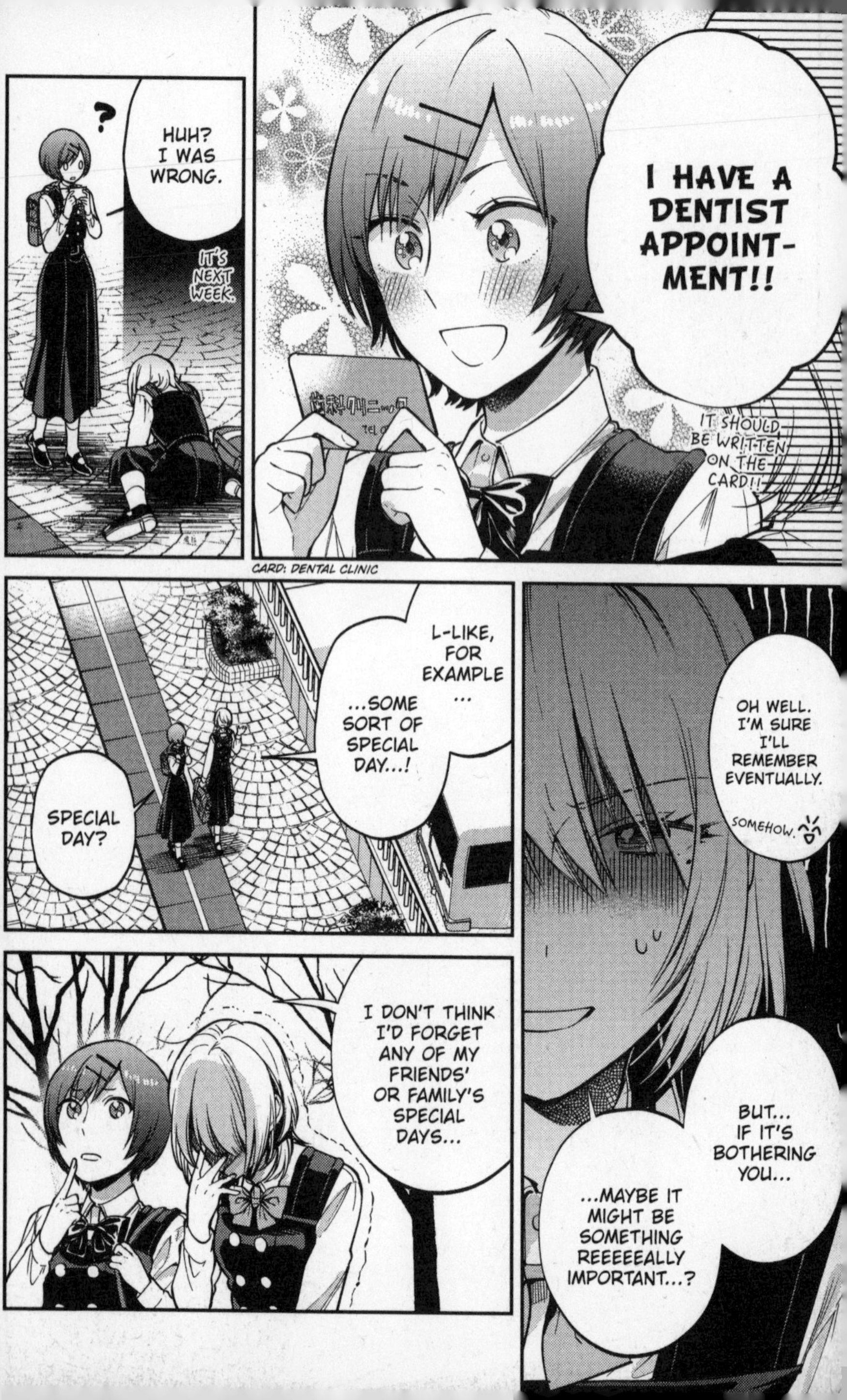
I HAVE A DENTIST APPOINTMENT!!
IT SHOULD BE WRITTEN ON THE CARD!!
HUH? I WAS WRONG.
IT'S NEXT WEEK.
CARD: DENTAL CLINIC
OH WELL. I'M SURE I'LL REMEMBER EVENTUALLY.
SOMEHOW.
BUT... IF IT'S BOTHERING YOU...
...MAYBE IT MIGHT BE SOMETHING REEEEEALLY IMPORTANT...?
L-LIKE, FOR EXAMPLE...
...SOME SORT OF SPECIAL DAY...!
SPECIAL DAY?
I DON'T THINK I'D FORGET ANY OF MY FRIENDS' OR FAMILY'S SPECIAL DAYS...

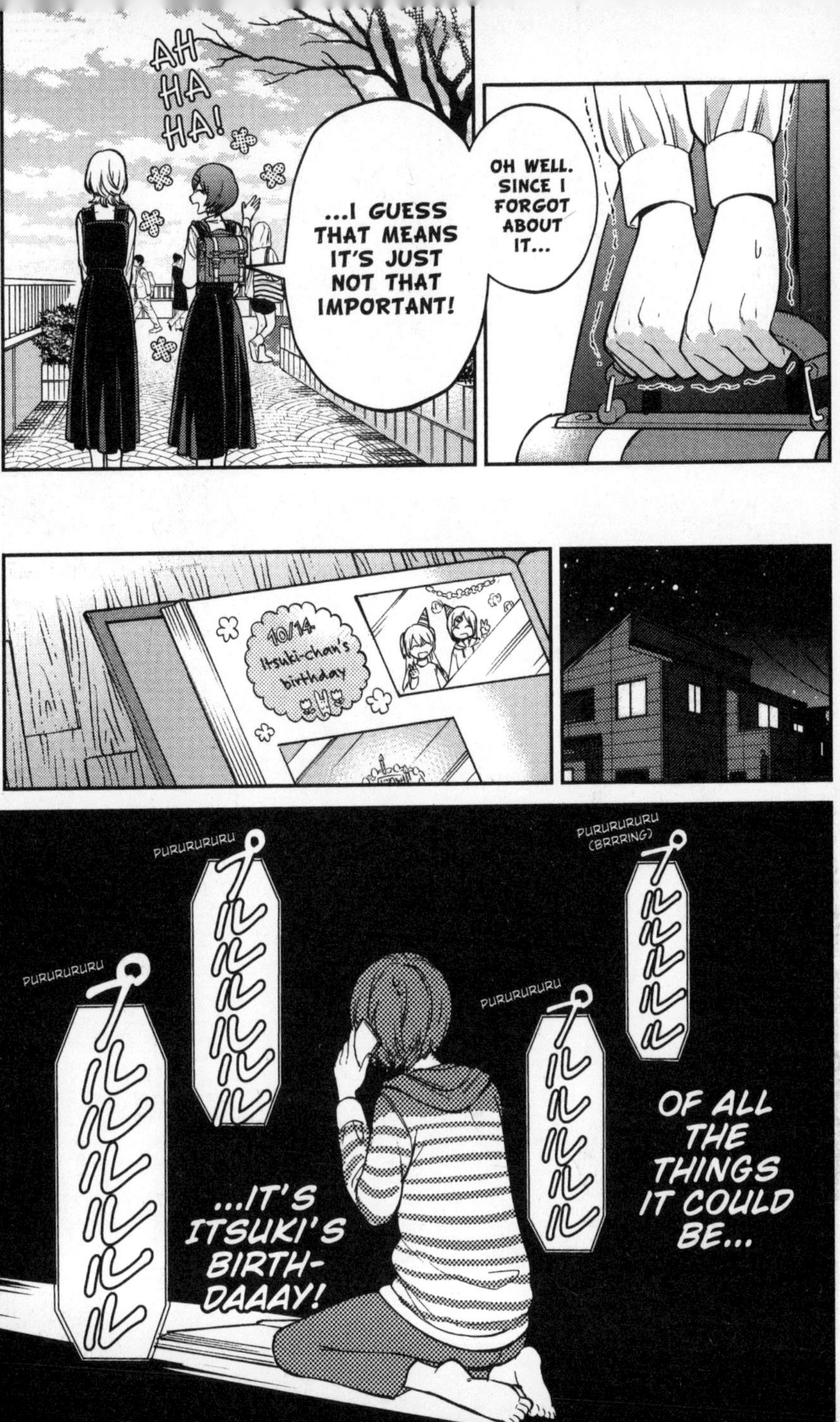
OH WELL. SINCE I FORGOT ABOUT IT...
...I GUESS THAT MEANS IT'S JUST NOT THAT IMPORTANT!
AH HA HA!
10/14 Itsuki-chan's birthday
PURURURURU (BRRRING)
OF ALL THE THINGS IT COULD BE...
PURURURURU
PURURURURU
...IT'S ITSUKI'S BIRTH-DAAAY!
PURURURURU

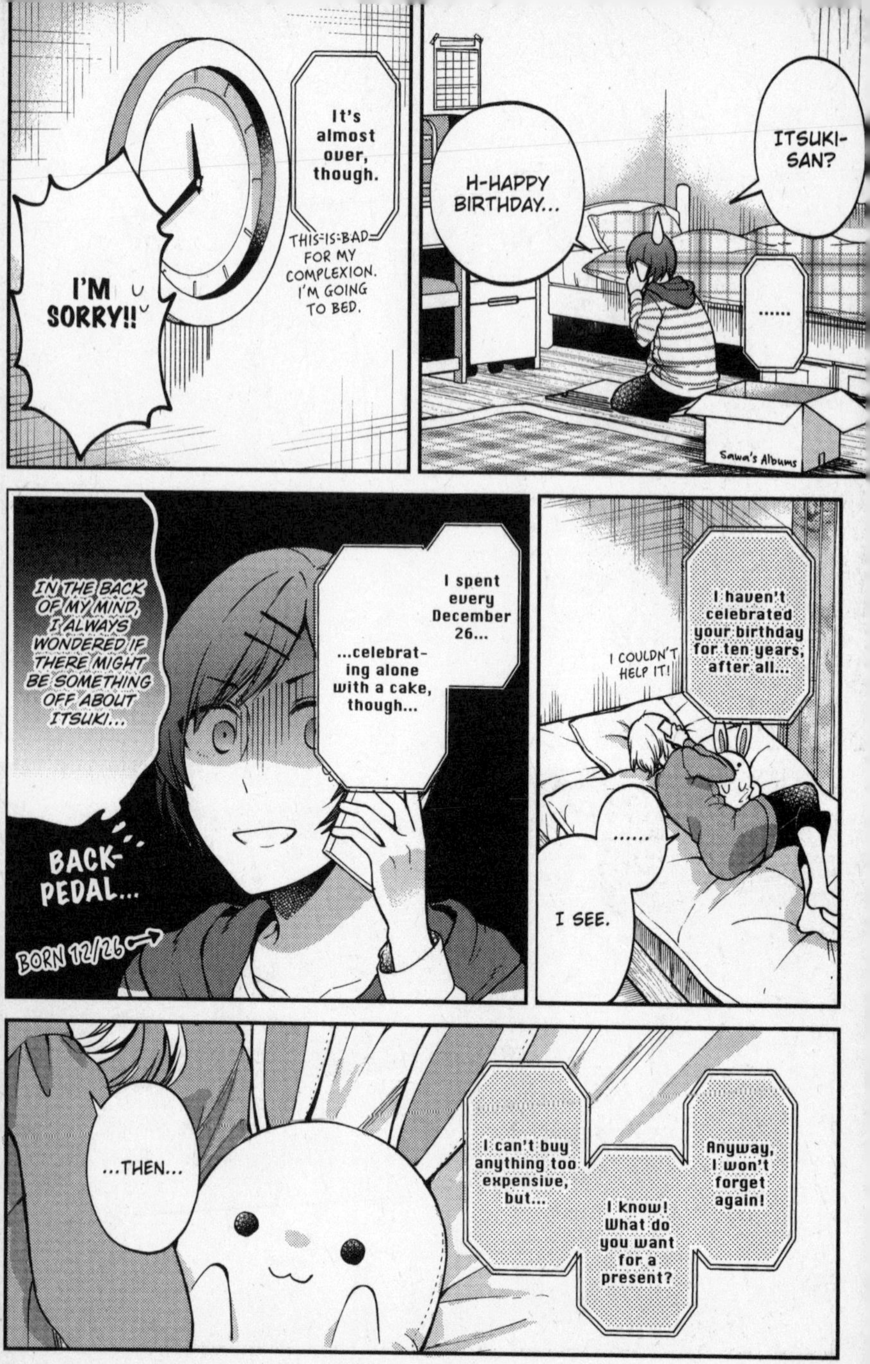
ITSUKI-SAN?
......
H-HAPPY BIRTHDAY...
Sawa's Albums
It's almost over, though.
THIS IS BAD FOR MY COMPLEXION. I'M GOING TO BED.
I'M SORRY!!
I haven't celebrated your birthday for ten years, after all...
I COULDN'T HELP IT!
......
I SEE.
I spent every December 26...
...celebrat-ing alone with a cake, though...
IN THE BACK OF MY MIND, I ALWAYS WONDERED IF THERE MIGHT BE SOMETHING OFF ABOUT ITSUKI...
BACK-PEDAL...
BORN 12/26
Anyway, I won't forget again!
I know! What do you want for a present?
I can't buy anything too expensive, but...
...THEN...

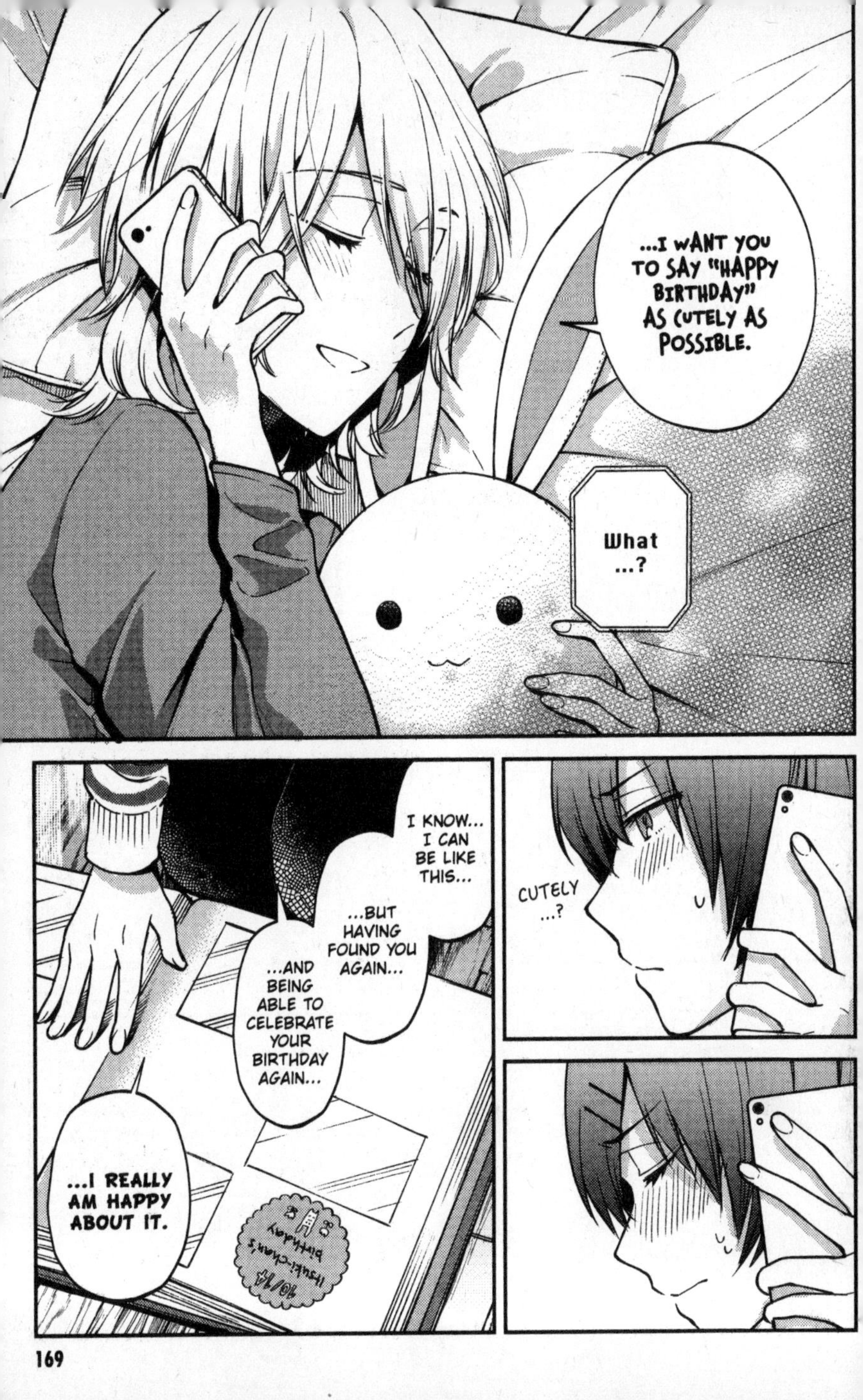
...I WANT YOU TO SAY "HAPPY BIRTHDAY" AS CUTELY AS POSSIBLE.
What ...?
CUTELY ...?
I KNOW... I CAN BE LIKE THIS...
...BUT HAVING FOUND YOU AGAIN...
...AND BEING ABLE TO CELEBRATE YOUR BIRTHDAY AGAIN...
10/14 Itsuki-chan's birthday
...I REALLY AM HAPPY ABOUT IT.

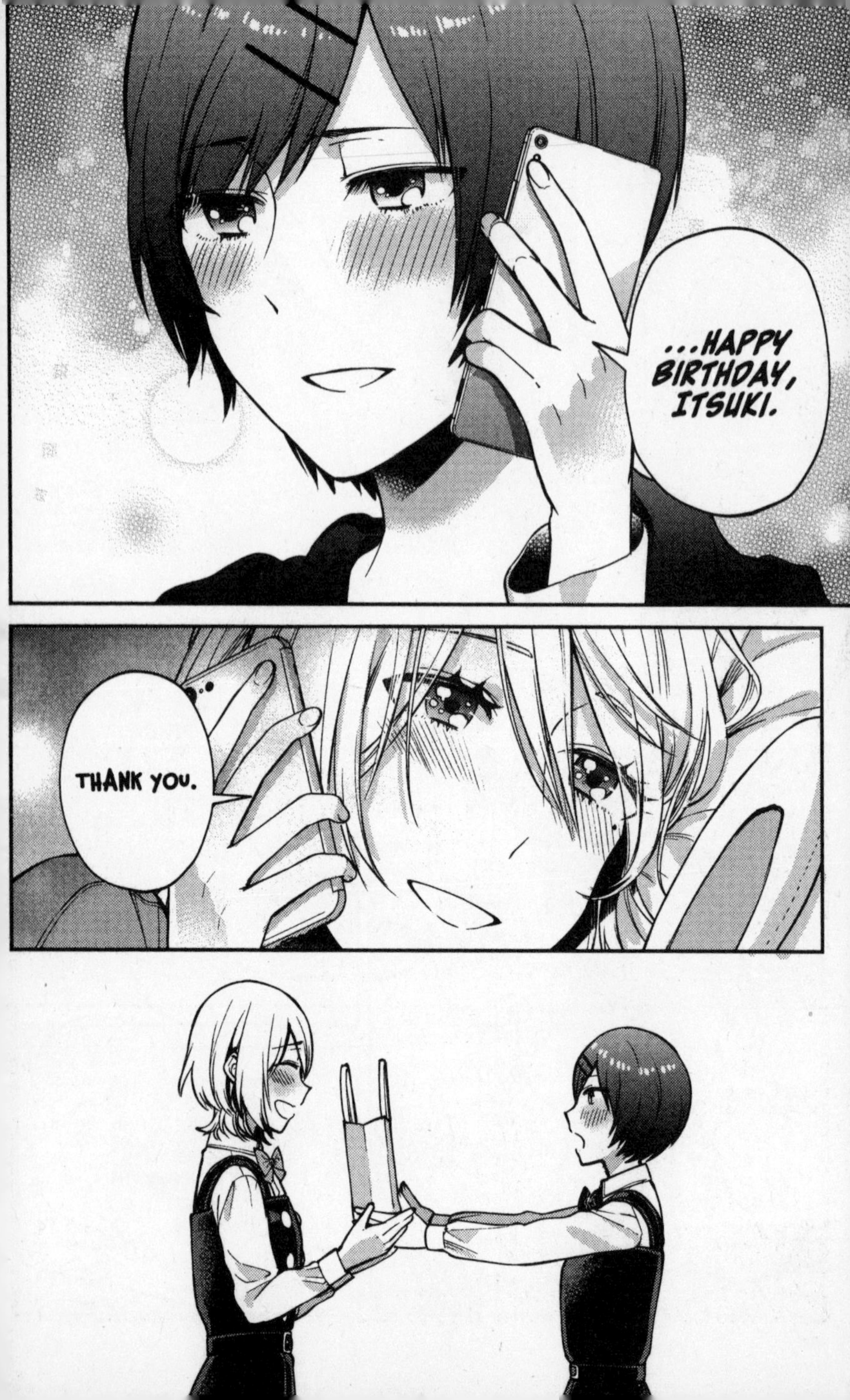
...HAPPY BIRTHDAY, ITSUKI.
THANK YOU.

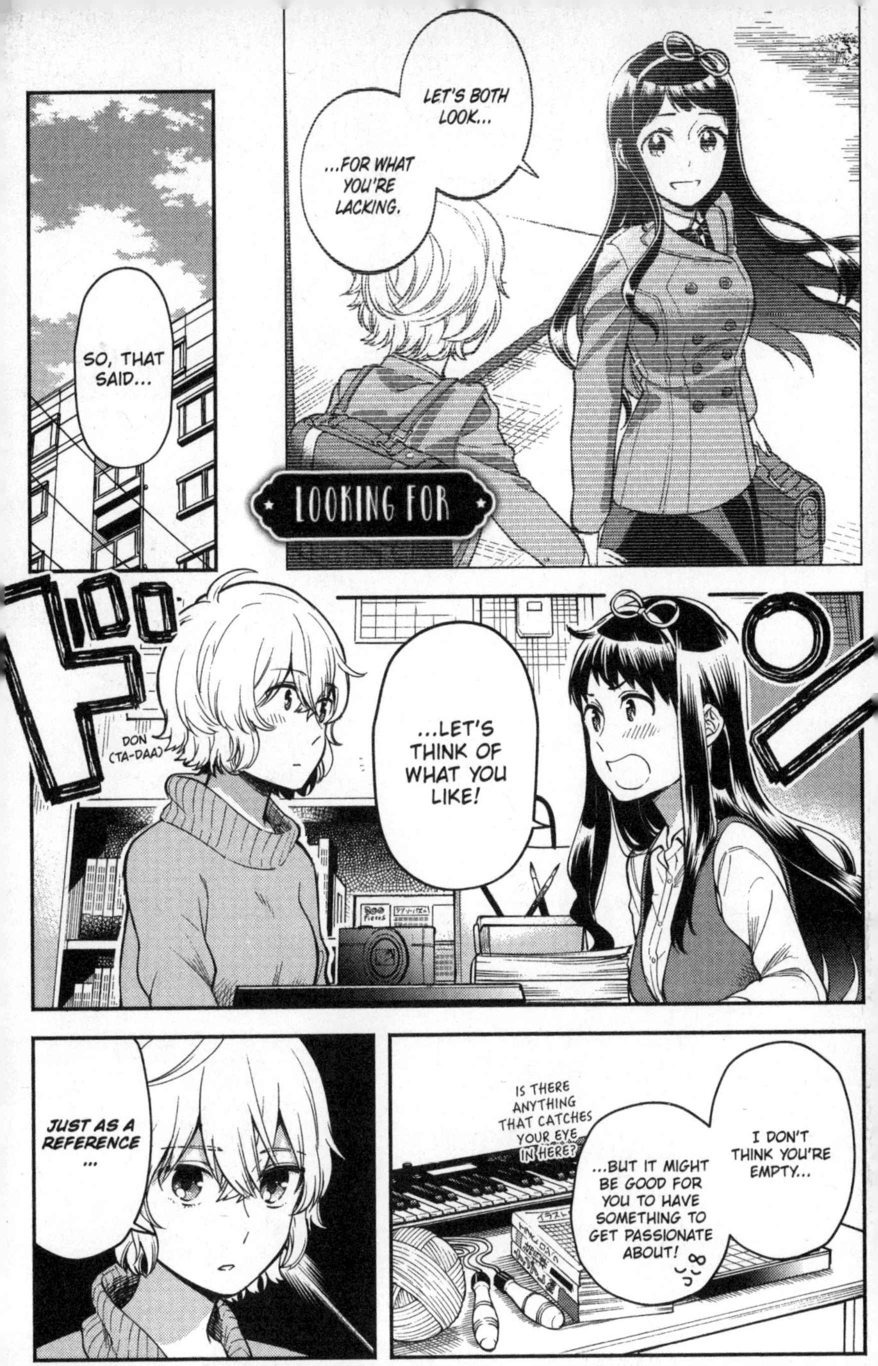
LET'S BOTH LOOK...
...FOR WHAT YOU'RE LACKING.
LOOKING FOR
SO, THAT SAID...
DON (TA-DAA)
...LET'S THINK OF WHAT YOU LIKE!
I DON'T THINK YOU'RE EMPTY...
...BUT IT MIGHT BE GOOD FOR YOU TO HAVE SOMETHING TO GET PASSIONATE ABOUT!
IS THERE ANYTHING THAT CATCHES YOUR EYE IN HERE?
JUST AS A REFERENCE ...

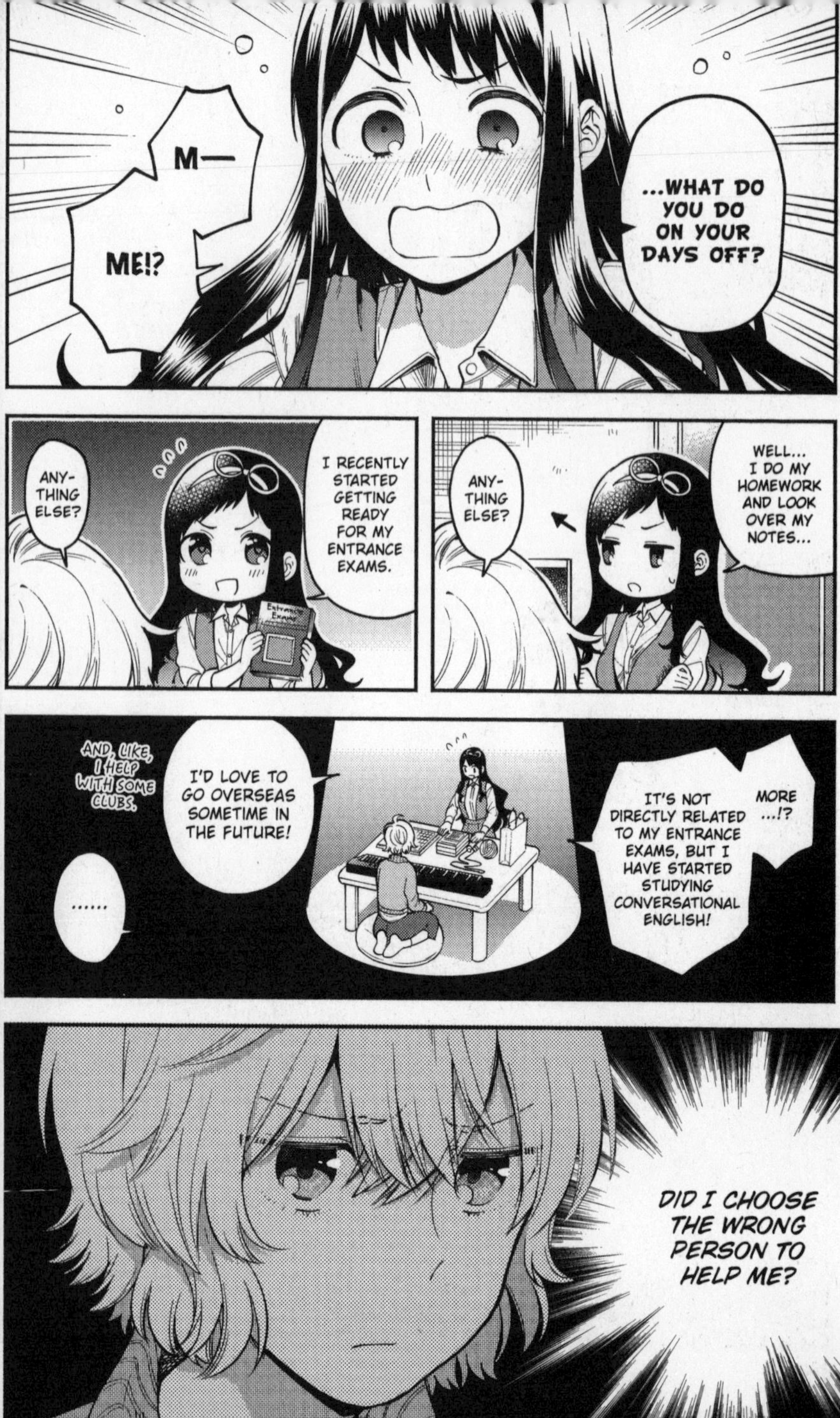
...WHAT DO YOU DO ON YOUR DAYS OFF?
M—
ME!?
WELL... I DO MY HOMEWORK AND LOOK OVER MY NOTES...
ANY-THING ELSE?
I RECENTLY STARTED GETTING READY FOR MY ENTRANCE EXAMS.
ANY-THING ELSE?
MORE ...!?
IT'S NOT DIRECTLY RELATED TO MY ENTRANCE EXAMS, BUT I HAVE STARTED STUDYING CONVERSATIONAL ENGLISH!
I'D LOVE TO GO OVERSEAS SOMETIME IN THE FUTURE!
AND, LIKE, I HELP WITH SOME CLUBS.
......
DID I CHOOSE THE WRONG PERSON TO HELP ME?

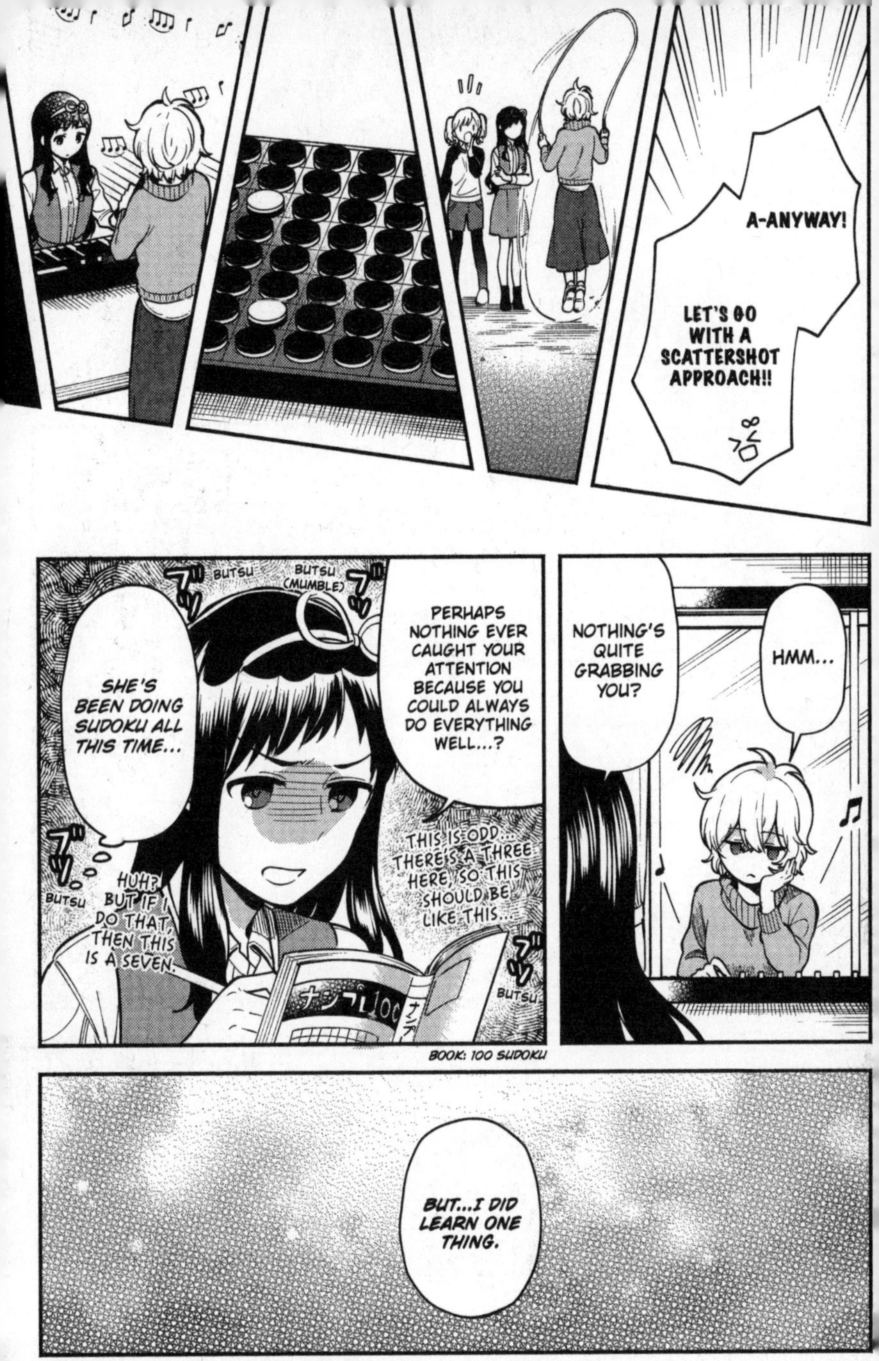
A-ANYWAY!
LET'S GO WITH A SCATTERSHOT APPROACH!!
HMM...
NOTHING'S QUITE GRABBING YOU?
PERHAPS NOTHING EVER CAUGHT YOUR ATTENTION BECAUSE YOU COULD ALWAYS DO EVERYTHING WELL...?
BUTSU (MUMBLE)
BUTSU
SHE'S BEEN DOING SUDOKU ALL THIS TIME...
THIS IS ODD... THERE'S A THREE HERE, SO THIS SHOULD BE LIKE THIS...
HUH? BUT IF I DO THAT, THEN THIS IS A SEVEN.
BUTSU
BUTSU
BUT...I DID LEARN ONE THING.
BOOK: 100 SUDOKU

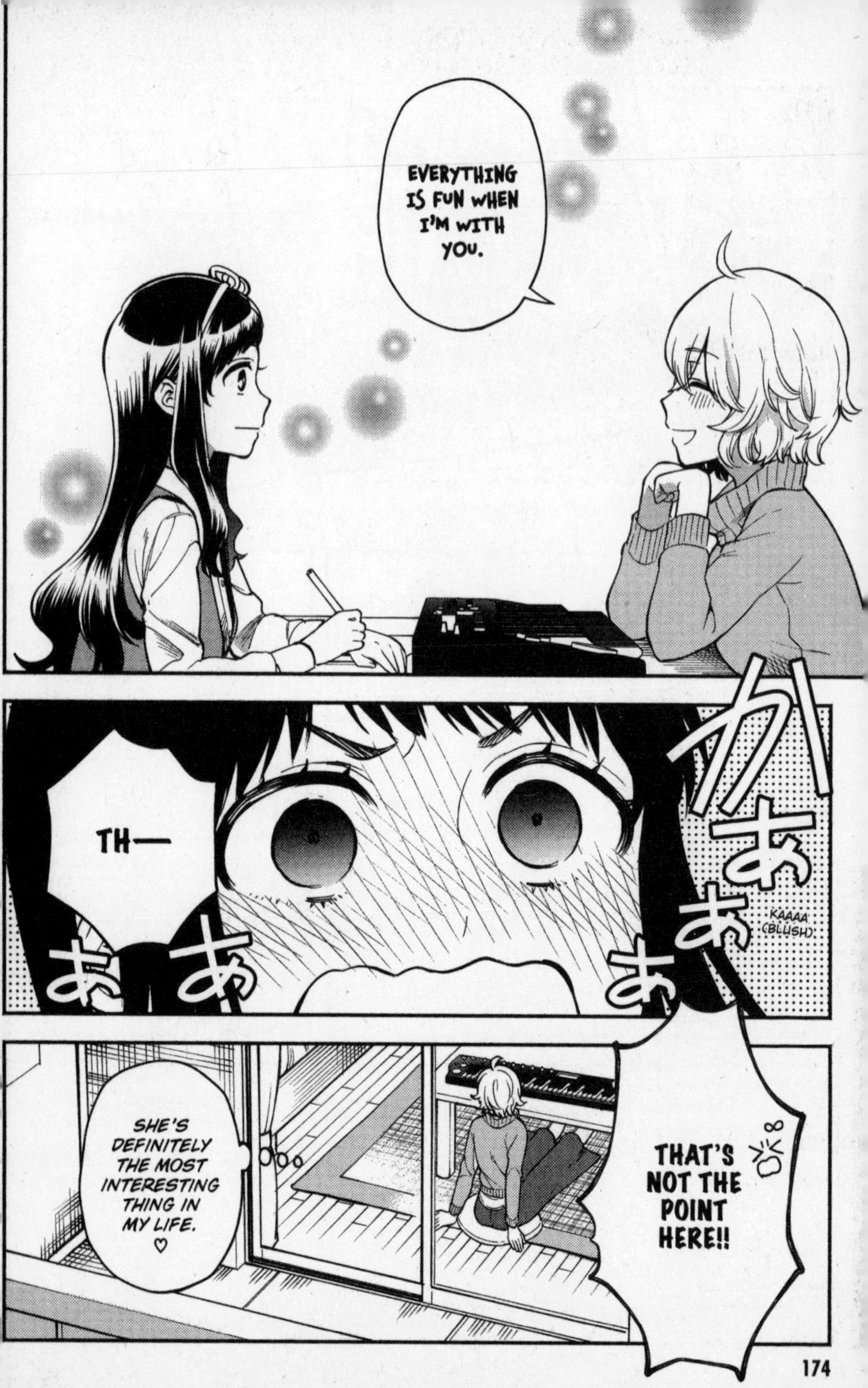
EVERYTHING IS FUN WHEN I'M WITH YOU.
かあああ
KAAAA (BLUSH)
TH—
ああ
THAT'S NOT THE POINT HERE!!
SHE'S DEFINITELY THE MOST INTERESTING THING IN MY LIFE. ♡

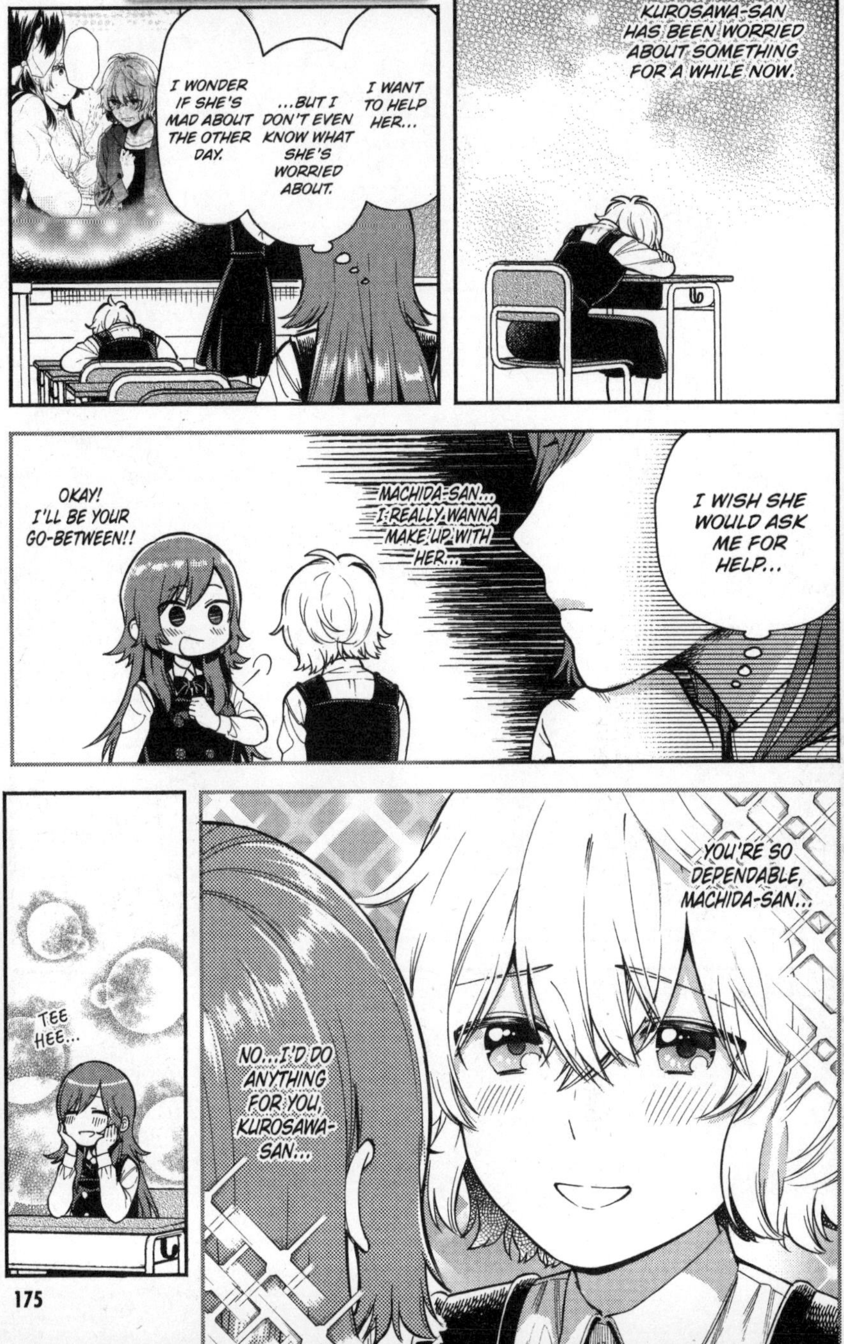
KUROSAWA-SAN HAS BEEN WORRIED ABOUT SOMETHING FOR A WHILE NOW.
I WANT TO HELP HER...
...BUT I DON'T EVEN KNOW WHAT SHE'S WORRIED ABOUT.
I WONDER IF SHE'S MAD ABOUT THE OTHER DAY.
I WISH SHE WOULD ASK ME FOR HELP...
MACHIDA-SAN... I REALLY WANNA MAKE UP WITH HER...
OKAY! I'LL BE YOUR GO-BETWEEN!!
YOU'RE SO DEPENDABLE, MACHIDA-SAN...
NO...I'D DO ANYTHING FOR YOU, KUROSAWA-SAN...
TEE HEE...

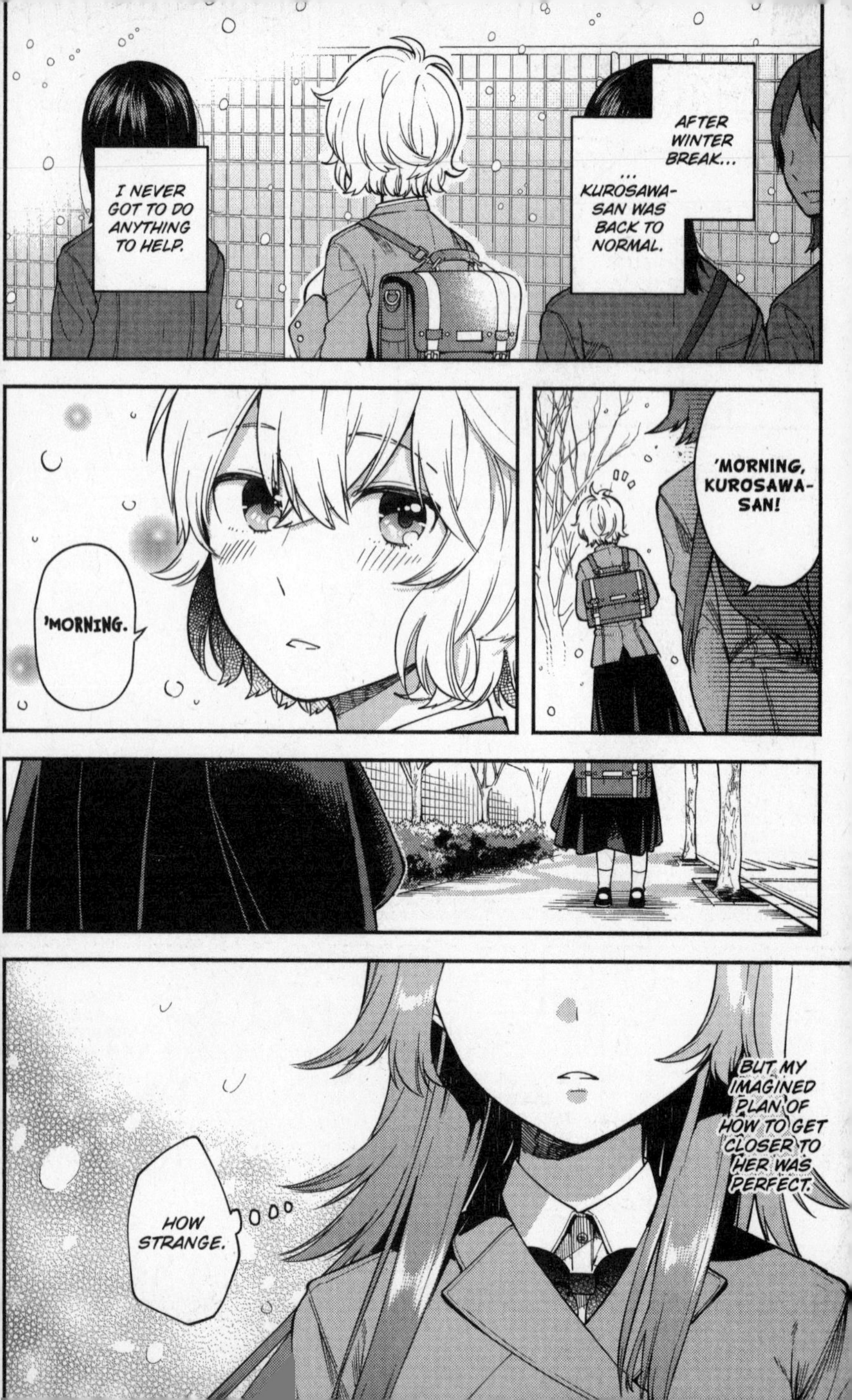
AFTER WINTER BREAK...
...KUROSAWA-SAN WAS BACK TO NORMAL.
I NEVER GOT TO DO ANYTHING TO HELP.
'MORNING, KUROSAWA-SAN!
'MORNING.
BUT MY IMAGINED PLAN OF HOW TO GET CLOSER TO HER WAS PERFECT.
HOW STRANGE.

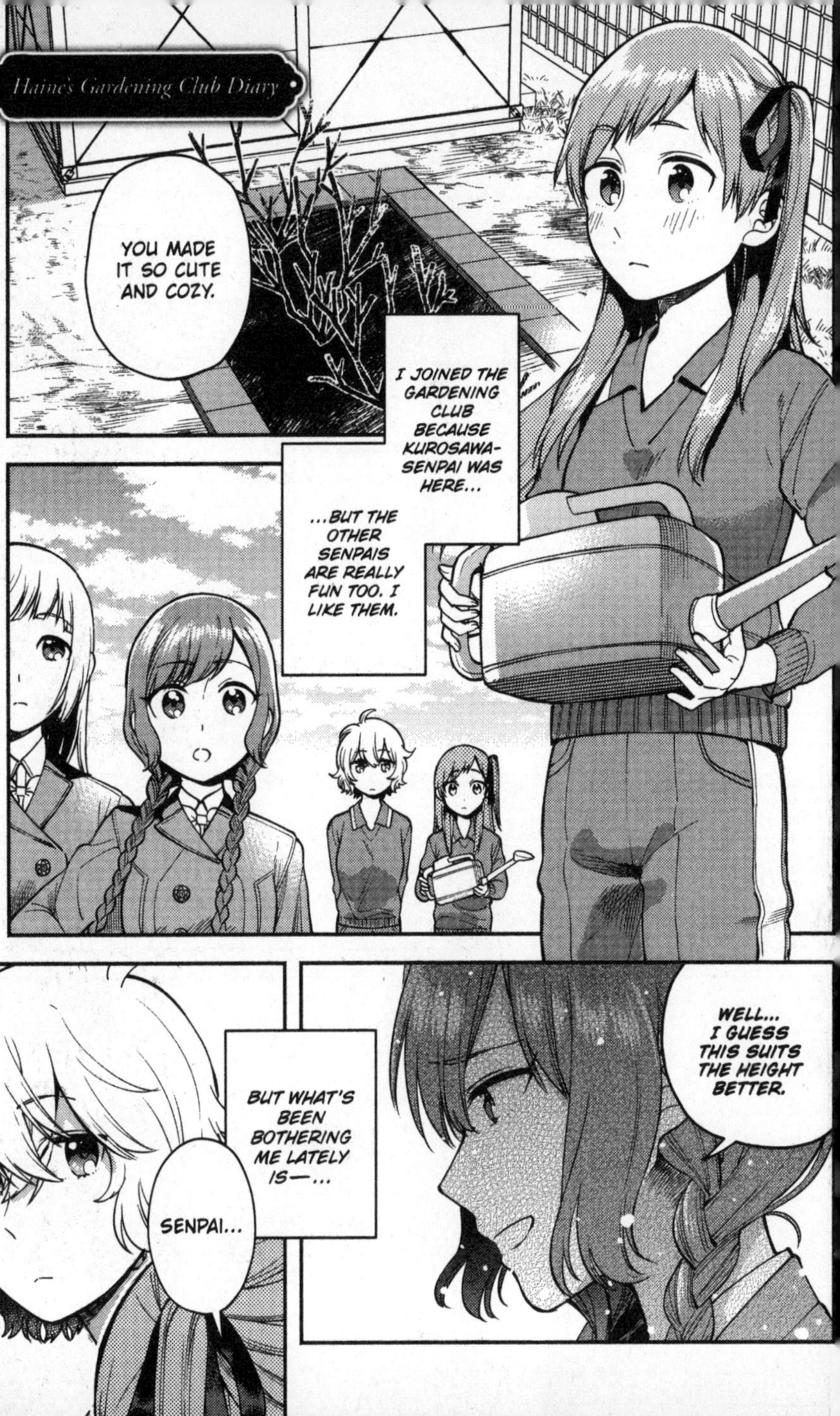
Haine's Gardening Club Diary
I JOINED THE GARDENING CLUB BECAUSE KUROSAWA-SENPAI WAS HERE...
...BUT THE OTHER SENPAIS ARE REALLY FUN TOO. I LIKE THEM.
YOU MADE IT SO CUTE AND COZY.
WELL... I GUESS THIS SUITS THE HEIGHT BETTER.
BUT WHAT'S BEEN BOTHERING ME LATELY IS—...
SENPAI...

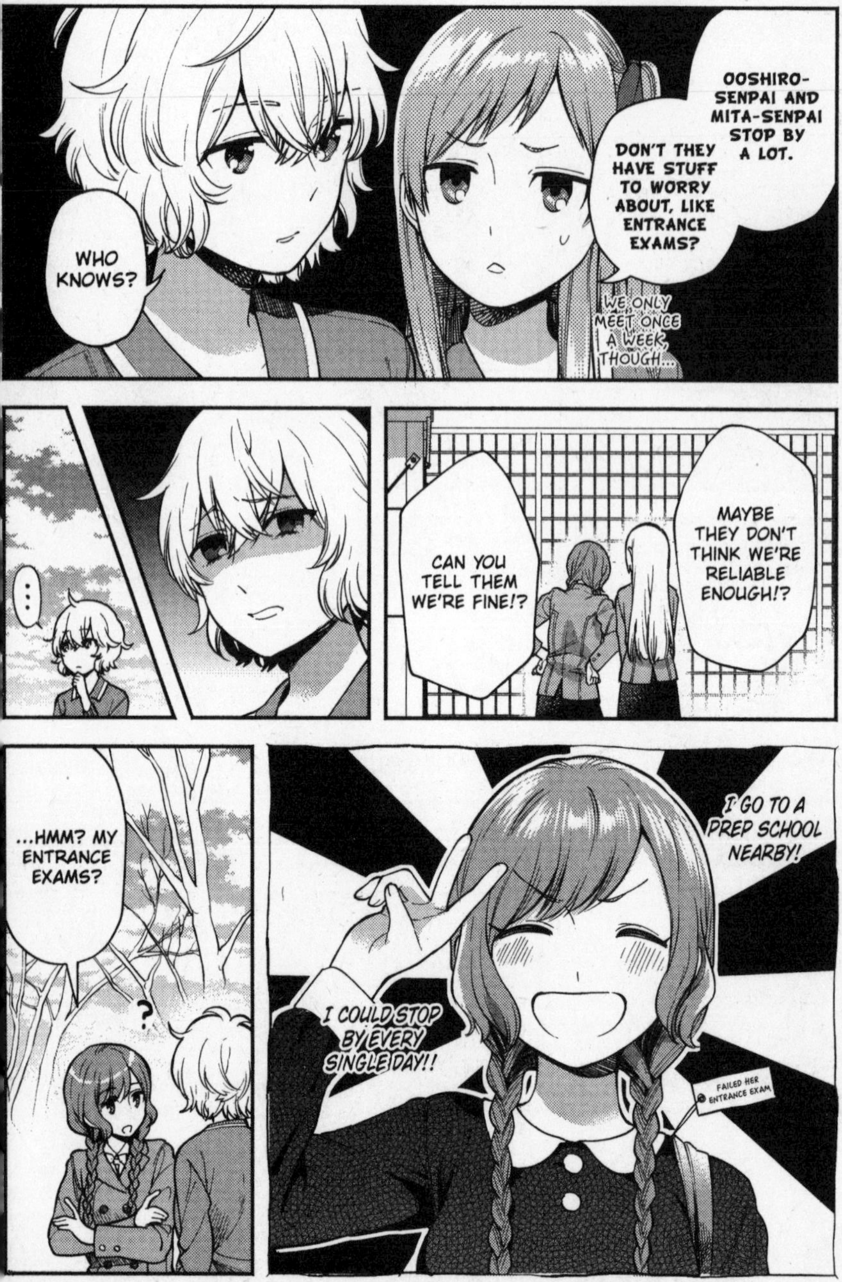
OOSHIRO-SENPAI AND MITA-SENPAI STOP BY A LOT.
DON'T THEY HAVE STUFF TO WORRY ABOUT, LIKE ENTRANCE EXAMS?
WE ONLY MEET ONCE A WEEK, THOUGH...
WHO KNOWS?
MAYBE THEY DON'T THINK WE'RE RELIABLE ENOUGH!?
CAN YOU TELL THEM WE'RE FINE!?
...
I GO TO A PREP SCHOOL NEARBY!
I COULD STOP BY EVERY SINGLE DAY!!
FAILED HER ENTRANCE EXAM
...HMM? MY ENTRANCE EXAMS?
?

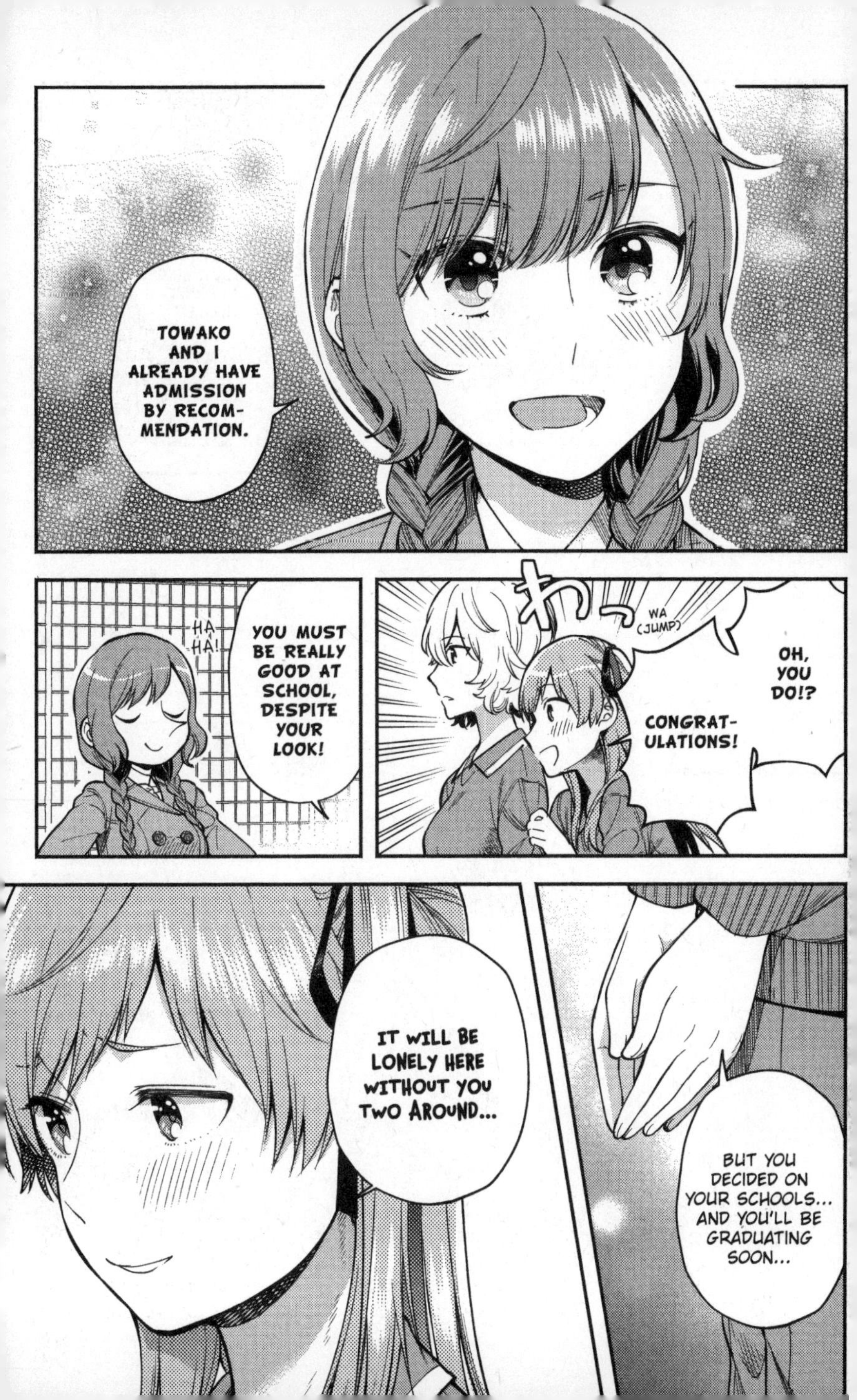
TOWAKO AND I ALREADY HAVE ADMISSION BY RECOM-MENDATION.
わっ
WA (JUMP)
OH, YOU DO!?
CONGRAT-ULATIONS!
YOU MUST BE REALLY GOOD AT SCHOOL, DESPITE YOUR LOOK!
HA HA!
BUT YOU DECIDED ON YOUR SCHOOLS... AND YOU'LL BE GRADUATING SOON...
IT WILL BE LONELY HERE WITHOUT YOU TWO AROUND...

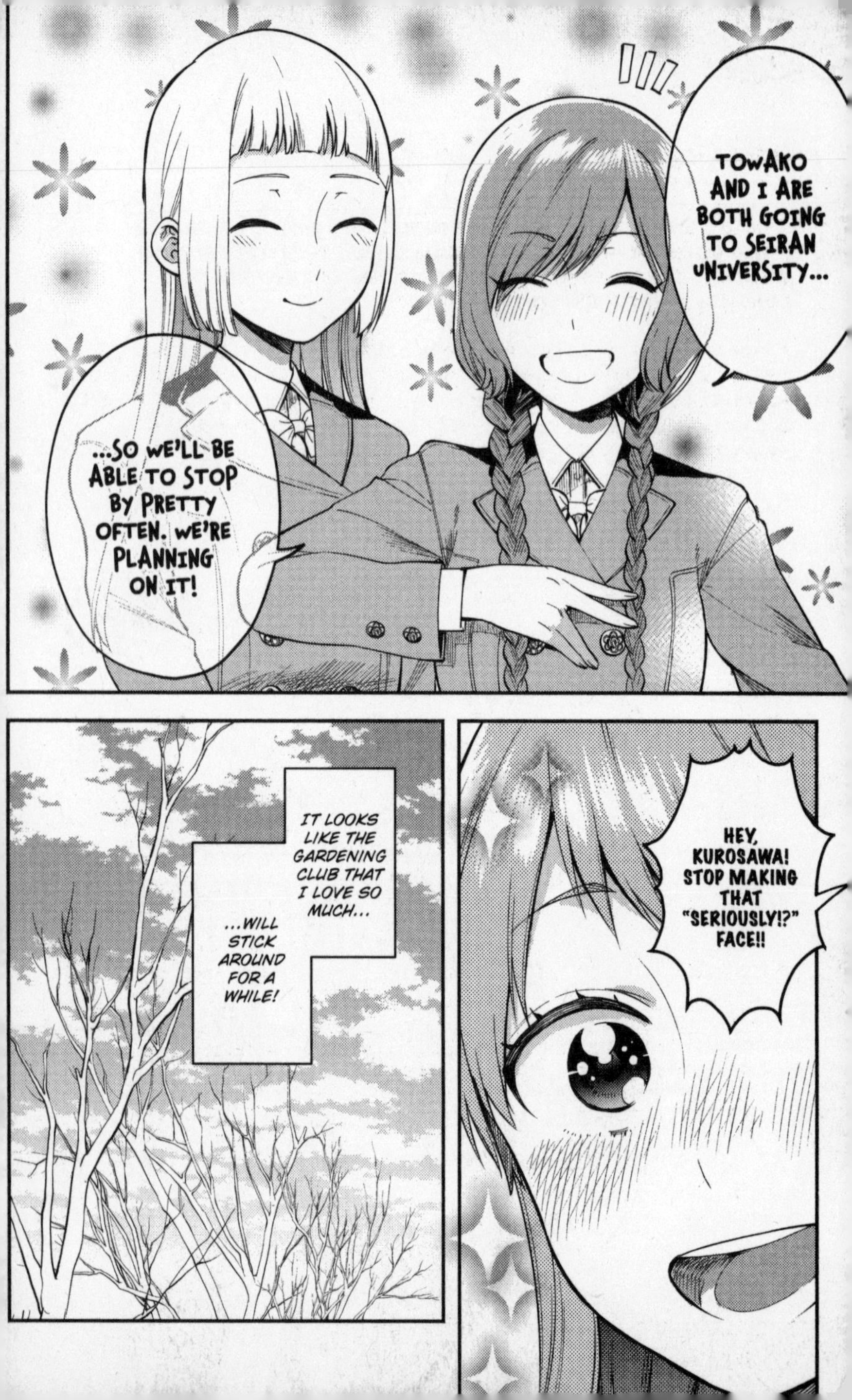
TOWAKO AND I ARE BOTH GOING TO SEIRAN UNIVERSITY...
...SO WE'LL BE ABLE TO STOP BY PRETTY OFTEN. WE'RE PLANNING ON IT!
HEY, KUROSAWA! STOP MAKING THAT "SERIOUSLY!?" FACE!!
IT LOOKS LIKE THE GARDENING CLUB THAT I LOVE SO MUCH...
...WILL STICK AROUND FOR A WHILE!

AFTERWORD

I'VE JUST SORT OF JUMPED OVER ALL THE BIG SEASONAL EVENTS SO FAR (I'VE MADE IT UP IN THE SIDE STORIES, THOUGH), SO I DECIDED TO PROVE THAT I CAN DO A SPECIAL-EVENT STORY THIS TIME. SO THAT'S WHAT WENT INTO THIS CHRISTMAS STORY. CANNO HERE. I DIDN'T HAVE TO SAY THAT, DID I???

ONCE AGAIN, THANK YOU SO MUCH TO EVERYONE IN THE ALIVE EDITORIAL DEPARTMENT; THE DESIGNER SEKI-SAN; YUI-SAN AND SAKI-SAN, WHO WERE SO HELPFUL; NAKAMURA-SAN, WHO TAUGHT ME ABOUT THE PIANO; AND EVERYONE INVOLVED WHO HELPED GET THIS BOOK OUT SUCCESSFULLY. BUT MOST IMPORTANTLY, EVERYONE WHO'S READ THIS FAR. THANK YOU SO MUCH. I THINK VOLUME 8 IS GOING TO BE ABOUT SHIRAMINE/KUROSAWA AGAIN. ANYWAY, I HOPE TO SEE YOU THEN.

CANNO

Kiss & White Lily for My Dearest Girl

7

{CANNO}

TRANSLATION: LEIGHANN HARVEY
LETTERING: ALEXIS ECKERMAN

ANOKO NI KISS TO SHIRAYURI WO Vol. 7
©Canno 2017
First published in Japan in 2017 by KADOKAWA CORPORATION, Tokyo.
English translation rights arranged with KADOKAWA CORPORATION, Tokyo
through Tuttle-Mori Agency, Inc., Tokyo.

English translation © 2018 by Yen Press, LLC

Yen Press
1290 Avenue of the Americas
New York, NY 10104

Visit us at yenpress.com
facebook.com/yenpress
instagram.com/yenpress

twitter.com/yenpress
yenpress.tumblr.com

First Yen Press Edition: October 2018

Yen Press is an imprint of Yen Press, LLC.
The Yen Press name and logo are trademarks of Yen Press, LLC.

Library of Congress Control Number: 2016958499

ISBNs: 978-1-9753-8099-1 (paperback)
978-1-9753-0215-3 (ebook)

10 9 8 7 6 5 4 3 2 1

WOR

Printed in the United States of America